Military Honour and the Conduct of War

This book examines the influence of ideas of honour on the causes, conduct, and ending of wars from Ancient Greece to the present day. Opening with a theoretical examination of the concept of honour, it explains the many contradictions and tensions inherent within honour systems, as honour has often paradoxical effects on the conduct of war. Using a wealth of sources including original archival research and interviews with serving military officers, Paul Robinson then illustrates this thesis through seven case studies: Classical Greece; Ancient Rome; mediaeval chivalry; Elizabethan England; the American Civil War; the British Empire; and the Western world after the Second World War (including the Vietnam War and the current conflict in Iraq). Highlighting both the differences and similarities between the various eras the author shows that honour has played an important and complex role in the ignition, conduct and end of wars throughout history and how it remains a vital influence on modern warfare.

This volume will be of interest to students of military history, military ethics, security studies, and international relations.

Paul Robinson is a lecturer in Security Studies at the University of Hull. He is the author of numerous works on military history, ethics, and international affairs, most notably: *The White Russian Army in Exile, 1920–1941* (2002) and *Just War in Comparative Perspective* (2003). He has served as an officer in both the British and Canadian armies and writes regularly for the international press.

Routledge Military Studies

Rose Mary Sheldon, *Intelligence Activities in Ancient Rome: Trust in the Gods, But Verify*

Isabelle Duyvesteyn, *Clausewitz and African War: Politics and Strategy in Liberia and Somalia*

Michael Cohen, *Strategy and Politics in the Middle East, 1954–60: Defending the Northern Tier*

Edward George, *The Cuban Intervention in Angola, 1965–1991: From Che Guevara to Cuito Cuanavale*

Stanley Carpenter, *Military Leadership in the British Civil Wars, 1642–1651: 'The Genius of this Age'*

Ze'ev Drory, *Israel's Reprisal Policy, 1953–1956: The Dynamics of Military Retaliation*

Enver Redzic, *Bosnia and Herzegovina in the Second World War*

Frederick Kagan and Christian Kubik (eds), *Leaders in War: West Point Remembers the 1991 Gulf War*

John Dunn, *Khedive Ismail's Army*

Amadeo Watkins, *Yugoslav Military Industry 1918–1991*

John Williams, *Corporal Hitler and the Great War 1914–1918: The List Regiment*

Brian Murphy, *Rostov in the Russian Civil War, 1917–1920: The Key to Victory*

Jake Blood, *The Tet Effect, Intelligence and the Public Perception of War*

Sam C. Sarkesian and Robert E. Connor, Jr. (eds), *The US Military Profession into the 21st Century: War, Peace and Politics*

Hans Born, Marina Caparini, Karl Haltiner and Jürgen Kuhlmann (eds), *Civil-Military Relations in Europe: Learning from Crisis and Institutional Change*

Lawrence Sondhaus, *Strategic Culture and Ways of War*

Richard Bartle and Lindy Heinecken (eds), *Military Unionism in the Post Cold War Era: A Future Reality?*

Charles A. Stevenson, *Warriors and Politicians: U.S. Civil-Military Relations under Stress*

Paul Robinson, *Military Honour and the Conduct of War: From Ancient Greece to Iraq*

Timothy D. Hoyt, *Military Industry and Regional Defense Policy: India, Iraq and Israel*

Laura R. Cleary and Teri McConville (eds), *Managing Defence in a Democracy*

Military Honour and the Conduct of War

From Ancient Greece to Iraq

Paul Robinson

Routledge
Taylor & Francis Group
LONDON AND NEW YORK

First published 2006
by Routledge
2 Park Square, Milton Park,
Abingdon, Oxon OX14 4RN

Simultaneously published in the USA and Canada
by Routledge
270 Madison Ave, New York, NY 10016

Routledge is an imprint of the Taylor & Francis Group, an informa business

Transferred to Digital Printing 2009

Typeset in Times by Keyword Group Ltd

British Library Cataloguing in Publication Data
A catalogue record for this book is available from the British Library

Library of Congress Cataloging in Publication Data
Robinson, Paul, 1966-
Military honour and the conduct of war: from ancient Greece to Iraq / Paul Robinson.
p. cm.—(Routledge military studies)
Includes bibliographical references and index.
ISBN 0-415-39201-2 (hardback)
1. Honor—Case studies. 2. Military ethics—History—Case studies. 3. Military art and science—History—Case studies. I. Title. II. Series
U22.R65 2006
355.1′12—dc22
2005031287

ISBN10: 0-415-39201-2 (hbk)
ISBN10: 0-415-54509-9 (pbk)
ISBN10: 0-203-96963-4 (ebk)

ISBN13: 978-0-415-39201-3 (hbk)
ISBN13: 978-0-415-54509-9 (pbk)
ISBN13: 978-0-203-96963-2 (ebk)

Contents

Acknowledgements

Many people have helped in the writing of this book. On the personal side, first thanks go to my wife, Chione, to my parents, Michael and Ann Robinson, and to my parents-in-law, Donald and Pattice Hughes. They have all been a great support throughout my writing career. I also wish to thank Luke and Ginny Vania of Menlo Park, California, and Iain and Kris Murray in Virginia, for providing me with accommodation and friendship during my travels, as well as Paul Dryden in Hampshire — who also lent me books about Elizabethan England.

On the academic side, the Institute of Applied Ethics and the Faculty of Arts and Social Sciences at the University of Hull have both provided me with generous financial aid to enable me to complete my research. I would like to express my gratitude to Richard Davies at Leeds University, for his aid in navigating the Liddle Archive; Kees Boterbloem, now at South Florida University; Michael Duffy for sending me a copy of his book *Man of Honour*; Pauletta Otis for sending me a copy of General Zinni's memoirs, *Battle Ready*; the staff of the British Museum for helping me analyse Greek war memorials, and showing me an example of a casualty list; Ruth Ann Coski and other staff at the Museum of the Confederacy for help in their archives and for showing me examples of Confederate battle flags; Captains Jim Campbell and Robert Schoultz, and various midshipmen, at the US Naval Academy Annapolis; Lieutenant Colonel Blair Tiger and the members of the Honor Committee at the US Military Academy West Point; the officers of Canada's 22 Wing, North Bay; various officers of the UK, US, and Canadian delegations to NATO Headquarters, Brussels; and finally to the lieutenant colonel who showed me the word 'honorificabilitudinity'. It has been an honour to work with you all.

1 Introduction

Researching an earlier book about White Russian officers who fought against the Bolsheviks in the Russian Civil War, 1917–1921,[1] I found in thousands of letters and published writings almost no evidence of any formalized political thought, no idea of what these officers would do with political power if ever they won it. One word did, however, appear again and again – *chest'*. Honour. The Whites' resistance to Bolshevism, I gradually realized, was much less about any specific material goal than about a desire to restore outraged honour.[2] That discovery impelled me to find out whether the Whites were unique. They were not. Honour and war are inseparable.

This book explores, through seven case studies, how honour has affected the causes, conduct, and ending of wars in the Western world over the last three thousand years. Each chapter looks at nine aspects of the relationship between honour and war in the era in question, namely: honour and virtue; honour as a cause of war; honour as a motivation for fighting; honours and rewards; honour and death; honour and the conduct of war; honour and the enemy; honour and the ending of war; and honour and women.

The case studies are all of Western societies. This is not because the experiences described in this book are unique to the West. Ancient China, for instance, had a code of chivalry. There are stories of Chinese commanders refusing to attack an enemy when he was disadvantaged crossing a river, and of charioteers helping enemy soldiers extricate stuck chariots to make their escape, on the grounds that it was dishonourable to attack an enemy who was helpless. Sixteenth- and seventeenth-century Russian warfare was influenced by a unique honour system known as *mestnichestvo*, and Russian nobles often refused to fight if subordinated to commanders of less prestigious ancestry. Honour also played an enormous role in the behaviour of Japanese soldiers during the Second World War, as seen in their attitude towards surrender, their treatment of enemy prisoners, and the tactics of the *kamikaze*. There is insufficient space in one book to do justice to so many cultures and eras. Instead, this book will trace one cultural strand from the beginning of the Western tradition to today.

Defining honour

The relationship between war and honour is full of tensions and contradictions which make it difficult to generalize. To understand why, it is necessary at this point to digress into an examination of what 'honour' is.[3]

Every human society wishes to prosper, and so rewards or 'honours' those who succeed, in order to encourage others to do likewise.[4] Societies also honour the display of those virtues which they consider conducive to success. At a third remove, individuals desire the marks of honour as ends in themselves, divorced from their original social function. This disconnect between the social and personal purposes of honour lies at the heart of many of the tensions within honour systems.

Definitions of honour normally split it into two types: external and internal. One behaves honourably either in order to win the praise of others or to live up to one's own standards of correct behaviour. In the first case, honour is similar to words such as reputation, prestige, face, and name. In the second case, it is closer to conscience or integrity.[5] Ideally, the two sorts of honour create the same demands, and individual morality coincides with what society desires and rewards. Often, however, the actions or virtues which win public repute oppose the demands of conscience. That said, one's conscience is in part a product of external influences, and in return, social norms are influenced by individual ideals. Honour, therefore, never quite corresponds to either external honour alone or internal honour alone. The two necessarily co-exist, and are in constant dialogue with one another.[6]

External honour is marked by rewards which set those who win them apart from others. Honour in this sense becomes synonymous with precedence.[7] Concern for precedence often results in belligerence. One loses precedence to anyone who insults one, so there is pressure to respond forcefully; this deters insulting behaviour, and thus acts as a form of para-legal protection of peoples' rights. For this reason, one definition of honour is as 'the right to respect',[8] and honour systems often flourish where official legal protection of rights is poor. All too often this results in people associating honour with violent defence of their reputation rather than with practising virtue.

In war, these contradictory ideas of honour have a complex impact. To win a battle, it helps to possess certain specific virtues – courage, strength, loyalty to one's comrades, a sense of duty, patriotism, and so on. As a result, the possession of those virtues is considered honourable, and they are inculcated into fighters, so that they become internally enforceable. Once a man has internalized them, though, he will often obey the dictates of the code of honour even when this is in neither his nor his society's interests. He will fight in such a way as to preserve his personal sense of honour rather than to win. At the same time, his society will continue to value and honour those who do win, and in consequence, other men may ignore the code of honour and behave in a dishonourable way as a shortcut to victory. Honour will thus simultaneously encourage fighters both to maintain and to discard the rules of honourable conduct.

Honour and virtue

Each of the seven case studies which follow looks first at the virtues associated with honour in the period in question. The four virtues of prowess, courage, loyalty, and truthfulness form the unchanging core of military honour, although, as later chapters will show, other virtues have also been prized to varying degrees in different eras – obedience, discipline, observance of religious ritual, respect for women, duty, service, mercy, generosity, and prudence, among others. Of all these, the prime virtue is prowess, a combination of physical strength and skill with a weapon. To be of use, though, prowess must be coupled with courage and with loyalty. Soldiers rely on each others' protection, and military cultures stress the virtue of loyalty to one's colleagues, and, at a higher level, to one's friends and allies. As for truthfulness, soldiers need to be able to trust one another if they are to operate effectively. In fact, enemies also need to be able to trust one another, at least on certain matters such as the fulfilment of the terms of peace treaties.[9]

Many societies create formal codes of behaviour which prescribe how to display the approved virtues. Unfortunately, in yet another complication, this means that honour can derive from rigid obedience of the code even when it is unhelpful or even clearly wrong. Established 'codes of honour' suffer from another defect, which is that they are products of past experience and social structures, as well as of past war-fighting techniques. As a result, they are often obsolete at the start of new wars. People will follow them still because they have been trained to do so, but the consequences may be at odds with practicality.

Honour and the causes of war

The numerous theories explaining mankind's propensity to wage war draw attention to two main types of motives: emotional and psychological ones – such as some innate inclination to violence; and material ones – the desire for safety and for profit.[10]

The pursuit of honour fits into both categories. The desire for honour is at one level an urge inherent in human nature, and at another something worth pursuing for the advantages that it brings. This is why questions of honour are so commonly present at the start of wars. It is, in fact, striking how regularly the rhetoric for war includes calls to protect both national security and national honour.[11]

Honour may be seen as a mechanism for validating self-worth. Questions of honour strike at one's very identity, and this is why they are so important. If honour is lost, identity is annihilated.[12] To restore one's sense of self, it can be worth risking death in a test of arms. Personal and national honour also serve a practical purpose. If one acquires a reputation for weakness and cowardice, future attacks on one's person become more likely. Honour and security are, therefore, linked.

Honour in the sense of precedence is another driver of conflict.[13] As people, institutions, and nations compete to excel and to gain precedence over one another, some will use all means, including force, to achieve their objectives. Those whom they subdue will in turn resent their loss of status and use whatever means they can to regain it. Sensitivity to insult is also dependent on security. Those who feel insecure are more likely to respond violently to attempts to denigrate them.[14]

The search for precedence encourages people to take risks in order to stand out from the crowd and acquire glory. In societies which feel insecure and in which war is a fairly normal phenomenon, military prowess is one of the most valued virtues. Glory-seekers will, therefore, go out of their way to look for opportunities to demonstrate their prowess in battle. On occasion, this can mean deliberately provoking wars just to have the chance to fight and win glory.

In addition, since one measures precedence not in absolute terms, but in relation to others, it is often much simpler to achieve honour by pushing somebody else down than by achieving anything oneself. The consequence of the pursuit of honour can be a continuous effort to humiliate others, which inevitably provokes resistance and thus violent conflict. Very often, moreover, the actual issue over which the conflict is fought is extremely trivial, a 'point of honour' – an issue or object whose value is primarily symbolic.

The final way in which honour helps to start wars is through the obligation which it imposes on people to fulfil their promises, for instance those made to allies, even in circumstances when remaining loyal provides no material benefit. Promises also come into play in coercive diplomacy. In trying to force concessions from a second party through threats of force, the aim is not to go to war, but to get the concession and avoid war. The problem is that the very act of coercion is demeaning from the second party's point of view. If he concedes, he will lose honour, so very possibly he will refuse. That leaves the coercer with two options: carry out his threat, which will most likely be disproportionate to the benefit he was hoping to achieve; or back down, and lose face. Either way, calculations of honour play a fundamental role.

Honour as a motivation for fighting

As a result of these dynamics, states sometimes find themselves at war for no obvious reason beyond meeting the demands of honour. Their soldiers will then have to fight on their behalf. Some will do so for purely negative reasons: those in authority have forced them to do so; to flee is too dangerous; and personal survival dictates that they kill their enemy before he kills them. Positive motivations may be mercenary – the pay, or the prospect of plunder and booty. A few men may fight because they enjoy it. Some will believe in the cause for which they are fighting. Others still will be driven by motives of personal or group honour. Most will respond to a mixture of some or all of the above.

Honour spurs men to fight in two ways: positively, through a desire to display virtue and win honour; and negatively, through a desire to avoid dishonour or shame. Shame is enforced both internally and externally. Most men will have internalized the idea that courage is a virtue, and cowardice a sin, and will wish to avoid the sense of shame that arises from failing to live up to what they believe are society's expectations. On the other hand, societies recognize that internal motivation is not always effective, and therefore develop methods of external enforcement of standards. In a military context, cowards may suffer any number of punishments, ranging from ostracism to death.

The group whose good opinion the soldier is trying to acquire (the 'honour group') may be society as a whole, family or friends, the opposite sex, or at the lowest level his immediate colleagues, and this may vary through time. When he is signing up, general social opinion may matter a great deal, but when the bullets are flying he may care more about the opinion of his comrades. As Joshua Chamberlain, a general in the American Civil War, described it, at this point, 'the instinct to seek safety is overcome by the instinct of honour.'[15]

Honours and rewards

Another inducement to fight is the prospect of winning tangible honours; money, booty, promotions, titles, statues, medals, and so forth. The value of these relates primarily to what they symbolize. Even booty and plunder are often valued as much for the honour they bestow as for their monetary worth. As John Pedersen says, 'the more gold, the more honour … wealth means more than material gain. … It fills and uplifts the soul, and so makes it grow in value; blessing acts in it, and honour swells.'[16]

Rewards such as medals serve two purposes. In the first place, they prove to the troops that good performance is recognized, a fact which is important in maintaining morale. In addition, they provide incentives for soldiers to perform specific acts of bravery in the hope of gaining a reward. The rewards may seem insignificant compared with the risks involved, but the incentive seems to work, and attempts to abolish military honours have invariably failed. After the Russian Revolution, the Soviets tried eliminating the trappings of 'bourgeois' honour – medals, fancy uniforms, gold braid, epaulettes, badges of rank, etc. – but once Germany invaded the USSR in 1941, Moscow soon reinstated them all. The example of the First World War veteran and author Ernst Junger indicates the importance which soldiers attach to these marks of honour. In his book *Storm of Steel* he describes how in the middle of a battle he realized that, 'my Iron Cross had become detached and fallen on the ground somewhere. Schrader, my servant, and I started looking for it, even though concealed snipers were shooting at us.'[17] Eventually they found it, Junger pinned it back on, and they returned to the battle. Clearly, for Junger, the honour granted by this little chunk of metal was not something he took lightly.

Death and honour

Societies honour not only the living, but also those who have died in war. Because the dead made the ultimate sacrifice, they acquire a hallowed status. From a practical point of view, it is also good for the morale of living soldiers to know that they will be thought of with respect once their lives are over. Nevertheless, honour in death tends to be unequally distributed. In hierarchical societies, the rank and file are generally dumped in mass graves and forgotten, and only higher ranking personnel are commemorated. In more egalitarian societies, each dead soldier is considered worthy of respect, and even the lowliest private receives his memorial. Thus there are strong parallels in the treatment of the dead by democracies as far separated in time as ancient Athens and modern Britain.

It can even become a matter of honour to recover the dead rather than let them fall into the hands of the enemy. From the Trojan War to the battle between Americans and Somalis in Mogadishu in 1993, soldiers have invested considerable effort into fighting over corpses. Practically speaking, this makes no sense. But, as so often in war, the dictates of honour rule.

That said, there is considerable room for manoeuvre within the framework of the popular military expression, 'death before dishonour'. Different cultures have interpreted this message more rigidly than others. The Roman historian Tacitus commented that among the Germans, 'To give ground, provided that you return to the attack, is considered good tactics rather than cowardice.'[18] Roman soldiers, by contrast, were expected to hold their ground in all circumstances and, if necessary, die in the process. Failure was severely punished.

If life was all that mattered, the only people who would fight would be those who feared for their lives if they did not. A conviction that death is not the worst fate a man can suffer is a vital tool in motivating soldiers.

Honour and the conduct of war

Ideas of honourable conduct restrict the options open to soldiers in battle. Sometimes, the competing demands of military necessity and honour lead men to resort to absurdities. At the battle of Fontenoy in 1745, British and French commanders reportedly invited each other to fire first. If one regards the point of war as being to defeat the enemy, such behaviour appears ridiculous. If one understands that war's real purpose is more often to provide men with an opportunity to win honour by displaying their courage (and at Fontenoy, also their courtesy), it is entirely rational.

If a war continues for a long time, demands for victory will cause tactics, weapons, and targets which were once considered out of bounds to gradually become acceptable. Many commentators see codes of honour as the most powerful force preventing excess on the battlefield.[19] Such codes limit not just the tactics one may use, but also the targets one may attack. Warriors gain honour through displaying their courage; massacring women and children and murdering enemy soldiers who have already surrendered requires no courage, and so brings no honour. Refusing to kill, on the other hand, allows a man to display honourable characteristics such as mercy, generosity, and magnanimity. The warrior who triumphs, and then spares those he has vanquished, wins honour twice over.

As always, though, the impact of honour is contradictory. Honour can limit excess in war; it can also encourage it. As previously noted, an easy way to gain precedence is to humiliate others. Furthermore, ideas associated with honour, such as loyalty, duty, and obedience, can lead men to carry out actions they might otherwise consider wrong. During the Second World War, Captain Wolfgang Hoffmann had a tendency to disappear sick when his unit, Police Battalion 101, was massacring Polish Jews. His superior, Major Trapp, noted his absences and reported him for having a 'deficient sense of service'. In response, Hoffmann stated that his 'honour as an officer and a soldier had been most deeply hurt'.[20] To him, murdering civilians was not dishonourable, but being seen to lack the fortitude to do so certainly was.

Honour and the enemy

Ideas of honour also affect soldiers' concept of the enemy. The treatment of prisoners provides a clear example. Today, soldiers are expected to treat their captives with respect. In the past this was not always the case. The ancient Assyrians, for instance, shamed their prisoners by stripping them and leading them,

> naked and bound, a practice which can be seen in the war reliefs of Assyria and Babylon. ... Humiliating captive warriors lowered them and their nation to an inferior position and raised up the victors in status. Consequently, captive warriors or kings were made to walk naked, to grovel in the dust abjectly, or to feel helpless and defenceless.[21]

Modern thinkers tend rather to idealize the attitude expressed by Odysseus about his rival Ajax in Sophocles' play *Ajax*: 'He was my enemy, but he was noble.'[22] One of the most important aspects of honouring one's opponent is seen in the historical institution of parole, in which captured soldiers gave their word ('parole' in French) that if they were freed, they would not bear arms once more against their former captors. The whole system was obviously dependent on trusting captive soldiers to keep their promises. Should they fail to do so, captors would find other ways of dealing with prisoners, such as killing them. Keeping one's word is to this day a central aspect of most military honour codes.

One must bear in mind, though, that soldiers who honour an enemy still aim to kill him. The officers at Fontenoy, while willing to let the other side shoot first, were in no doubt that if they survived the first volley they would fire back.

Honour and the ending of wars

Attitudes towards the enemy take on particular importance when one is trying to bring a war to a close. As a general rule, wars end in one of two ways: one side is completely exterminated, or completely loses its physical ability to resist; or else one side recognizes that it is beaten, loses its will to resist, and agrees to give up the struggle. The first of these is rare. Few wars result in the total destruction of the enemy. Most wars end in the second way. Oddly enough, what this means is that it is the loser and not the winner who decides when a war ends – 'war is pressed by the victor, but peace is made by the vanquished.'[23]

In making the decision to quit, the loser will weigh two things against each other: the likelihood of further losses if the war continues; and the positive inducements offered by the enemy in return for surrender. This is where questions of honour become vitally important. If the victor insists on humiliating his opponent, the latter may well decide that it is less painful to continue the war. If the victor finds some ways for his enemy to save face, the latter may accept the terms despite their material cost.

The chapters which follow contain numerous examples of this. Where honour was granted to defeated enemies, as at the end of the American Civil War, the transition to peace took place remarkably smoothly. Where it was not, as so often in Ancient Greece, war was unnecessarily protracted.

Women and honour

This book, it must be said, is almost exclusively about men. Men have always done most of the fighting in wars, military codes of honour are based on traditionally male values, and when men speak of honour in the context of war, very often what they are talking about is their desire to prove their 'manliness'.

Anthropologists have noted that in traditional societies female honour is narrowly defined in terms of sexual chastity.[24] Nevertheless, even in these societies, women do play a role in questions of martial honour. When men go to war, the people whose good opinion they are seeking are often their mothers, wives, and lovers. Likewise, from the time when the Sabine women legendarily placed themselves between the Roman and Sabine armies and forced them to stop fighting, women have often been cited as a cause of the end of wars. As Chapter 6 shows, in the American Civil War Southern soldiers went to war to avoid shaming their families, but once their wives told them to come home again, many abandoned the colours and did so.

Women also enforce standards of behaviour during war. As William Miller comments, in ancient heroic cultures it was the women who were 'the arbiters of male competence in combat and competition … it was the female gaze through which so much of male honour and reputations for courage and cowardice were filtered.'[25] Tacitus gave an example, describing how German women accompanied their men into battle, and saying that, 'It stands on record that armies already wavering and on the point of collapse have been rallied by the women, pleading heroically with their men, thrusting forward their bared breasts.'[26]

In all of this, the role of women is as non-combatants. Only at the very end of this book am I able to include some analysis of women as fighters. The evolution of the role of women in war in the last one hundred years is one of the most significant changes we will encounter in the history which now follows.

Notes

1 See my earlier book, Robinson, Paul, *The White Russian Army in Exile, 1920–1941*, Oxford: Clarendon Press, 2002.

2 I have outlined this thesis in more detail elsewhere: Robinson, Paul, '"Always with Honour": The Code of the White Russian Officers', *Canadian Slavonic Papers*, 1999, vol. 41, no. 2, 121–41.

3 A full bibliography of works on the subject of honour can be found at the back of this book. All the works listed contributed in some fashion to the discussion of honour in this section.

4 The simplest definition of honour is, therefore, that of Aristotle, who defined it as 'the reward for virtue'. Aristotle, *Ethics*, trans. J.A.K. Thomson, revised by Hugh Tredennick, London: Penguin, 1976, p. 284.

5 For a definition of honour which rests on the distinction between internal and external measurements of worth, see, among others: Peristiany, J.G., *Honour and Shame: The Values of a Mediterranean Society*, Chicago, University of Chicago Press, 1968, p. 30. For a critique of this definition see Stewart, Frank Henderson, *Honor*, Chicago: Chicago University Press, 1994.

6 This is a somewhat controversial assertion. For explanations, see among others: Cairns, Douglas, *Aidos: The Psychology and Ethics of Honour and Shame in Ancient Greek Literature*, Oxford: Oxford University Press, 1992, p. 40; Gray, J. Glenn, 'Ending with Honor', in Luck, Edward C. and Albert, Stuart (eds), *On the Ending of Wars*, Port Washington, NY: Kennikat Press Corp., 1980, pp. 145–56; and Kollmann, Nancy Shields, *By Honor Bound: State and Society in Early Modern Russia*, Ithaca and London: Cornell University Press, 1999, p. 27.

7 For an analysis of the conflict between honour as virtue and honour as precedence, see Peristiany (ed.), *Honour and Shame*; and Peristiany, J.G. and Pitt- Rivers, J. (eds), *Honor and Grace in Anthropology*, Cambridge: Cambridge University Press, 1992.

8 Stewart, *Honor*, p. 21.

9 For comments on these virtues, see: Pitt-Rivers, Julian, 'Honor', in *Encyclopedia of the Social Sciences*, vol. 6, New York: Macmillan, 1968, p. 505; Axinn, Sidney, *A Moral Military*, Philadelphia: Temple University Press, 1989, p. 42; and O'Neill, Barry, *Honor, Symbols, and War*, Ann Arbor: University of Michigan Press, 2001, p. 87.

10 For a discussion of these issues, see Brown, Seyom, *The Causes and Prevention of War*, New York: St. Martin's Press, 1987; Cashman, Greg, *What Causes Wars? An Introduction to Theories of International Conflict*, San Francisco: Lexington, 1993; and Suganami, Hidemi, *On the Causes of War*, Oxford: Clarendon Press, 1996.

11 For a comment to this effect, see Kagan, Donald, *On the Origins of War and the Preservation of Peace*, New York: Anchor, 1995, p. 8.

12 For a statement on this, see Scheider, Richard, 'Honor and Conflict in a Sicilian Town', *Anthropological Quarterly*, 1969, vol. 42, 153.

13 Peristiany, *Honour and Shame*, p. 24.

14 Campbell, J.K., *Honour, Family, and Patronage: A Study of Institutions and Moral Values in a Greek Mountain Village*, Oxford: Clarendon Press, 1964, p. 267.

15 Cited in Hastings, Max, *Warriors: Extraordinary Tales from the Battlefield*, London: HarperCollins, 2005, p. 50. For other comments on the influence of honour on men's willingness to fight, see Holmes, Richard, *Acts of War: The Behavior of Men in Battle*, New York: The Free Press, 1985, p. 301, and Grossman, Dave, *On Killing: The Psychological Cost of Learning to Kill in War and Society*, Boston and London: Little Brown, 1995, p. 89.

16 Pedersen, John, *Israel: Its Life and Culture*, London: Oxford University Press, 1946, pp. 228–9.

17 Junger, Ernst, *Storm of Steel*, trans. Michael Hoffmann, London: Allen Lane, 2003, p. 281.

18 Tacitus, *The Germania*, trans. H. Mattingly, revised S.A. Handford, Harmondsworth: Penguin, 1970, p. 106.

19 For instance, Osiel, Mark J., *Obeying Orders: Atrocity, Military Discipline, and the Law of War*, New Brunswick: Transaction, 2002, p. 23.

20 Browning, Christopher R., *Ordinary Men: Reserve Police Battalion 101 and the Final Solution in Poland*, London: Penguin, 2001, p. 119.

21 Bechtel, Lyn M., 'Shame as a Sanction of Social Control in Biblical Israel: Judicial, Political, and Social Shaming', *Journal for the Study of the Old Testament*, 1991, issue 49, 63–5.
22 Sophocles, *Electra and Other Plays*, trans. E.F. Watling, Harmondsworth: Penguin, 1953, p. 64.
23 Calahan, H.A., *What Makes a War End?*, New York: Vanguard Press, 1944, pp. 18–19, cited in Robinson, Chione, 'A Theory of War Termination for Peacemakers', *Canadian Forces College Review*, 2000, p. 84.
24 See, for instance, Pitt-Rivers, Julian, 'Postscript: The Place of Grace in Anthropology', in Peristiany and Pitt-Rivers, *Honor and Grace*, p. 226.
25 Miller, William Ian, *Humiliation and Other Essays on Honor, Social Discomfort, and Violence*, Ithaca: Cornell Unversity Press, 1993, pp. 238–9.
26 Tacitus, *Germania*, pp. 107–8.

2 Classical Greece

Background

The Classical Greece of the fourth and fifth centuries BC was dominated by the city-states of Athens and Sparta. The Classical era ended with the rise to supremacy of Macedon under Philip II and Alexander the Great. Its importance to the heritage of the Western world is so great as to make it the logical starting point of the case studies in this book.

Honour (*time*) and shame (*aidos*) were the two magnetic poles of ancient Greek society. Love of honour (*philotimia*), according to the general and historian Xenophon, was the very feature that distinguished men from beasts.[1] In the marketplace of Athens stood three altars: 'one to Shamefastness, one to Rumour, and one to Effort'.[2] Together these illustrate what motivated the ancient Greeks: a pervasive fear of shame; an obsession with what others were saying about them; and the resulting competitive drive to ensure that whatever people were saying, it was nothing one need feel ashamed about.

Individuals strove for dominance within a state, and states strove for dominance over one another. The consequence was almost continual inter-state war. In a rare example of unity, the Greeks combined their resources to defeat two Persian invasions in 490 BC and 480–479 BC. Thereafter they concentrated on fighting each another. Victory over Persia left Athens the major power in the Greek world. Its primary rival was Sparta. The rivalry between these two states and their allies eventually turned into a prolonged conflict, known as the Peloponnesian War, which lasted from 431 to 404 BC. Athens initially had the advantage, but suffered a terrible defeat when it attacked the city of Syracuse in Sicily in 416 BC, and never fully recovered. After the Athenian fleet was destroyed at the battle of Aegospotami, Athens was forced to surrender, and Sparta became the primary power in Greece. As always, though, when one Greek state gained a dominant position, others rose up against it. Sparta had to fight continual wars to maintain its position. Eventually, at Leuktra in 372 BC, the Theban army crushed the Spartans, and ended Spartan pre-eminence for good.

Thebes, in turn, was not able to enjoy its power for long. By 360 BC, a new force was gaining ground. This was the state of Macedon, which, led by King Philip II, eventually brought the whole of Greece under its heel, destroying a combined Theban-Athenian army at Chaeronea in 338 BC. Four years later, in 334 BC, Philip's son Alexander the Great set out on a journey of conquest which established him as master of most of the known world. After Alexander's early death in 325 BC, his kingdom split up into several smaller states. These then waged war on each other during the subsequent 'Hellenistic' age until their conquest by the Romans a century later.

Honour and virtue in ancient Greece

The Greeks believed that a society prospered by honouring those who prospered. Through love of honour and fear of disgrace, society impelled men to compete for success, benefiting all through the pursuit of their own self-interest. Plato wrote that without the 'values that produce feelings of shame for disgraceful actions and ambition for excellence … neither a city-state nor a private person can accomplish great and excellent things.'[3]

Aristotle, agreeing that honour 'is clearly the greatest external good',[4] argued that just as it was wrong to demand more honour than one deserved, it was equally wrong to insist on receiving too little. The former suggested 'vanity', the latter 'pusillanimity'. The ideal was 'magnanimity'.[5] As Aristotle wrote:

> A person is considered magnanimous if he thinks he is worthy of great things, provided that he *is* worthy of them … the magnanimous man has the right attitude towards honours and dishonours. Indeed it is apparent even without argument that magnanimous people are concerned with honour, because it is honour above all else that they claim as their due, and deservedly.[6]

Classical Greek societies, therefore, encouraged a love of honour in all their citizens. The Spartans took this to the farthest extreme. According to Plutarch:

> The Spartan law-giver Lycurgus seems to have introduced the spirit of ambition and contention into the country's constitution as an incitement to virtue: evidently he was anxious that good citizens should always be conscious of differences between each other.[7]

To encourage this attitude, while young Spartans ate their meals the prefects would 'pose questions to boys such as: "Who among the men is best?", or "What is your opinion of so-and-so's action?" Thereby boys grew accustomed to judging excellence and to making a critical appraisal of the citizens right from the start.'[8]

The ancient Greeks did indeed grow to love honour and this had a significant impact on their behaviour. As merit was considered only in relative terms, it had to be established through competition. This was then pursued well past the point of any possible advantage to society. 'Honour in life, or honour in death; there is no other thing a nobleman can ask for. That is all,' says Ajax in a play by Sophocles.[9]

The love of honour motivated Greek states as well as individuals. The Athenian statesman Demosthenes wrote that:

> The Athenian people has never exerted itself to acquire money, but more than anything to acquire reputation. The proof of this is that although it once had more money than any other Greek state, it spent all for the sake of *philotimia*, and it never yet refused any danger when reputation was at stake.[10]

In turn, the Athenian Thucydides wrote of the Spartans that, 'military honour is the be-all and end-all of their existence.'[11]

The people of the ancient world lived in small societies with little privacy, and were consequently open all the time to the gaze of others. How others saw them defined their own identity, and was of the utmost importance. The people who mattered varied according to the era in question and the context. In the earlier Homeric age, the family home, the *oikos*, appears to have been the focus of loyalty.[12] By the Classical era, however, the Greek citizen would have been concerned not just with his family but also with his fellow-citizens, and with the honour of the city-state itself.

Some historians interpret Greeks' endless talk of external forms as meaning that the ancient Greeks lacked any concept of sin or internal conscience, and measured themselves and their acts purely in terms of others' opinions.[13] This idea does not stand up to close scrutiny. As Douglas Cairns points out in a study of honour and shame in Greek literature, members of every society internalize that society's values at least to some extent, and the Greeks were no exception.[14] In fact, Greek honour demanded adherence to an internally enforceable set of rules which defined 'virtue' (*arete* – often translated instead as 'excellence', as it may imply excellence at some technical skill rather than a moral quality).

Aristotle defined honour as 'the reward for virtue',[15] and listed the elements of virtue as being: 'Justice, courage, restraint, splendour, magnanimity, liberality, prudence and wisdom'.[16] In a military context the most important virtues were courage and prowess. In Homer's *Iliad*, the hero Achilles is in many ways an unattractive figure: he is moody and selfish. But he is still the greatest of the Greeks, for the simple reason that no man is a match for him in battle. That fact outweighs everything else. The Spartan poet Tyrtaeus encapsulated the relative priorities well in one of his marching songs:

> I would not commemorate a man for his excellent running or wrestling, not
> If he had the size and strength of the Cyclopes, beat Thracian Boreas running,
> Was fairer of form than Tithanus, richer than Midas and Cinyras, more kingly
> Than Tantalid Pelops, had a tongue that spoke sweet as Adrastus and every
> Other distinction, but lacked furious courage. In war no man is good
> Unless he faces blood and death, taking a stand in every reach.
> *That* is excellence; *that* is the noblest contest a young man can win.[17]

Another, though lesser, virtue was truthfulness. 'I hate like Hades the man who hides one thing in his mind and speaks another,'[18] Achilles says in the *Iliad* to Odysseus, a man whose own flexibility on such matters made him a somewhat ambiguous figure in Greek literature. By the Classical period, after long experience of reckless glory-seeking, collective duty and patriotism had also become important parts of the honour code. This was especially true in Sparta, where Tyrtaeus wrote, 'It is a beautiful thing when a good man falls and dies fighting for his country.'[19] By this date, when a warrior was killed, his comrades felt honour-bound to give him a decent burial. Protecting the dead thus formed another important part of the Classical honour code.

Honour and the causes of war

Early in the third century BC, Tarentum, a city at the southern tip of Italy, invited Pyrrhus, king of Epirus in Greece, to help it combat the growing power of Rome. According to the historian Plutarch, when Pyrrhus was preparing to sail to Italy, his advisor Cineas asked him what he would do if he defeated the Romans. He replied that he would conquer all of Italy. And 'After that?' asked Cineas. Conquer Sicily. After that? Carthage. After that? Greece and Macedonia. After that? Finally, Pyrrhus replied, 'Why, then we shall relax. We shall drink, my dear fellow, every day, and talk and amuse one another.' But we can do that already, Cineas protested: 'what prevents us from relaxing and drinking and entertaining each other now? ... the very prizes which we propose to win with all this bloodshed and toil and danger ... we could enjoy them without taking another step!'[20]

Cineas' protests had no effect. Pyrrhus went to Italy, where he won several victories over the Romans at such exorbitant cost that his name has ever since been associated with the 'Pyrrhic' victory which is so costly that it harms the winner almost as much as the loser. It is unlikely that the conversation with Cineas ever took place. Most such conversations and speeches in ancient histories are fabrications. It encapsulates neatly, however, the causes of many of the Greek wars. They were all about glory.

War was almost a permanent condition in the Classical era. As mentioned, the Greek states only united in a common cause twice, when they combined their forces to defeat the Persians. The rest of the time, they competed endlessly for precedence among each other. When one became too powerful, others formed temporary alliances of spite against it to cut it down to size. From 490 to 338 BC, the city of Athens was at war for two out of every three years.[21]

Paradoxically, this resulted not so much from mutual antipathy as from shared values. The Greeks, according to the modern classical scholar Hans van Wees, were united 'not only by a common language and religion, but also by a common rivalry to be the best'.[22] 'Rivalry and conflict between city-states', claims van Wees, was 'largely inspired by the wish to defend and enhance the intangible *honour* of the community. ... more than anything else, the states in question sought to gain prestige by demonstrating their superiority over their neighbours.'[23]

This is not to say that one can entirely ignore other factors as causes of wars. There has to be some pretext, something which engages the sense of honour, in order to initiate fighting. A typical example is the Peloponnesian War. According to Thucydides, who was a contemporary observer of the war, 'what made war inevitable was the growth of Athenian power and the fear which this caused in

Sparta.'[24] Sparta and Athens had been allies against Persia, but thereafter Athens had acquired a position of dominance in the Greek world. When Athens achieved clear precedence above all Greek states, including Sparta, the latter deemed this intolerable. After an earthquake in Sparta, the Spartan slave population, the Helots, rose up in revolt, and Sparta asked Athens for help in putting down the rebellion. Then, having second thoughts, it worried that if an Athenian army entered Spartan territory it might start spreading dangerous revolutionary and democratic ideas. Sparta therefore withdrew its request for support. The Athenians took this as a grave insult to their honour. As Thucydides wrote, 'They were deeply offended … and allied themselves with Sparta's enemy, Argos.'[25]

The final spark came when a third city, Corinth, quarrelled with its colony at Corcyra. Thucydides explains that the Corinthians 'hated the Corcyreans because they failed to show Corinth the respect due from a colony to the mother city. … the Corcyreans did not give to Corinthians the usual rights and honours at public festivals … Indeed they looked down upon their mother city.'[26] Corcyra appealed to Athens for help, and when the Athenians sent a positive response, the Spartans joined the fray, complaining that this constituted a breach of the Spartan-Athenian alliance. Negotiations followed, and all the issues between Sparta and Athens were discussed. Agreement seemed within reach until the negotiations got stuck on a single point of honour – the Athenians' insistence that traders from the port of Megara be excluded from all ports in the Athenian empire. The Spartans were willing to keep the peace if this order was revoked, but the Athenians were adamant. Athenian leader Pericles is recorded by Thucydides as saying that one should not give in over a trifle. Although made up by Thucydides rather than said by Pericles himself, the following speech is a classic exposition of how the point of honour, however trivial, becomes a *casus belli*:

> For you this trifle is both the assurance and the proof of your determination. If you give in, you will be immediately confronted with some greater demand, since they will think that you only gave way on this point through fear. But if you take a firm stand you will make it clear to them that they have to treat you properly as equals … When one's equals, before resorting to arbitration, make claims on their neighbours and put those claims in the form of commands, it would be slavish to give in to them, however big or small such claims may be.[27]

Following this logic, the Athenians refused to cede over Megara. The Spartans declared war, and eventually defeated Athens 27 years later.

Two generations further on, a still belligerent, though much weakened, Athens took on the Macedon of King Philip II. We are fortunate that the speeches of the foremost Athenian 'war hawk', Demosthenes, have survived. These provide great insight into Athenian motivations.

Demosthenes built his career around efforts to persuade his fellow Athenians to wage war against Philip's growing power. Plutarch points out that in doing so, he followed a consistent line of policy:

> In most of these speeches ... we can trace the conviction that honour ought to be pursued for its own sake. In all these orations Demosthenes does not try to persuade his fellow-citizens to do what is most agreeable, or easy, or profitable, but time and again he argues that they ought to place their honour and their obligations before their safety or self-preservation.[28]

The specific charge which Demosthenes levelled against Philip was that he was guilty of 'hubris'. This term, of such importance in Greek warfare, is much misunderstood in the modern world. People often associate ancient Greek hubris with arrogance, and particularly with challenges to the gods (which were invariably punished, leading to another common Classical experience, that of 'nemesis'). For instance, in Sophocles' play *Ajax*, the eponymous hero disdains the help of the goddess Athena in battle. Told by his father, 'win, but win with God beside you', Ajax responds smartly, 'any fool can win with God beside him; I intend to win glory and honour on my own account.'[29] Ajax pays for his presumption when the gods drive him into insanity and eventually suicide.

Undoubtedly such arrogance constituted irreligious behaviour, but it was not what the Greeks meant by 'hubris'. Hubris, wrote Aristotle:

> consists of doing or saying such things as involve shame for the victim, not for some advantage for oneself other than that these have been done, but for the fun of it. ... The cause of pleasure for those insulting is that they think that by treating others badly they are themselves the superior.[30]

Given the importance Greeks attached to their personal honour, not surprisingly they considered hubris to be intolerable. Nonetheless, it was extremely common, for the simple reason that dishonouring others was such an obvious way of raising one's own relative status.

Philip was insolent, said Demosthenes, and his hubris had to be punished:

> Mark the situation, men of Athens: mark the pitch which the man's [Philip's] outrageous insolence has reached, when he does not even give you a choice between action and inaction, but threatens you, and utters haughty language. ... When, then, men of Athens, when, I say, will you take the action that is required? What are you waiting for? 'We are waiting', you say, 'till it is necessary.' But what must we think of all that is happening at this present time? Surely the strongest necessity that a free people can experience is the shame which they must feel at their position.[31]

> If he [Philip] were content to remain at peace, in possession of all that he has won by conquest or by forestalling us – if he had no further plans – even then, the record against us as a people, a record of shame and cowardice and all that is most dishonourable, would, I think, seem complete enough to some of you. But now he is always making some new attempt, always grasping after something more.[32]

Athens went to war against Macedon, and suffered a terrible defeat. Even afterwards, though, Demosthenes was still confident that he had been right. In a speech near the end of his life, he justified himself, saying, 'From the very first, I chose the straight and honest path in public life. I chose to foster the honour, the supremacy, the good name of my country, to seek to enhance them, and to stand or fall with them.'[33] Athens had been defeated, but had won honour by fighting:

> Had she [Athens] surrendered without a struggle … with what faces should we have looked upon those who came to visit the city, if events had come round to the same conclusion as they now have … it was not tolerable … Throughout all time she [Athens] has maintained her perilous struggle for pre-eminence, honour, and glory.[34]

Hubris manifested itself at both the collective and the individual level. Throughout most of the period, it is clear that Greek states deliberately insulted and demeaned others for no better reason than the satisfaction to be derived from their own resultant relative elevation. Athens, for instance, undertook the subjugation of Melos when it refused to join its alliance because: 'if we were on friendly terms with you, our subjects would regard that as a sign of weakness, whereas your hatred is evidence of our power.'[35] The Athenians did this even though they knew perfectly well that Melos had no hostile intentions against them. Eventually, they attacked somebody whom they could not beat, and nemesis caught up with them.

This happened in 416 BC when Athens took on the city of Syracuse in Sicily, launching a disastrous expedition which was sparked off partly by rivalry between the Athenian politicians Alcibiades and Nicias. After Nicias had arranged a peace with Sparta and won great fame, Alcibiades, writes Plutarch, 'was vexed beyond measure at his rival's success and out of sheer jealousy began to plot a way of violating the treaty.' He urged his fellow-citizens to support an attack on Sicily, hoping to win command of the expedition, and gain glory for himself.[36] His tactic worked up to a point; war was declared, but he lost his command after some of his other rivals accused him of drunkenly defacing religious statues.

In this instance, an ambitious man provoked fighting in order to provide himself with an opportunity for glory. In Greece's Classical period, which had moved to mainly state-state rather than leader-leader relations, this was something of a rarity. Wars were more often a matter of inter-state status rivalry than the product of individual ambition. From the mid-fourth century BC, and into the Hellenistic period, there was a slide back into personal glory, with more wars being caused by and for individuals. This was perhaps a result of the decline of democratic government, and also of the rise of mercenary armies, which gave rulers more leeway to indulge their ambitions.

Alexander the Great is the prime example of a ruler whose campaigns cannot be adequately explained in terms of material gain, state interest, or questions of security. His conquests so exceeded what was necessary for those purposes that only considerations of honour could have motivated him. It would appear that Alexander was driven by an unquenchable thirst for glory, and sought continuous war in order to win recognition as the foremost warrior in the world. This is certainly how ancient historians saw his actions. According to Arrian, Alexander 'longed to equal the fame of Perseus and Heracles';[37] 'his passion was for glory only, and in that he was insatiable.'[38] Plutarch claims that during the crossing of the River Hydaspes in 326 BC in the face of the army of the Indian King Porus, Alexander said, 'O you Athenians, will you ever believe what risks I am running just to earn your praise?'[39] These and other recorded or invented sayings of Alexander's indicate that the Greeks considered his main war aim to have been the pursuit of honour and glory.

After Alexander's death, his empire was split into several smaller Hellenistic kingdoms. Although the rulers of these waged almost continuous internecine war, they avoided eliminating each other altogether. Kings wished to gain acknowledgement of their superiority from other kings, and therefore did not wish to kill them.[40] Thus in 312 BC, when one of Alexander's successors, Ptolemy, defeated another, Demetrius, Ptolemy restored to Demetrius all his possessions, adding 'the courteous message that they were not engaged in a struggle for life or death, but only for honour and power.'[41] Determined not to remain in Ptolemy's debt, Demetrius subsequently defeated one of Ptolemy's generals, Cilles, and returned the favour. He 'loaded Cilles and his companions with gifts and sent them back to Ptolemy'.[42] War of this sort had little purpose other than to satisfy men's pride.

Honour as a motivation for fighting

For much of the Classical era, citizen armies dominated Greek wars. All freeborn men were expected to fight as the price of their status. From around 400 BC, there was a growth in mercenary forces and purely monetary motivations became a factor in recruiting soldiers. Nonetheless, honour remained an important element in impelling men both to participate in wars and to stay in the ranks once fighting had begun. It also had a substantial impact on the ways in which they fought.

Glory-seeking trumped tactical commonsense time after time. At Thermopylae, the Spartan King Leonidas ordered most of his allies to withdraw before the battle, 'but said that he himself could not draw back with honour, knowing that, if he stayed, glory awaited him.' He wanted the allies to leave so that he could keep 'the whole glory for the Spartans', and not have to share it with them.[43] This fixation on monopolizing the glory often caused disaster. During the siege of Syracuse, the Athenian commander Nicias wanted to avoid a naval battle before the arrival of reinforcements. On the other hand, wrote Plutarch,

> The newly promoted Euthydemus and Menander were strongly tempted to risk a battle, partly through personal ambition and partly through their jealousy of the other two generals; they hoped to outshine Nicias on the spot and to distinguish themselves before [the reinforcements] could arrive. They therefore made great play with the prestige of Athens, which they maintained would be irretrievably damaged if they refused battle with the Syracusan

> fleet, and on this pretext they overruled Nicias and forced a decision to fight by sea. In the action that followed, they … were defeated with heavy loss.[44]

Ostentatious displays of courage were also a perennial feature of Greek tactics. For instance, when the Persian king defeated Cyrus, a pretender to his throne, Cyrus' army of Greek mercenaries, under the command of Xenophon, had to fight their way back to safety through what is now Turkey. Xenophon records that on the march, during an attack on a barbarian stronghold, a soldier named Callimachus ran forward to draw the enemy's fire and make them use up the supply of stones which they were rolling down the cliff on to the only approach. He kept running forward and then quickly back again, each time provoking more stones and using them up. But, wrote Xenophon:

> When Agasias saw what Callimachus was doing, and with the whole army for spectators, he became fearful that he would not be the first to make the run across to the stronghold; so … he dashed forward himself and proceeded to go past everybody. Callimachus, however, when he saw him going by, seized the rim of his shield; and at that moment Aristonymus of Methydrium ran past both of them, and upon his heels Eurylochus of Lusi. For all these four were rivals in valour and continually striving with one another; and in thus contending they captured the stronghold.[45]

In a similar vein, when the army of Alexander the Great was besieging the city of Hallicarnassus, Arrian claims that:

> Two Macedonian infantrymen of Perdicass' battalion were drinking together in their tent and telling each other what stout fellows they were; as they warmed up with the drink, each bragging as hard as he could go, it soon developed into a competition between the pair of them, until at last they seized their weapons and, … simply to prove to each other what mighty fellows they were, sallied out on their own to attack the wall of the town.[46]

According to Arrian, other members of their unit then had to come to their aid, and a major battle ensued, in which 'the town itself was nearly taken.'

Excess of heroism was spurred on by fear of shame as well as a desire for honour. The Spartans in particular had very extreme methods of shaming those who performed poorly in battle. According to Plutarch, disgraced soldiers could neither hold office nor marry, had to wear dishevelled clothes, and were obliged to shave one half of their beards while leaving the other half uncut.[47] Xenophon, who became a friend of the Spartan monarch Agesilaus, and a great admirer of Spartan society, commented that 'at Sparta everyone would be ashamed to be associated with a coward in his mess or to have him as a wrestling partner.' He continued:

> When sides are being picked for a ball game that sort of man is often left out with no position assigned, and in dances he is banished to the insulting

> places. Moreover in the streets he is required to give way, as well as to give up his seat even to younger men. The girls of his family he has to support at home, and must explain to them why they cannot get husbands. He must endure having a household with no wife, and at the same time has to pay a fine for this. He must not walk around with a cheerful face, nor must he imitate men of impeccable reputation: otherwise he must submit to being beaten by his betters.[48]

Punishments like these were inflicted even on men who failed through no fault of their own. According to Herodotus, two Spartans were sick before the battle at Thermopylae and Leonidas ordered them to leave the camp. Once the battle started, one sick man, Eurytus, rushed to join in, while the other, Aristodemus, did not. As a result, Aristodemus survived the slaughter of all 300 members of the Spartan force. On his return to Sparta, he was disgraced: 'no Spartan would give him a light to kindle his fire, or so much as address a word to him … all spoke of him as "the craven".' Herodotus also claimed that, 'Another of the three hundred is likewise said to have survived the battle, a man named Pantites, whom Leonidas had sent on an embassy into Thessaly. He, they say, on his return to Sparta, found himself in such disesteem that he hanged himself.'[49]

Xenophon concluded that, 'When disgrace of this kind is imposed on cowards I am certainly not at all surprised that death is preferred there to a life of such dishonour and ignominy.'[50] In the case of Aristodemus, he felt his dishonour so powerfully that, one year later at the battle of Plataea, he performed acts of great bravery, openly courting death, in order to wipe out his shame.[51]

These values were so accepted that most Spartans had internalized them. One suspects that after a lifetime's exposure to propaganda of this sort, most of them would have agreed fully with Tyrtaeus and sought to emulate the ideal warrior he portrayed:

> Though he may fall and die, struck
> in the chest a hundred times
> despite his shield and breastplate, he leaves his fame
> to his city, people, and father.
> …
> his tomb and children are famous, even his children's
> children and later descendants.
> His name and legend never die. Lying
> in the earth, he becomes immortal.
> …
> Climb the hill of virtue, soldier – never
> soften your warrior's heart.[52]

In theory, the pursuit of individual honour was supposed to enhance the collective honour. In practice, the two often clashed. During the ill-fated expedition to Syracuse, Nicias was urged to withdraw the Athenian army from Sicily while it was still possible. But Nicias was afraid of what the people in Athens would say about him if he did. He had, after all, opposed the expedition, and so might be accused of deliberately sabotaging it. By the time he agreed to withdraw, the Syracusans had defeated the Athenian fleet, and withdrawal was no longer possible.

To try to protect the interests of the collective, honour came to be intimately connected with patriotism, in which the honour of the citizen was dependent on the honour of his city-state. If his city lost honour, so did he. This was especially true of the Spartans. Plutarch wrote that, 'the Spartans, whenever any question of honour arises, always give first place to their country's interest; they refuse to learn or understand any other concept of justice, except for such action as they believe will make Sparta great.'[53] Athenians thought along similar lines. Demosthenes stated in his speech *On the Crown* that:

> He who thinks that he was born for his parents alone awaits the death which destiny assigns him in the course of nature: but he who thinks he was born for his country also will be willing to die that he may not see her in bondage, and will look upon the outrages and the indignities that he must needs bear in a city that is in bondage as more to be dreaded than death.[54]

Generals who, for the common good, put aside opportunities for personal glory, were regarded as particularly worthy of honour. A prime example of this is the Athenian Aristides, known as 'the Just'. When the Athenians fought the Persians at the battle of Marathon, the Athenian army was under the command of ten generals, one for each of the tribes which made up the population of Athens. Command rotated between them, each general holding it for one day at a time. But, 'when Aristides' turn arrived, he handed over authority to Miltiades.' The others followed suit, thus giving Miltiades 'undivided authority', and enabling him to win the battle.[55] To Aristides at least, the honour of the collective appears to have meant more than the opportunity for self-promotion.

Despite this, it was possible to switch sides and betray one's city without incurring total dishonour. The Athenian commander Themistocles patriotically surrendered his command and his chance at maximum glory to another at the battle of Salamis against the Persians, but a few years later was exiled from Athens 'to humble his great reputation', and went to work for his former enemy, the Persians.[56] Similarly, Alcibiades, after losing his chance to command the Athenian expedition to Sicily, fled to Sparta and took up arms against his own city. He next switched sides again, and went to work for the King of Persia, then finally betrayed the Persians as well and went back to Athens,[57] where he was welcomed as a potential saviour during a grave crisis near the end of the Peloponnesian War. While patriotism was a virtue, it seems to have been rather a mobile one.

Honours and rewards

In many cases the reward for success or virtuous behaviour was no more than a good name, but there could also be tangible rewards: money, prizes, booty, promotion, crowns, statues, and inscriptions. The first three of these were of use not merely for their monetary value, but as status symbols and levers to gain further honour by displaying generosity through gift-giving. The recipient of any gift was placed in a subordinate position, thus boosting the giver's status. All prizes, in fact, had worth beyond their material value, since they gave proof of honour and status.

Loot being an important matter, Greek armies exercised considerable control over the distribution of the spoils of war. Soldiers were meant to hand over booty, as it was considered common property. Often a tenth was then set aside for the gods, to fund construction of temples and statues of the gods. For instance, the Athenians used a tenth of the booty from their victory over the Persians at the battle of Eurymedon to erect a statue at Delphi of a 'bronze tree crowned by a gilded statue of Athena'.[58]

Commanders distributed the rest of the booty so as to provide pay for their soldiers, to reward those who had performed gallantly, and to reward themselves. As in most cultures, rank seems to have played a part, with those in senior positions being entitled to a greater share of the spoils.

Bringing home seized armour was good proof of having vanquished an opponent. Even senior Greek officers readily stripped the armour off their defeated opponents, live or dead. Arrian describes Ptolemy, one of Alexander's most senior commanders, killing an Indian warleader and stripping his body. This action resulted in a fierce battle with the Indians for possession of the corpse.[59]

Some of the armour thus gained became public property. Cities marked their victories by dedicating complete suits ('panoplies') of enemy armour to the gods, and hanging them in their temples. After defeating the Persians at Granicus, Alexander 'sent to Athens 300 full suits of Persian armour, with the following inscription: Alexander, son of Philip, and the Greeks (except the Lacedaemonians) dedicate these spoils, taken from the Persians who dwell in Asia'.[60] (The spiteful reference to the Lacedaemonians – the Greek name for the Spartans – was because they had refused to join the army Alexander had led into Persia.)

As it happens, the Spartans did not share the habit of hanging panoplies in temples anyway. Asked why, the Spartan King Cleomenes reputedly replied, 'Because they come from cowards.'[61]

Temples full of captured equipment testified to the greatness of a city. Individual symbolic displays were equally important. A common reward was a crown of olive leaves. Other soldiers were rewarded with promotions. Statues were yet another form of commemoration. These might be either statues of the gods, with inscriptions explaining the reason for their dedication, or statues of the winning generals themselves. Thus we learn from Plutarch that after defeating Athens at the naval battle of Aegospotami, and forcing the Athenians to surrender, 'Lysander set up bronze statues of himself and each of his two admirals at Delphi.'[62] More modestly, after Cimon captured the city of Eion from the Persians, the Athenians 'authorized him to dedicate three stone statues of Hermes at Athens' with inscriptions celebrating the victory. 'Although Cimon's name does not appear in any of these inscriptions, his contemporaries regarded this memorial as a supreme mark of honour for him.'[63]

At the battle site, victorious armies recorded their honour by setting up trophies, a custom possibly developed from a way of thanking the gods. Strict conventions governed trophies. They consisted of captured arms and armour set out in human form on a tree, and were intended to decay with time and fall apart. A permanent trophy would have acted as a continual reminder to the defeated party of its inferiority, and to humiliate an enemy in this way would have been an unwise act of hubris. Greeks did not, therefore, erect permanent monuments of their victories over other Greeks, although they did do so to celebrate their battles against the Persians, setting up permanent memorials at both Marathon and Thermopylae. Only once was this rule broken, when the Thebans built a permanent trophy on the battlefield of Leuktra to celebrate their overwhelming victory over the Spartans there. The Spartans protested that such a monument broke the rules of honourable behaviour, but were too weak to do anything about it.[64] The base of the monument stands to this day.

The importance of trophies was such that they became a battle aim in themselves. The right to set up a trophy belonged to the side which, at the end of a battle, controlled the ground on which the battle had been fought.[65] The reason for this was that possession of the battlefield gave one control over the bodies of the dead who lay there. To bury their dead, those who had withdrawn from the site would have to ask for a truce to recover them, and in so doing, they put themselves in a position of indebtedness and inferiority.[66] The result of this rule was that possession of the battlefield became the primary aim of combat, regardless of other tactical or strategic considerations.

In consequence, Greek battles tended to stop as soon as one side broke and fled. At that point the victors had done enough to merit a trophy and felt no need to do any more. Plutarch claims that after the Spartans had beaten their enemies, 'they gave chase only far enough to confirm their victory by their opponents' flight, and then at once pulled back.'[67] Inevitably, this made victories rather inconclusive, as victors lost opportunities to destroy retreating enemies.

The defeated commander would, in any case, have problems enough of his own. The Greeks were very unforgiving of defeat, which they regarded as a great disgrace. Those who failed to perform as expected were very often put on trial and punished. Thucydides, for instance, went into exile for some unknown failing as a general.

Surprisingly, the Greeks did not merely punish those who failed – they often also punished those who succeeded! Envy was the reason.[68] Honour in the sense of precedence is a limited good, since not all can be first among men. Those who do not come first tend to be extremely jealous of those who do, and to want to humble them. Successful generals had to face the possibility that their fellow-citizens would greet their triumphs not with joy but with consternation, and would immediately look for some excuse to take them down a peg or two. Even the most brilliant commanders experienced this. The Theban generals Epaminondas and Pelopidas, who were responsible for destroying the Spartan army at Leuktra, had to extend their year in command to carry the war into Spartan territory. 'As their fame grew', writes Plutarch, 'so did the envy of their compatriots. … On their return both Pelopidas and Epaminondas were put on trial for their lives', for not having resigned their commands.[69] They were acquitted, but others were not so lucky. The Athenian admirals who defeated the Spartan fleet at Arginusae were sentenced to death for choosing to pursue the enemy fleet rather than pick up survivors, and the Athenian general Paches 'killed himself in open court' when he was forced to account for his actions after capturing the island of Lesbos.[70]

In Athens, the formal mechanism to limit the influence of those who gathered too much honour was ostracism. Under this system, the Athenians could vote to exile for ten years anybody they wished. The person ostracized did not have to have committed any crime; indeed, he rarely had. Ostracism was a punishment reserved for the honourable. Athenians used it to get rid of those who had excelled too much. Those exiled in this way included great leaders such as Themistocles and Aristides. The practice continued until Nicias and Alcibiades, after campaigning to ostracize one another, decided to save themselves by ganging up on a weaker third party, Hyperbolus. Athenians considered that the ostracizing of such an unimportant figure had degraded the entire institution, and the practice thereafter ceased.

Honour-envy had real consequences for military operations. Fear of provoking it made some generals worried about winning too much honour, and prompted them to act with caution. Nicias is a prime example of this. Plutarch says that Nicias 'noticed that while the people were ready to make use of men who excelled in eloquence or intellectual power, they still looked on them with suspicion and constantly strove to humble their pride or detract from their reputation.' As a result, 'whenever he was a general he played for safety.'[71] This may well have contributed to his catastrophic handling of the Sicilian expedition.

Death and honour

As in nearly all cultures, in ancient Greece people believed that it was better to die than to be dishonoured. This did not mean that the ancient Greeks sought death. In Homer's *Odyssey*, when Odysseus meets Achilles in the underworld, the latter wishes he were living the lowliest life on earth rather than being dead with glory. The Greek attitude was clearly expressed by Euripides in his play *The Women of Troy*:

> Any sensible man must hate war,
> He does his best to avoid it. But if it should come,
> Even if it should end like this, it is no shame
> For a city, indeed, it is a crown of honour
> To die nobly, with dignity. The really shameful thing
> Is to die dishonourably, ignobly, without pride.[72]

In the face of total disgrace, suicide was an option. At the end of the Sicilian expedition, for instance, the Athenian commander Demosthenes attempted suicide but was captured before he could die. His colleague Nicias chose to surrender voluntarily. The Syracusans later executed both men, but Athenians viewed Demosthenes as the more honourable. The memorial outside Athens to the dead of the Sicilian expedition bore the names of all those who fell, including Demosthenes, and excepting only Nicias, because the latter was 'condemned a voluntary prisoner and an unworthy soldier'.[73] Nonetheless, Demosthenes' attempt at suicide was quite a rare example, and suicide does not appear often in Greek histories, especially when compared with Roman ones.

The treatment of the dead was a matter of prime importance. Greek religion required that each man receive a proper burial, and it became not just a religious obligation but also a matter of honour to ensure that this happened. One had either to recapture bodies during battle, or ask for a truce and thereby concede defeat. Cunning enemies could exploit this by making it difficult for bodies to be retrieved. For instance, when Corinth beat off a Theban attack in 369 BC, the Corinthians placed the bodies of the dead Thebans directly under their walls (where anybody trying to collect them would come under heavy fire), so that Thebes would have to sue for a truce to regain them.

To prevent this sort of thing from happening, as well as to prevent the desecration of the dead, Greek armies would expend very considerable efforts on keeping their dead from falling into enemy hands. Thus in the *Iliad* the Trojan Glaukos urges his comrades to defend the body of his dead colleague Sarpedon, telling them, 'Come then, friends, stand by him, with shame and anger in your hearts to stop the Myrmidons [Achilles' troops] stripping his armour and dishonouring his body.'[74]

The Athenians and Thebans may have attached rather more importance to recovering the dead than the Spartans, who seem to have placed a greater emphasis on victory. During the Peloponnesian War, Nicias undertook an amphibious raid against Corinthian territory. When his soldiers re-embarked on their ships afterwards they realized that the bodies of two men had been left behind. In military terms the raid was a success and the Corinthians had suffered heavy losses. Asking for a truce to recover the two bodies would, under the rules of war, be an admission of defeat. Nevertheless, Nicias did just that, and in this way 'preferred to renounce the victory and his personal triumph rather than allow two of his fellow-countrymen to lie unburied.' In a similar fashion, the Athenian admiral Chabrias, possibly bearing in mind what had happened to his colleagues after their victory at Arginusae, failed to destroy a Spartan fleet when he had the opportunity to do so, because he stopped his attack to pick up survivors and the bodies of the dead.[75] In contrast, when the Spartan leader Pausanias agreed to a truce to collect the bodies of comrades killed outside Thebes, he was sentenced to death upon his return to Sparta for 'taking the bodies of the dead under a truce, instead of trying to recover them in battle'.[76] The difference between the Spartans and the Athenians may have been due to the fact that Athens was a democracy and so placed greater emphasis on the rights of the individual, even in death.

Different cities also buried their dead differently. The Spartans buried theirs at the site where they fell in combat. The Athenians normally brought theirs home, sometimes after cremating them. The one exception was Marathon, that victory being considered so important that the dead could best be honoured by being left there. Burial mounds on battle sites advertised the sacrifices made by a city and thus brought it honour. Herodotus claimed that those cities who lost no citizens in the decisive battle of Plataea against the Persians 'erected empty barrows upon the field, to obtain credit with those who should come after them'.[77]

Collective graves on battlefields were often inscribed with suitable epitaphs. The most famous is that written by Simonides for the Spartan dead at Thermopylae:

> Tell them in Sparta, passer-by,
> That here, obedient to their words, we lie.[78]

Spartan epitaphs tended to emphasize dying for one's country, Athenian ones liberty. Thus the difference between the following two epitaphs written by Simonides for those killed fighting the Persians at Plataea:

For the Spartans:

> Into the dark death they passed, to set
> Fame on their own dear land for fadeless wreath,
> And dying died not. Valour lifts them yet
> Into the splendour from the night beneath.

And for the Athenians:

> If Valour's best be gallantly to die
> Fortune to us of all men grant it now.
> We to set Freedom's crown on Hellas' brow
> Laboured, and here in ageless honour lie.[79]

After bringing the bodies or ashes home, the Athenians buried their war dead on both sides of the road leading out of the city to the Academy. The ashes were stored in individual urns, and the name of every dead soldier was inscribed on a stone 'casualty list'. Each tribe put up a separate such list every year.[80] Pausanias recorded a similar method of honouring the dead at the grave at Marathon, which he said had on it 'slabs giving the names of the killed according to their tribe'.[81] These sort of monuments strongly resemble the type of war memorial which became common in Western Europe and North America in the twentieth century, also listing the name of every soldier however humble.

Honour and the conduct of war

The Greeks had firm ideas on acceptable conduct in war. Fleeing from the battlefield was clearly dishonourable. Tyrtaeus wrote, 'You, young men, keep together, hold the line, do not start panic, or disgraceful rout',[82] and Xenophon commented that 'to retire before an enemy is not fitting for any man of honour.'[83] Loss of one's shield was a particular mark of dishonour. A shield was heavy, and easily disposed of, so a soldier in flight would drop it. This explains the famous exhortation of Spartan mothers to their children to come home with their shields, or on them (although in reality Spartan women are most unlikely to have said this since Spartans were buried where they fell and would never have been brought back on their shields). Legend had it that Epaminondas, dying on the battlefield of Mantinea, ordered 'the javelin to be plucked from his body only after he had been told in answer to his question that his shield was safe, so that even in the agony of his wound he could meet an honourable death with mind at ease.'[84]

Nonetheless, some Greeks seem to have felt that discretion was the better part of valour. In the *Iliad*, Agamemnon comments that 'there is no shame in running from disaster, even by night: better to run and escape disaster than be caught in it.'[85] In the *Odyssey*, Odysseus argues that there is no defence against Scylla, 'and valour lies in flight'.[86] The soldier-poet Archilochus put it in rather more flippant tones:

> A perfect shield bedecks some Thracian now;
> I had no choice: I left it in a wood.
> Ah, well, I saved my skin, so let it go!
> A new one's just as good.[87]

The Greeks were ambivalent about the use of ruses in war. Their attitude towards Odysseus, the arch-deceiver in Greek mythology, is characteristic. On the one hand, he is undoubtedly a hero, and his cunning is a source of admiration. On the other hand, there is sometimes a sense that he does not play fair. Thus in the *Odyssey*, he is lauded as 'the admirable Odysseus, who in every kind of strategy proved himself supreme',[88] but in Euripides' *Women of Troy* he is described as 'a man without morality, a liar, a deceiver, to whom the laws of gods and men mean nothing.'[89]

Greek warfare reflected this ambiguity concerning deception. Xenophon's *Anabasis* is full of examples of sly barbarians, and Xenophon comments that 'if men are seen to practise truth, their words, if they desire anything, have power to accomplish no less than force in the hands of other men.'[90] Thucydides cites the Spartan leader Brasidas as saying:

> It is more disgraceful, at least for those who have a name to lose, to gain one's end by deceit which pretends to be morality than by open violence. Straightforward aggression has a certain justification in the strength that is given us by fortune; but the other form of attack comes simply from the treacherous devices of an evil mind.[91]

Overall, the Greeks did show a preference for open battle and face-to-face combat. The dominant force in combat was the hoplite – a heavily armed infantryman – and hoplites sought to preserve their dominance by restricting fighting to situations where they were at their strongest, namely set-piece battles on open terrain. They discouraged other forms of combat by suggesting that these were somehow dishonourable because they did not require real courage. As Euripides wrote: 'the bow is no proof of manly courage; no, your real man stands firm in the ranks and dares to face the gash the spear makes.'[92]

That said, Greek histories are full of examples of unabashed treachery. Numerous cities were captured when the gates were opened by traitors within the walls. Greek armies often used ambushes, deception, and other *ruses de guerre* to achieve their objectives. The great Spartan commander Lysander, for instance, defeated the Athenian fleet at Aegospotami by launching his fleet and then withdrawing it every day without attacking, until he had lured the Athenians into a false sense of security. When he at last launched the real attack, he took the Athenians entirely by surprise. Before the battle of Salamis, Themistocles sent a message by one of his slaves to the Persian king stating that he wished to defect, and advising him that the Greeks were quarrelling and an immediate attack would serve him well. This led the Persians into a trap prepared by the Greeks, and resulted in the destruction of their fleet.[93] The Spartan admiral Erybiades, who disapproved of Themistocles' underhand methods, supposedly told him: 'You know, Themistocles, at the games they thrash anybody who starts before the signal'; to which came the reply: 'Yes, but they do not crown anybody who gets left at the post.'[94]

Another aspect of honour on the battlefield was the Greek habit of posting their best units on the far right of the line of battle. This was the place of greatest honour, followed by the left half of the left wing, the right half of the left wing, and then the left half of the right wing. The centre was the least honourable position.[95] Accordingly, the Spartans always placed themselves on the right, with their allies to their left. Alexander the Great similarly always led from the right, and all his great victories featured assaults on the enemy's left by him and his elite Royal Guards. This practice contrasted with that of the Persians, whose king led from the centre.

When coalitions of Greek cities were fighting together, disputes over the position of honour could cause serious problems. Before the battle of Plataea, for instance, the Tegeans and Athenians argued over who should take the second place in precedence after the Spartans. Eventually, Aristides agreed to sacrifice the place in favour of Tegea, a decision which so impressed the other nations that they immediately gave it to Athens instead.[96]

It is not clear why the right of the line was so prestigious. One explanation lies in the tendency, described by Thucydides, of Greek armies to drift to the right. This happened because as the troops advanced in formation, with a spear in their right hand and a shield in their left, each man took shelter behind the shield of his neighbour. As they advanced, reasons of self-preservation made every man shuffle just a little bit further under the shield to his right, so gradually moving the formation rightwards. It followed that one wanted one's bravest men on the far right, where they would have no shield protecting them, and yet would advance straight forward, resisting the pressure from those on their left to move right.

Whether this is the true explanation or not, the practice had peculiar consequences in Greek battles. Sometimes both sides triumphed on their right wings and lost on their left, and in consequence, the whole battle would swivel round in an anti-clockwise direction. The great Theban leader Epaminondas exploited this to defeat the Spartans at the battle of Leuktra. Knowing that the Spartans would take the right wing, and their allies the left, Epaminondas reversed normal practice and placed his own elite forces, the Sacred Band, on his left, and then strengthened them by making the formation several ranks deeper than normal. The idea was that this would enable him to smash the Spartans, after which their allies would collapse. Epaminondas's strategy worked perfectly, and Spartan power was shattered, never to recover.

Honour and the enemy

Some Greeks undoubtedly regarded granting mercy as a mark of honour. Xenophon, for instance, records that the inhabitants of Philus,

> When they made a prisoner of Proxenus, from Pellene, they let him go without a ransom, even though they themselves were short of everything. There is no question that men who did deeds like this must be called noble men and great warriors.[97]

Xenophon, though, was exceptionally moralistic in tone, and his chosen example does not seem representative of normal Greek warfare.[98] Greek warriors regularly slaughtered those at their mercy. In the *Iliad* Achilles cuts the throats of 12 Trojan children as a sacrifice at the funeral of his friend Patroclus. When Menelaos considers ransoming a prisoner, Agamemnon reproaches him: 'why this concern for men's lives? … Not one of them must escape stark destruction at our hands, even the boys still carried in their mothers' wombs – even they must not escape.'[99] Such attitudes carried over into real warfare in the Classical age. The Athenians massacred all the adult males of Melos, and sold the women and children into slavery.[100] It must be said, though, that such massacres only took place after sieges, and not after pitched battles.[101] This reflects a common pattern in warfare in which different rules apply to sieges and battles, and those who are defeated in the former suffer much more harshly than in the latter.

In addition, non-Greeks suffered harsher treatment than Greeks, so confirming another general rule of war: that the laws of war tend to apply only to people of the same culture. Greeks did not massacre each other after pitched battles, but did slaughter Persians after both Marathon and Plataea. In the Peloponnesian War, however, the laws of intra-Greek warfare broke down, and atrocities which would previously have been unthinkable took place on a regular basis. Thucydides complained that as the situation deteriorated:

> Neither side had any use for conscientious motive; more interest was shown in those who could produce attractive arguments to justify some disgraceful action … no guarantee could be given that could be trusted, no oath sworn that people would fear to break.[102]

The Peloponnesian War was an unusually prolonged one, and in general the longer war lasts, the harder it becomes to maintain the initial code of honour.

Honour and the ending of wars

Because Greeks so often interpreted victory very narrowly in terms of gaining the battlefield and the right to set up a trophy, many wars were short and easily ended. One side won a quick victory in a pitched battle, thereby proving its pre-eminence, and the war was concluded. Sometimes, though, hubristic behaviour extended the length of conflicts because those who had gained a dominant position enjoyed humiliating their opponents too much to allow peace to last long.

Thucydides was aware of the problems that this caused. He describes the situation which arose in the Peloponnesian War on the island of Sphacteria, where the Athenians had trapped 400 Spartan soldiers. This was a highly unusual event, since people were very rarely able to capture Spartans, let alone such large numbers of them. The Athenians were in an extremely strong position to make peace with Sparta in return for the freedom of the men trapped on Sphacteria. However, their determination to impose intolerable terms in a humiliating fashion ensured that Sparta could not accept them. The most insufferable demand made by the Athenian commander Cleon was that negotiations be conducted 'in front of everyone', not in secret. The Spartans refused this hubristic suggestion, stating that 'even if they did decide to make concessions in their present difficult position, they might well speak and still not get what they wanted, and find that what they had said would give them a bad name with their allies.'[103] Questions of honour thus ensured that this opportunity for peace was lost.

In describing the incident, Thucydides puts words into the mouths of the Spartans which powerfully portray the need for those wanting peace to treat their enemies with honour:

> In our view, where great hatreds exist, no lasting settlement can be made in a spirit of revenge when one side gets the better of things in war and forces its opponent to swear to carry out the terms of an unequal treaty; what will make the settlement lasting is when the party that has it in its power to act like this takes instead a more reasonable point of view, overcomes his adversary in generosity, and makes peace on more moderate terms than his enemy expected. In such a case, so far from wanting to get his own back for the violence that has been done to him, the enemy is already under an obligation to pay back good for good, and so is the more ready, from a sense of honour, to abide by the terms that have been made.[104]

Numerous failed peace efforts in the past two and half thousand years have borne out the wisdom of Thucydides' comments.

Women and honour

Ancient Greece was a male-dominated society. Histories of Greek wars barely mention women, and when they do, it is normally as passive victims. It would appear, however, that at least in Sparta women did play an important role in provoking men to war and enforcing the code of honour.

Spartan women were fiercely independent. Many owned property, and as their husbands ate and spent much of their time in soldiers' messes, they did not have the same domestic burdens as women in other cities. They had few qualms about pushing themselves forward and telling men how to behave, but they tended to support the status quo. As one study of Spartan women concludes, 'not only did women sanction the official ideology of motherhood, but several, in fact, were architects of it.' Thus, when the traitor Pausanias took refuge in the temple of Athena, his mother Theano 'placed a brick at the door of the temple and left. Following her example, [others] then blocked up the doors, leaving Pausanias inside.'[105]

Deeds like this find a reflection in the *Sayings of Spartan Women*. These sayings were collected many years after Sparta's era of dominance, and may be entirely apocryphal. Still, they indicate what other Greeks imagined typical Spartan women would say and do:

> After hearing that her son was a coward and unworthy of her, Damatia killed him when he made his appearance.
>
> Another Spartan woman killed her son, who had deserted, as unworthy of his country, saying 'He's not my offspring.'
>
> When some woman had heard that her son had been saved and had escaped from the enemy, she wrote to him: 'You've been tarnished by a bad reputation. Either wipe it out or cease to exist.'
>
> Another woman, in reply to her son who declared that the sword he had was a small one, said: 'Then extend it by a stride.'[106]

With mothers like these, it is hardly surprising that the Spartans made tough soldiers. In 272 BC, Pyrrhus marched on Sparta and the Spartans considered sending their women away to safety. At that point, 'Archidamia walked into the Senate with a sword in her hand and reproached the Senators for proposing that the wives and daughters should survive while Sparta itself perished.' The women stayed and helped dig a trench to defend the city. They then handed the men their weapons, and 'reminded them that it would be sweet to conquer in sight of the whole country and glorious to die in the arms of their wives and mothers.' For two days, Pyrrhus' forces attempted to take the city by assault. 'The women too were in the thick of the action, handing the men arrows and javelins, bringing food and drink whenever they needed, and carrying away the wounded.'[107] In the end, the attackers retreated. The women of Sparta had saved their city.

Conclusion

Honour was central to the values of Classical Greece. In a culture which had only newly evolved from family/tribe groupings to the city-state, the concept of personal ranking in society carried over into inter-state relations. This led the Greeks into constant wars, most of them rather pointless.

The endless competition kept Greece permanently divided and weakened its ability to resist external enemies. Close by, in Italy, a disciplined and single-minded force was being built that would bring Greek dominance of the ancient world to an end. It is to Rome that we now turn.

Notes

1 Xenophon, *Hiero*, 7.3. Cited in Neyrey, Jerome H., *Honor and Shame in the Gospel of Matthew*, Louisville: Westminster John Knox Press, 1998, p. 17.
2 Pausanias, *Descriptions of Ancient Greece*, vol. 1, London: William Heinemann, 1918, p. 81.
3 Cited in Martin, Thomas R., *Ancient Greece: From Prehistoric to Hellenistic Times*, New Haven and London: Yale Nota Bene, 2000, p. 141.
4 Aristotle, *Ethics*, trans. J.A.K. Thompson, revised Hugh Tredennick, London: Penguin, 1976, p. 154.
5 Ibid, p. 104.
6 Ibid, pp. 153–4.
7 Plutarch, 'Agesilaus', in *The Age of Alexander: Nine Greek Lives*, trans. Ian Scott-Kilvert, London: Penguin, 1973, p. 29.
8 Plutarch, 'Lycurgus', in *Plutarch on Sparta*, trans. R.J.A. Talbert. London: Penguin, 1988, p. 30.
9 Sophocles, 'Ajax', in *Electra and Other Plays*, trans. E.F. Watling, Harmondsworth: Penguin, 1953, p. 34.
10 Demosthenes, *Prosecution of Androtion*, 75. Cited in Dover, K.J., *Greek Popular Morality in the Time of Plato and Aristotle*, Oxford: Basil Blackwell, 1974, p. 236.
11 Thucydides, *History of the Peloponnesian War*, trans Rex Warner, London: Penguin, 1972, p. 416.
12 Finley, M.I., *The World of Odysseus*, London: Pimlico, 1999, p. 57.
13 See, for instance, Dover, *Greek Popular Morality*, p. 226, and Dodds, E.R., *The Greeks and the Irrational*, Berkeley: University of California Press, 1951, p. 37.
14 Cairns, Douglas, *Aidos: The Psychology and Ethics of Honour and Shame in Ancient Greek Literature*, Oxford: Oxford University Press, 1992, p. 39. See also Lloyd-Jones, Hugh, 'Honour and Shame in Ancient Greek Culture', in *Greek Comedy, Hellenistic Literature, Greek Religion, and Miscellanea*, Oxford: Clarendon Press, 1990, p. 258.
15 Aristotle, *Ethics*, p. 284.
16 Aristotle, *The Art of Rhetoric*, trans. Hugh Lawson-Tancred, London: Penguin, 1991, p. 105.
17 Tyrtaeus, in Mulroy, David, *Early Greek Lyric Poetry*, Ann Arbor: University of Michigan Press, 1992, pp. 51–2.
18 Homer, *The Iliad: A New Prose Translation*, trans. Martin Hammond, Harmondsworth: Penguin, 1987, p. 172.
19 Mulroy, *Early Greek Lyric Poetry*, p. 48.
20 Plutarch, 'Pyrrhus', in *The Age of Alexander*, pp. 399–400.
21 Garlan, Yvon, *War in the Ancient World: A Social History*, London: Chatto & Windus, 1975, p. 15.
22 van Wees, Hans, *Status Warriors: War, Violence and Society in Homer and History*, Amsterdam: J.C. Gieben, 1992, p. 255.
23 Ibid, pp. 254–5.
24 Thucydides, *History of the Peloponnesian War*, p. 49.
25 Ibid, p. 95.
26 Ibid, p. 50.
27 Ibid, p. 119.

28 Plutarch, 'Demosthenes', in *The Age of Alexander*, p. 199.
29 Sophocles, 'Ajax', p. 43.
30 Aristotle, *The Art of Rhetoric*, p. 143. For a full analysis of Greek hubris, see Fisher, N.R.E., *Hybris: A Study in the Values of Honour and Shame in Ancient Greece*, Warminster: Aris & Phillips, 1992.
31 Demosthenes, 'The First Philippic', in *Demosthenes' Public Orations*, trans. A.W. Pickard-Cambridge, London: Dent, 1963, pp. 73–4.
32 Ibid, p. 83.
33 Demosthenes, 'On the Crown', in *Demosthenes' Public Orations*, pp. 409–10.
34 Ibid, p. 372.
35 Thucydides, *History of the Peloponnesian War*, p. 402.
36 Ibid, p. 418.
37 Arrian, *The Campaigns of Alexander*, trans. Aubrey de Selincourt, London: Penguin, 1971, p. 151.
38 Ibid, p. 395.
39 Plutarch, 'Alexander', in *The Age of Alexander*, p. 317.
40 Goldsworthy, Adrian, *Roman Warfare*, London: Cassell, 2002, p. 71.
41 Plutarch, 'Demetrius', in *The Age of Alexander*, p. 339.
42 Ibid, p. 340.
43 Herodotus, *The Histories*, trans. George Rawlinson, New York: Alfred A. Knopf Inc., 1997, p. 600.
44 Plutarch, 'Nicias', in *The Rise and Fall of Athens: Nine Greek Lives*, trans. Ian Scott-Kilvert, Harmondsworth: Penguin, 1973, p. 233.
45 Xenophon, *Anabasis*, trans. Carleton L. Browson, Cambridge, Mass.: Harvard University Press, 1998, pp. 359–61.
46 Arrian, *The Campaigns of Alexander*, p. 86.
47 Plutarch, 'Agesilaus', pp. 56–7.
48 Xenophon, 'Spartan Society', in *Plutarch on Sparta*, p. 176.
49 Herodotus, *The Histories*, p. 604.
50 Xenophon, 'Spartan Society', p. 176.
51 Herodotus, *The Histories*, p. 704.
52 Tyrtaeus, in Mulroy, *Early Greek Lyric Poetry*, p. 53.
53 Plutarch, 'Agesilaus', p. 65.
54 Demosthenes, 'On the Crown', p. 373.
55 Ibid, p. 114.
56 Plutarch, 'Themistocles', in *The Rise and Fall of Athens*, p. 98.
57 Plutarch, 'Alcibiades', in *The Rise and Fall of Athens*, pp. 265–72.
58 Pritchett, W. Kendrick, *The Greek State at War*, Part I, Berkeley: University of California Press, 1971, pp. 54–67.
59 Arrian, *The Campaigns of Alexander*, p. 242.
60 Ibid, p. 76.
61 Plutarch, 'Cleomenes', in *Plutarch on Sparta*, p. 141.
62 Plutarch, 'Lysander', in *The Rise and Fall of Athens*, p. 303.
63 Plutarch, 'Cimon', in *The Rise and Fall of Athens*, pp. 148–9.
64 Pritchett, Kendrick, *The Greek State at War*, Part II, p. 254.
65 Ibid, p. 259.
66 Plutarch, 'Nicias', p. 215.
67 Plutarch, 'Lycurgus', p. 35.
68 For a detailed analysis of this subject, see Walcot, Peter, *Envy and the Greeks: A Study in Human Behaviour*, Warminster: Aris & Phillips, 1978.
69 Plutarch, 'Pelopidas', in *The Age of Alexander*, pp. 90–1.
70 Plutarch, 'Nicias', p. 214.
71 Ibid, pp. 213–4.

72 Euripides, 'The Women of Troy', in *Euripides. Plays: Two*, London: Methuen, 1991, p. 64.
73 Pausanias, *Descriptions of Ancient Greece*, pp. 161–3.
74 Homer, *The Iliad*, pp. 279–80.
75 Pritchett, Kendrick, *The Greek State at War*, Part II, p. 31.
76 Xenophon, *A History of My Times*, pp. 180–1.
77 Herodotus, *The Histories*, p. 710.
78 Simonides, in Bowra, C.M., *Early Greek Elegists*, London: Oxford University Press, 1938, p. 193.
79 Ibid, pp. 196–7.
80 Garland, Robert, *The Greek Way of Death*, London: Duckworth, 1985, p. 90. Also, Stupperich, Reinhard, 'The Iconography of Athenian State Burials in the Classical Period', in Coulston, W.D.E. et al., *The Archeology of Athens and Attica under the Democracy*, Oxford: Oxbow, 1994, pp. 93–103.
81 Pausanias, *Descriptions of Ancient Greece*, p. 175.
82 Tyrtaeus, cited in Tritle, Lawrence A., *From Melos to My Lai: War and Survival*, London and New York: Routledge, 2000, p. 39.
83 Xenophon, *Anabasis*, p. 515.
84 Cicero, 'Letter to Lucceius', cited in Carter, John, 'Introduction', in Appian, *The Civil Wars*, trans. John Carter, London: Penguin, 1996, p. xix.
85 Homer, *The Iliad*, p. 245.
86 Homer, *The Odyssey*, trans. E.V. Rieu, Harmondsworth: Penguin, 1978, p. 192.
87 Archilochus, cited in Bowra, *Early Greek Elegists*, p. 10.
88 Homer, *The Odyssey*, p. 53.
89 Euripides, 'The Women of Troy', p. 60.
90 Xenophon, *Anabasis*, p. 629.
91 Thucydides, *History of the Peloponnesian War*, p. 317.
92 Euripides, 'Heracles', cited in Garlan, *War in the Ancient World*, p. 128.
93 Herodotus, *The Histories*, pp. 637–8.
94 Plutarch, 'Themistocles', p. 88.
95 Pritchett, Kendrick, *The Greek State at War*, Part II, p. 190.
96 Plutarch, 'Aristides', p. 123.
97 Xenophon, *A History of My Times*, pp. 374–5.
98 Pritchett, Kendrick, *The Greek State at War*, Part V, p. 208.
99 Homer, *The Iliad*, p. 131.
100 Thucydides, *History of the Peloponnesian War*, p. 408.
101 Kern, Paul Bentley, *Ancient Siege Warfare*, Bloomington and Indianapolis: Indiana University Press, 1999, p. 153.
102 Thucydides, *History of the Peloponnesian War*, p. 244.
103 Ibid, p. 277.
104 Ibid, pp. 275–6.
105 Pomeroy, Sarah B., *Spartan Women*, Oxford: Oxford University Press, 2002, p. 58.
106 'Sayings of Spartan Women', in *Plutarch on Sparta*, pp. 159–61.
107 Plutarch, 'Pyrrhus', pp. 417–9.

3 Ancient Rome

Background

According to Roman mythology, the brothers Romulus and Remus founded the city of Rome in the eighth century BC. For several centuries thereafter, the city remained a minor power on the Italian peninsula. The First Punic War against Carthage (264–241 BC) saw the Romans conquer territory outside the Italian mainland for the first time. In the Second Punic War (218–202 BC), Rome was almost crushed by the great Carthaginian general Hannibal, but ultimately prevailed and established its dominance over the Western Mediterranean. Rome's expansion continued relentlessly until it reached its territorial peak in the second century AD. Along the way, the original republican form of government collapsed as a result of prolonged civil wars, most notably those between Lucius Cornelius Sulla and Gaius Marius, Julius Caesar and Gnaeus Pompeius Magnus (Pompey the Great), and Mark Antony and Octavian. The Republic gave way to an Empire which lasted from the establishment of Octavian as the Emperor Augustus at the end of the first century BC to the collapse of Rome in the fifth century AD. The focus of this chapter is on the Republic and the years between the start of the First Punic War and the creation of the Empire (although some reference is made to earlier and later periods for the sake of comparison).

Roman honour was rather more complicated than Greek honour. The Romans were simultaneously merciful and brutal; exceedingly moralistic and callously indifferent to moral equations; and repeated aggressors yet firm believers that wars should only be fought in self-defence. Like the Greeks, they were highly competitive and encouraged the pursuit of external honour, but they were also given to very sophisticated moral reasoning. They managed in many ways to be startlingly modern, while in others still undeniably ancient.

The historian Sallust remarked that:

> Every man who wishes to rise superior to the lower animals should strive his hardest to avoid living all his days in silent obscurity, like the beasts of the field. Since only a short span of life has been vouchsafed us, we must make ourselves remembered as may be by those who come after us.[1]

Like the Greeks, Romans saw the pursuit of honour as useful to the common good. The Republic depended on this drive to get men to serve in and lead its armies, to staff the Senate and courts, and to fill the magistracies which governed the city.[2] Its political system both promoted and restrained ambition. Legislative power lay with the Senate of notables and an Assembly of citizens, whose representatives, the Tribunes, had a power of veto. Executive power belonged to a small group of magistrates (quaestors, praetors, aediles, censors, and consuls), who were elected for a one-year term of office by the people, but through a system of elections which gave the overwhelming share of the vote to the wealthiest propertied classes. Only a very few people could hope to rise to the top and become one of the two consuls who traditionally commanded Rome's field armies. This meant that great honour attached to these offices and men competed fiercely to acquire them.

Because their terms of office were limited to one year (and officially, one could only hold the post of consul at ten-year intervals, although this rule was sometimes broken), consuls felt impelled to carry out bold acts in the short time available to them so as to exploit the opportunity to win glory. This encouraged some of them to provoke enemies into war. On the other hand, because office was elective, terms were limited, power was always shared, and other competitive men were always keeping an eye out for reasons to bring down the mighty, there were factors constraining what an ambitious Roman might do. Eventually, these constraints proved insufficient, and popular generals began to amass increasing power in their own hands. In due course this led to civil war and eventually to the collapse of the Republic.

Honour and virtue in ancient Rome

There were Romans who were scornful of glory and believed that true honour lay only in virtue, that it was internal to the individual. This was especially true of followers of the philosophy of Stoicism, which taught that the road to happiness lay through the improvement of the inner self. The Emperor Marcus Aurelius, for instance, wrote that, 'honour and dishonour … are equally the lot of good men and bad. Things like these neither elevate nor degrade; and therefore they are no more good than bad.'[3] Equally, the satirist Juvenal beseeched a friend not to bother suing somebody who had wronged him, because that person would not escape punishment – he would be tormented by his conscience: 'No guilty person, although he may have suborned some judge to award him a rigged verdict can ever win acquittal at the bar of his own conscience.'[4] 'There is', he continued, 'one path, and only one, to a life of peace – through virtue.'[5] The great orator and statesman Cicero similarly urged Romans to ignore human fame, and to 'instead let Virtue herself, by her own unaided allurements summon you to a glory that is genuine and real.'[6] Despite such fine sentiments, few men were in fact ready to forego public acknowledgement of their virtues.

The values embodied in Roman virtue were 'overwhelmingly those of a warrior culture'.[7] As Plutarch wrote: 'there is only one word in the Latin vocabulary which signifies virtue, and its meaning is *manly valour*: thus the Romans made courage stand for virtue in all its aspects, although it only denotes one of them.'[8] Over time prowess gave way somewhat to obedience and discipline,[9] as Roman military tactics depended less on displays of individual courage and more on coordinated troop movements. Wild dashes of Greek-style competitive zeal could be counterproductive to good order, and generals now had other jobs to do than simply lead by example. 'There is nothing worse in an army than insubordination,' wrote Appian, purportedly citing words spoken by L. Calpurnius Piso Caesonius in the Senate.[10] Foreign observers like Appian (who was Greek) were well aware of the importance of discipline in the Romans' victories. Josephus, a Jew who had fought both against and alongside the Romans, wrote that he 'knew that the invincible might of Rome was chiefly due to unhesitating obedience and to practice in arms.'[11]

One of the main demands of discipline for the Roman soldier was that he hold his place in his formation in battle. Firmness of purpose (*constantia*) and tenacity (*firmitas*) were prime attributes of the honourable Roman both on and off the battlefield. Polybius noted that:

> In general the Romans rely upon force in all their undertakings, and consider that having set themselves a task they are bound to carry it through, and similarly that nothing is impossible once they have decided to attempt it. It often happens that this spirit inspires them to succeed, but sometimes it involves them in total disaster.[12]

The emphasis on discipline and fortitude reflected the Romans' insistence that personal honour should be subordinated to the collective honour of Rome. Connected with this was the idea of duty. Prime examples of the Roman model of selfless duty were the two Catos. Cato the Elder, according to Plutarch, 'believed that a good citizen should not accept even the praise that he had earned, unless this could benefit the state.'[13] The creed of Cato the Younger, according to the poet Lucan, was 'to devote his life to his country, to believe that he was born not for himself but for all the world. … his goodness was for the state.'[14]

Lucius Quinctius Cincinnatus was another example of this ideal of state service. In times of crisis, the Romans appointed a temporary dictator who had absolute power. Livy tells how in 458 BC Cincinnatus was appointed dictator after the neighbouring Aequian tribe surrounded and besieged an army commanded by consul Lucius Minucius. Cincinnatus called together a relief force, rescued Minucius, and despite having been granted absolute power for six months, resigned just 15 days after taking office, and went back to his farm.[15]

Romans liked to view themselves as upright warriors who kept their word and fought openly without recourse to deceit or treachery. In Virgil's *Aeneid* Aeneas denounces the 'perfidy' of the strategy used by the Greeks to capture Troy (the Trojan horse).[16] The implication seems to be that Romans would not use such methods. Livy similarly deplored Hannibal's un-Roman conduct as 'a more than Punic perfidy, a total disregard of truth, honour, and religion',[17] and complained that at the battle of Lake Trasimene, the Carthaginians promised to let the

Romans go free if they surrendered, but afterwards, 'with a truly Punic disregard for the sanctity of a promise, put them all into chains'.[18]

Keeping one's word included respecting promises made to the enemy, and keeping to the terms of treaties. For instance, when the African King Jugurtha first surrendered to Rome under an offer of immunity, some in Rome demanded his execution, but, according to Sallust, Gaius Memmius, who held the important post of Tribune, 'had more regard for Roman honour than for their anger, [and] tried to calm their excited feelings, declaring that he would not do anything to encourage a violation of Rome's plighted word.'[19] Subsequently, Jugurtha returned to Africa and resumed his war against the Romans.

It was equally important to keep pledges given to friends. Livy wrote that, 'Loyalty is the strongest bond of an ally.'[20] This was true for pragmatic reasons – if one was loyal to allies, they would be loyal in return. But loyalty (*fides*) also became a virtue in and of itself. Rome started several wars in order to fulfil obligations to allies.

A final virtue which deserves mention is that of clemency. Seneca commented that clemency brought glory: 'Not to destroy, when one could do so easily, was a noble act.'[21] It is hard to reconcile this belief with the Romans' notorious brutality, but as will become clear, clemency and brutality often went hand in hand.

Overall, Romans reacted less predictably than Greeks in matters of honour. For instance, they were, like the Greeks, sensitive to insult. This applied not merely to individuals but also to the Roman state, which fought many wars in order to respond to perceived attacks on national honour. However, a Roman had the option, not obviously open to a Greek, to display *gravitas* and treat an insult with disdain. Thus, Marcus Aurelius wrote that, 'interference, ingratitude, insolence, disloyalty ... none of these things can injure me, for nobody can implicate me in what is degrading.'[22] 'Reject your sense of injury', he advised, 'and the injury itself disappears.'[23] As we shall see, some generals followed this advice in war; others did not.

Similarly, when faced with a choice between inward virtue and outward success, Romans might pick either one. Cicero claimed that if there was a conflict between morality and expediency, the former must win,[24] but also wrote that 'when it comes to war one should choose the stronger side and reckon the safer course the better.'[25] This was certainly the view of many Roman military commanders. For instance, when suppressing the Jewish revolt in Palestine, the future Emperor Vespasian held a court-martial to determine the fate of those who had been captured in the town of Tarichaeae. Having considered that morality meant they should spare the prisoners, in the end the Romans decided to kill them anyway on the grounds 'that expediency must be preferred to conventional morality whenever the two were in conflict.'[26]

On the other hand, another Roman commander in Palestine made a different choice. Ordered by the Emperor Caligula, 'to march to Jerusalem and erect his [Caligula's] statues in the Temple', the general Petronius refused to do so, recognizing that such a provocative act would lead to resistance and enormous bloodshed. According to Josephus, he told the Jews, 'With God's help I shall convince Caesar and we can all breathe again: if he is exasperated, I will gladly give my life to save so many.'[27] Fortunately for Petronius, Caligula died before he learnt of his officer's disobedience. Still, forced to choose between glory and conscience, Romans were more likely to pick glory. The pressure to win honour for Rome and for oneself was very strong.

Honour and the causes of war

In the 150 years between 415 and 265 BC, Rome enjoyed only 13 years in which we know of no war; in the 211 years between 240 and 29 BC, only seven years.[28] In some cases, enemies forced war upon the Romans. In most cases war was a matter of choice. Quite why the Romans continually sought to expand their territory is the subject of considerable historical debate.

Material goals, namely the desire for land and slaves, played an important part in Rome's military aggressiveness.[29] These motives, though, may have applied more to individuals than to the Roman state itself – in other words, these may have persuaded individuals to participate in wars more than they encouraged Rome itself to wage wars.[30] Profits were a fortunate side effect of warfare, rather than its aim.[31] War and expansion were rarely, if ever, the results of a desire to commercially exploit conquered territories (as opposed to plundering them).[32]

An alternative theory posits that fear of invasion – above all by Celts and Carthaginians, who both invaded Italy – made Rome expand in order to protect its home base.[33] When Rome did annex land, this theory states, it did so solely because of the persistently aggressive behaviour of the previous owners. There are too many examples of outright aggression for this to be plausible. In 238 BC, for instance, the Romans seized Sardinia in outright violation of their treaty with Carthage, and under the Emperor Claudius they invaded and conquered Britain, which posed no threat to the Empire.

What is interesting is that Romans felt that they needed to justify aggression in terms of self-defence. It was not acceptable to wage war without just cause. Under the Republic at least, it was necessary to persuade the Senate and the people to agree to war (generals in the field could, and often did, pre-empt that decision by starting one anyway and presenting Rome with a *fait accompli*, but they ran the risk of being punished if their decision was unpopular). If the people felt that there was not a just cause, and that the war was not compatible with the honour of Rome, then it would not be permitted.

The only three just causes in Roman eyes were defence of oneself, defence of one's allies, and response to provocation or insult. In early Rome, a specific procedure laid down by the 'fetial law' had to be followed to make a war 'just'. First there had to be some grievance, and an envoy should be sent to the enemy to demand redress. If none was given after 33 days, the people of Rome would debate whether they wanted war. If they voted in favour, they would send a priest, called a *fetial*, to make the formal declaration of war by throwing a spear across the frontier.[34]

By the late Republic the fetial law had fallen into disuse. Nonetheless, despite some argument to the contrary,[35] it had had the effect of conditioning Romans to the idea that there was a distinction between just and unjust wars.[36] This had practical consequences. An unjust war brought dishonour upon Rome, and so Senators occasionally punished those who waged one. For instance, when in 270 BC the people of Rhegium in the toe of Italy requested Roman protection against Pyrrhus, the Romans provided a garrison. The soldiers, envious of the wealth of the city, 'expelled or massacred the citizens and took possession of the place'. Back in Rome, according to Polybius, 'the people were outraged at their compatriots' action.' They sent an army which laid siege to Rhegium, retook the city, and executed the guilty troops. The object of this, says Polybius, 'was to restore, so far as possible, the good name of Rome among the allies. The city and territory of Rhegium were immediately restored to the inhabitants.'[37]

A century later, in 172 BC, the Senate restored freedom to a tribe of Ligurians whom the consul Caius Cicereius had attacked without good reason.[38] Similarly, when the general Lucius Hortensius stormed and sacked the Greek city of Abdera, the Senate determined that Hortensius had waged an unjust war, freed all those whom he had enslaved, and restored to Abdera its freedom and independence.[39]

It is true that in such cases, other factors also motivated the Senate. Romans, like Greeks, were extremely envious of successful colleagues. The Senate may have restored freedom to the people of Abdera, and so on, primarily in order to humiliate the generals responsible. But had the framework of justice not existed, it would not have been possible to call upon it for this purpose.

Roman generals had to be wary of this framework when making the decision to start a war, but it was not an insurmountable deterrent. Constitutionally, in the Republic the right to make the decision to go to war belonged to the Senate and the Assembly of the people in Rome. In practice, the Senate had by far the greater say. As Rome's territory grew, decision-making inevitably devolved to distant commanders in the field, to whose judgement Senators generally deferred.[40] Under the Republic, men normally held military command for only one year at a time. The window of opportunity for winning glory was thus limited, so if no war was already underway, there was a strong temptation to start one. There is some evidence to suggest that until the first century BC, the habit of provoking wars to gain glory was rare except in the more remote provinces.[41] In the last century of the Republic, however, it became quite common.

Julius Caesar is a prime example. In his memoirs he gives a variety of justifications for his attacks on the Gauls, Germans, and Britons, but none of them are convincing. Caesar's own desire for glory seems a more credible explanation for his actions.

The conquest of Gaul, for instance, began with a strike against the Helvetii, a tribe which had announced its intention to migrate from what is now Switzerland to what is now Western France. The Helvetii asked Caesar, who was governor of the Roman province in southern Gaul, for permission to transit Roman territory. Caesar refused, and so the Helvetii decided to cross through land further north. Caesar then intercepted and slaughtered them anyway. His justification was based on matters of both security and honour: first, the Helvetii were untrustworthy and he could not be sure that they would not do harm *en route* to their new home; and second, 50 years earlier, the Helvetii had routed a Roman army under the consul Lucius Cassius and forced its men to pass under the yoke, an insult which had to be avenged. Caesar claimed that he felt unable to ignore the Helvetians' 'fresh insults – their attempt to force a passage … in defiance of his prohibition'.[42]

After crushing the Helvetii, Caesar turned on Germans who had settled in Gaul, led by the chieftain Ariovistus. Caesar claimed that:

> If the Germans formed a habit of crossing the Rhine and entering Gaul in large numbers, he saw how dangerous it would be for the Romans. If those fierce barbarians occupied the whole of Gaul, the temptation would be too strong: they would cross the frontier into the Province … and march on Italy … This danger, he considered, must be provided against immediately. Moreover, Ariovistus personally had behaved with quite intolerable arrogance and pride.[43]

Caesar hardly bothered justifying his next attacks, on Britain. When, after that, he crossed the river Rhine into what is now Germany, that campaign achieved nothing in purely military terms except to give a demonstration of his power and win him fame as the first Roman to lead troops into German territory. Caesar left Germany after only 18 days, saying that, 'he considered that he had done all that honour or interest required.'[44]

The wars fought by Caesar's rivals for honour were similar. Marcus Crassus launched an unprovoked invasion of Parthia, Rome's great enemy in the East. The only possible explanation for this campaign, which resulted in the death of Crassus and the destruction of his army, was Crassus's desire for military glory. As Plutarch explains, 'the glorious exploits of Caesar made Crassus also long for trophies and triumphs – the one field of activity in which he was not, he considered, Caesar's superior. This passion of his gave him no rest or peace.'[45]

The great struggle for pre-eminence between Crassus, Caesar, and Pompey ended in civil war. When Caesar's term in command of the Roman armies in Gaul was due to end, Caesar was unwilling to hand over his forces to the Senate, as required by law, and demanded that he first receive a new office. Roman magistrates were immune from prosecution, and Caesar, in the course of his political career, had committed many crimes. He may have feared that were he to have no army at his back and no guarantee of immunity, his enemies might prosecute him.[46] He did, however, express his willingness to surrender his command if Pompey did the same. Pompey refused. He had been a great man long before Caesar and, while he was willing to make some concessions to him and was keen to avoid war, he was not willing to accept equality of status. As Lucan put it in his poem about the civil war: 'Rivalry in excellence spurs them on. … Caesar cannot now bear anyone ahead nor Pompey any equal.'[47] Caesar, therefore, marched on Rome.

In his memoirs, Caesar stressed the importance of issues of honour as a cause of the civil war. His prime complaint was that, 'Pompey … was reluctant to let anyone stand on the same pinnacle of prestige as himself.'[48] Assembling his men before crossing the Rubicon into Italy, he asked them 'to defend my reputation and standing against the assaults of my enemies'.[49] Later he defended his actions by saying, 'I alone have been denied the right always accepted to all commanders – that is, the right of coming home, after a successful campaign, with some honour, or at least without disgrace.'[50]

Similar disputes over honour and precedence had lain behind an earlier civil war, that between Marius and Sulla. Plutarch described Marius as a man 'who had the keenest sense of his own honour, no notion of sharing glory with anyone else, and was quite quick to take offence'.[51] Marius had sought command of a Roman army being prepared to fight the Asian king Mithridates. When Sulla received the command instead, Marius considered this a 'humiliation', and pulled political strings to replace Sulla with himself. Sulla then refused to hand over his command, as that would have been equally humiliating for him. Instead, he marched on Rome, and drove Marius into exile.[52]

Rivalries of this sort eventually brought the Republic to its knees. Sooner or later, one man was bound to win a position of unassailable power and consolidate it. This happened when Octavian defeated Mark Antony and thereafter established a new system of government, the Empire. Under the Empire, glory-seeking continued to play an important role in causing wars, but with some subtle differences.

Emperors held their position on the basis of having more honour than anyone else. A general who could challenge an Emperor in honour was a threat to the latter's survival, and Emperors, therefore, were not keen on generals who started wars to win glory for themselves. Some still did anyway. According to Tacitus, the imperial commander in Britain, Gaius Suetonius Paulinus, attacked Anglesey primarily in order to win for himself the same fame that another general, Corbulo, had won in Armenia.[53] This sort of action was still so common in the early Empire that the troops of the Emperor Claudius asked him to honour all his generals *before* they took up command, as otherwise they 'would try to win it [honour] in the field by provoking hostilities'![54]

Thereafter, the habit seems to have declined among generals, but some Emperors did continue to start wars for their own glory. Claudius's invasion of Britain and Trajan's conquest of Dacia are clear examples. Most Emperors, however, were more defensively minded, perhaps because they had already won honour for themselves in battle, or because a defensive strategy provided a good means of preventing their generals from getting above themselves.

What did cause wars in the Empire, as in the Republic, was insult. In both periods, this included both insults to individual generals or rulers and to Rome itself. Despite Stoic suggestions of forbearance, most Romans seem to have felt that honour demanded a violent response to insults. Cicero, for instance, said that Caesar started civil war 'to repel insult from himself'.[55] Indeed, Caesar often used the word *iniuria* (insult) when explaining his decisions to fight. He therefore referred to the *iniuriae* made against him by the Helvetii and Ariovistus, as well as by Pompey.

At a national level, insults to Rome's honour often provoked war. For instance, Rome went to war against Queen Teuta of Illyria in 230 BC over a dispute about pirates operating against Roman ships from Illyrian territory. The Romans had been willing to negotiate over the matter, but after one of the Roman envoys offended the Queen, she 'sent agents to assassinate' him. This so outraged Roman public opinion that the people demanded war.[56] In this instance, the genuine issues of trade and security raised by the pirates were important, but not sufficient to justify war without the insult of the assassination.

The honour Rome was defending in these cases was of the 'intrinsic' kind, that is to say, it was valued for itself. Honour of the 'instrumental' kind, that is to say, honour viewed as an instrument for the achievement of some other goal, was also an important cause of war. This was especially true in the Empire, when maintaining the Empire's honour was essential for its security. Rome had an enormous territory to defend, and only about 300,000 troops with which to do the job. To achieve security, Rome had to give the impression of even greater power than it had, and to do this felt a need to respond vigorously to any slights to Roman prestige. According to one recent history, preserving national honour was the 'most important policy goal' of Roman foreign policy.[57]

Roman honour also prescribed total loyalty to allies. This was especially important in Rome's earlier history, when much of Italy was not yet fully incorporated into the Roman political system and consisted of allied states who provided a substantial element of the manpower in Roman armies. The reliability of these allies depended in part on force – anybody who deserted Rome was subject to fierce punishment – but also in part on Rome's reliability as a protector.

The First Punic War between Rome and Carthage began when a third party, the Mamertines, seized control of the city of Messana in the north-eastern tip of Sicily and forged an alliance with Rome. Syracuse, which considered itself the rightful master of Messana, called in Carthaginian help, and together Syracusan and Carthaginian forces laid siege to the city. The Romans felt that the Mamertines were in the wrong, but an attack on a Roman ally, even one which had behaved unjustly, was an attack on Rome.[58] War was declared, and lasted for 23 years.

The Second Punic War began similarly. Hannibal attacked another Roman ally, the town of Saguntum in Spain, and triggered another 16 years of fighting. In this case, the Romans took their obligations to their ally so seriously that after they retook Saguntum, they went to considerable effort and expense to track down all its former citizens whom Hannibal had sold as slaves, bought back their freedom, and restored the city to their possession.[59]

Honour as a motivation for fighting

The reasons men fought in Rome's wars were often the same as those which caused those wars, though operating at a lower level – the desire for profit, a sense of service or duty, and a sense of shame and honour. The armies of early Rome consisted of citizen-soldiers whose citizenship included an obligation to serve as and when necessary. As Rome's territory grew, the city increasingly needed troops to serve for prolonged periods in distant lands. This led to a gradual professionalization of the army in the late Republic. Thereafter troops served for three main reasons: for the pay and promises of land on retirement; because once in the army, they were subjected to its discipline and had no choice; and because they adopted and internalized a professional ethos which included devotion to the honour of the army and their unit.

From early times, the prospect of booty was one of the chief inducements to fight. For instance, at the start of the First Punic War, the consuls, eager for glory, persuaded the people to go to war by reminding them of the 'great gain which clearly accrues to every individual citizen from the spoils of war'.[60]

A sense of shame was also important. Caesar described the operation of shame as a factor in keeping men in the ranks, writing that during his civil war campaign in Spain, Pompeian commanders on one occasion ruled out a night march because:

> A night battle was to be avoided, since the soldiers in the panicky atmosphere of civil war were more likely to be swayed by their fears than their sense of duty; daylight, on the other hand, was apt of itself to impose a sense of shame, under the gaze of everyone ... It was by such circumstances that soldiers were usually kept in hand and maintained their loyalty.[61]

Linked to this was a desire for glory. In the higher echelons of society, family pressures were an important factor. Men were expected to continue the family traditions and add to its greatness. Polybius recounts that whenever a great man died, a mask was made bearing his likeness. Thereafter:

> When any distinguished member of the family dies, the masks are taken to the funeral, and there are worn by men who are considered to bear the closest resemblance to the original ... the speaker who pronounces the oration over the man who is about to be buried, when he has delivered his tribute, goes on to relate the successes and achievements of all the others whose images are displayed there, beginning with the oldest. By this constant renewal of the good report of brave men, the fame of those who have performed any noble deed is made immortal, and the renown of those who have served their country well becomes a matter of common knowledge and a heritage for posterity. But the most important consequence of the ceremony is that it inspires young men to endure the extremes of suffering for the common good in the hope of winning the glory that waits upon the brave.[62]

One way of winning glory was through single combat against an enemy champion in front of the army. There are numerous examples of this in Roman history. Most famously, in 222 BC the great Roman general Marcus Claudius Marcellus killed Vindomarus, a chieftain of the Gauls, in single combat.[63] Such duels seem to have been most common in the early days of the Republic. Their popularity then waned among those in high positions. By the civil wars of the first century BC, when the rebel general Quintus Sertorius challenged Q. Metellus Pius to single combat, Metellus refused, and according to Plutarch, 'he was right, for a general, as Theophrastus says, should die like a general and not like a common soldier.'[64]

Another way of displaying courage was to rush out of formation and charge the enemy. During the siege of Jerusalem, Roman soldiers were inspired to such feats by the presence of their commander, the future Emperor Titus. Josephus, a witness to these events, comments that, 'To show weakness when Caesar was there fighting at their side was unthinkable, while the man who fought valiantly did so before the eyes of the one who would reward him … As a result many showed courage beyond their strength.' One cavalryman, Longinus, 'leapt out of the Roman ranks and charged the very middle of the Jewish phalanx', killing two Jews before returning to his own ranks. 'When he had given this demonstration of his prowess, there were many who imitated his valour.'[65]

What is particularly interesting is what followed. For, according to Josephus, when Titus saw Longinus's exploit, he 'declared that incautious enthusiasm was utter madness, and heroism was heroic only when it went with prudent regard for the hero's safety. His men were forbidden to risk their own lives in order to display their own fearlessness.'[66]

This concern for prudence and discipline was a constant theme. In an extreme example, in 340 BC the consul Manlius Torquatus is reported to have ordered the execution of his own son 'for disobeying orders and engaging in single combat before a battle'. According to Plutarch, 'Manlius Torquatus … beheaded [his son] after he had been awarded the laurel crown for an act of the utmost gallantry.'[67]

Allied to the concept of discipline was a sense of collective honour. Soldiers developed a strong sense of identity with their unit, whose honour was embodied in its standard. The standard served a practical purpose as a marker to show troops where their unit was, and acted as a rallying point in times of trouble. Its role was also symbolic. 'The eagle [of a military unit]', wrote Appian, 'is the most august symbol of all for Romans.'[68] Its fate was a matter of considerable importance. We read in Appian's history of the civil wars that when Sulla attacked Rome and there was fighting in the city, 'Sulla's troops were being driven back, but he seized a standard and risked his life in the front line; this action immediately stayed their rout because of the awe in which they held their general and the dishonour they feared if they lost their standard.'[69]

Commanders could exploit troops' attachment to their standards by deliberately endangering the latter. In 446 BC, according to Livy, in a battle against the Aequians and Volscians the consul Furius Agrippa:

> snatched the standards from their bearers and pressed forward with them in his own hands – and even, to shame his men to greater efforts, flung one of them into the thick of the enemy ranks. The ruse succeeded: a furious onslaught followed, and victory along the whole front was won.[70]

The focus of Roman loyalty was not just military formations and their symbols, but also Rome itself. There are clear examples of Romans putting the interests of Rome above their own. For instance, when Sertorius was waging a war of rebellion in Spain, Mithridates contacted him and offered his support if 'Sertorius should confirm his title to the sovereignty of the whole province of Asia'. Mithridates's backing would have been a major boost to Sertorius' cause, but he refused it, for even though he was in rebellion against those in power in Rome, he still regarded himself as Roman. According to Plutarch, he believed that, 'he had no right to extend his own power at her [Rome's] expense. A man of noble spirit, he told them, welcomes victory if he can achieve it with honour, but he will not embrace dishonour even to save his own life.'[71]

All in all, the Roman army, with its emphasis on discipline and the collective honour of unit and country, was much closer to a modern professional force than were the armies of the more individualistic Greeks.

Honours and rewards

> Who would embrace poor Virtue naked
> Without the rewards she bestows? – Juvenal, Satire X, lines 141–2.[72]

The greatest, and rarest, honour that a Roman could win was the *spolia opima*. Only the commander of a Roman army could achieve this honour, and only by personally killing the commander of the enemy army in combat. The victorious Roman gained the right to bring the armour of his foe into Rome and lay it at the temple of Jupiter Feretrius. According to Livy, the first winner of the honour was the founder of Rome, Romulus, and the second was Aulus Cornelius Cossus, who killed the king of Veii, Lars Tolumnius, in 437 BC.[73] Thereafter, only one person ever won the honour – Marcus Claudius Marcellus, for killing Vindomarus, chieftain of the Gauls.[74] Others tried to emulate Marcellus, but with no success. One such hopeful was Decimus Drusus, the brother of the Emperor Tiberius, who, according to Suetonius, was 'eager for personal glory ... not content with gaining victories over the enemy, he had a long-standing ambition to win "The Noblest Spoils" [*spolia opima*], and used to chase German chieftains across the battlefield at great risk to himself.'[75]

Drusus failed in his ambition. One general who by rights should have succeeded was the consul Marcus Licinius Crassus, who, while commanding Roman forces in Macedonia in 29 BC, killed King Daldo of the Bastarnae tribe. It would seem as if this feat entitled him to the *spolia opima*, but the Emperor Augustus prevented him from receiving them.[76] Crassus would have gained too much honour, outstripping Augustus, so the Emperor cheated Crassus by saying that he was not a commander. Crassus had to be satisfied with the lesser (albeit substantial) honour of a triumph. Thereafter, there are no records of anybody either winning or claiming the *spolia opima*.

Given that it was almost impossible to win the *spolia opima*, in practice the greatest honour a Roman was ever likely to gain was a triumph. When a general won a great victory, he could ask the Senate to grant him this honour. If it did, the general would ride through Rome in a chariot, crowned with a laurel wreath, garbed in a purple tunic, and accompanied by a great procession.[77] If the Senate felt that a victory was of insufficient importance to merit a triumph, it could award a lesser honour known as an *ovatio*. This was very similar, except that the general did not ride on a chariot, but walked in the procession. Another, still lesser, honour was a vote by the Senate for a public day of thanksgiving (*supplicatio*). Caesar, for instance, recorded that the Senate voted him an unprecedented 15 such days after his victory against the Nervii in 57 BC.[78]

Successful generals were also given titles. Some took the name of the people they had conquered or the name of the site of a victory. The first example of this was P. Cornelius Scipio, who acquired the title 'Africanus' for his victories in Africa against the Carthaginians.[79] The title 'Emperor' itself derived from a tradition during the Republic of troops hailing successful generals as '*Imperator*'. However, allowing oneself to be hailed as *Imperator* for trivial victories was considered dishonourable. Appian claimed that the title was theoretically reserved for those who won victories resulting in at least 10,000 enemy dead.[80] Tacitus records that the last general to be hailed *Imperator* was Quintus Junius Blaesus in 22 AD. After this, he says, the title 'was never conferred again'.[81] It was now reserved for Emperors.

The narrowing of the title *Imperator* reflected a more general change in the system of honours in the Empire. Cornelius Balbus celebrated the last non-royal triumph in 19 BC, after which triumphs became exclusive to Emperors and members of their family.[82] Consequently, their frequency declined dramatically. Non-royals had to make do with *ornamenta*, which consisted of the insignia and other trappings associated with a triumph (statue, chariot, laurel crown, ivory staff, triumphal garments, etc.), but without the actual honour of a procession through Rome.[83] Emperors soon fell into the habit of giving out *ornamenta* for reasons other than military successes, thereby devaluing them, and eventually the honour disappeared entirely.[84]

Despite all the fanfare for victory, the Romans were remarkably forgiving of defeat.[85] An analysis of the political careers of defeated generals shows that they fared no worse in elections to magisterial offices than victorious ones.[86] What mattered to the Romans was not whether a general was defeated, but how he behaved if he was. As Polybius said, 'The test of true virtue in a man surely resides in his capacity to bear with spirit and with dignity the most complete transformations of fortune.'[87] The key thing was to show fortitude, and not admit failure.

Take the examples of Gaius Mancinus and Gaius Terentius Varro. Mancinus led a campaign against the Numantines in Africa in 137 BC. When his army was surrounded, and there was no means of escape, he negotiated terms of surrender and a peace treaty between the Numantines and Rome. On his return home, however, 'he found that the whole transaction had aroused a storm of indignation, and was being denounced as a disaster and a disgrace to the name of Rome.' As a result, the people voted not to ratify the treaty, and since this meant going back on what Mancinus had agreed with the Numantines, they also voted to hand him over to the enemy 'stripped and in chains'.[88]

Mancinus' crime was that he had admitted defeat. By contrast, Varro, after escaping from the disastrous battle of Cannae, in which Rome lost some 50,000 men to Hannibal, suffered no punishment for his defeat. On the contrary, when he returned to Rome, he was met by crowds who thanked him for 'not having despaired of the commonwealth'.[89] This was because after fleeing the battlefield, he rallied what survivors he could find, and attempted to reconstitute some form of army to continue the struggle.[90]

Romans generally blamed the ordinary soldiers, not their commanders, for military disasters. Defeated generals could even win honour, but soldiers who fled had disgraced themselves, regardless of the circumstances. So, whereas Varro went on to hold several other important commands after Cannae, those of his troops who survived with him were treated with contempt. The Senate deployed them to Sicily and ordered that they not be allowed to return to mainland Italy until the war with Carthage was over. It also gave instructions that regardless of their future actions they 'not be awarded any of the usual honours or prizes for valour'.[91]

The honours and prizes which the Cannae survivors were not allowed to win consisted of promotions, money, and decorations (the last of these comprising various awards which could be worn, such as crowns and medals). The Republic was more egalitarian in its awards of decorations (in the sense that anybody of merit could win them) than the Empire, which made a clear distinction between awards to officers and other ranks.[92]

The highest decoration a Roman could win was the siege crown (*corona obsidonalis*), given to a commander who relieved a besieged city. Pliny the Elder claimed that only eight of these were ever awarded. They were made of grass, and had gone out of use by the end of the Republic.

Next in honour was the civic crown (*corona civica*), made of oak leaves, which was given for saving the life of a Roman citizen in battle. The Romans appear to have continued using the civic crown up to at least the mid-first century AD.

In the Republic, a soldier won the *corona muralis* if he was the first to scale the walls of an enemy city, and the *corona vallaris* if he was the first to climb over the rampart of an enemy camp. In the Empire, however, these crowns seem to have been given for purely honorific purposes, and only to officers ranked centurion and above. In this way they lost their original meaning.

The lowest type of crown was the gold crown (*corona aurea*). Soldiers could also win spears (*hastae purae*), sometimes made of silver or gold and originally given for slaying an enemy in single combat. Decorations worn with formal uniforms were necklaces (*torques*), armbands (*armillae*), and medal-like disks called *phalerae*.[93] By the time of the Empire, these were all lesser decorations given to soldiers ranked centurion and below.

Soldiers were not the only ones who could win these honours. Entire units could be awarded titles such as *torquata* or *armillata*. They also acquired titles indicating places in which they had won victories, as well as names which displayed honourable attributes, such as *Victrix* (awarded to the 20th Legion after the suppression of Boudicca's revolt); *Felix* (given by Vespasian to the 4th Flavian Legion); and *Fortis* (granted by Trajan to the 2nd Parthica).[94] Equally, if a unit disgraced itself, it could lose its titles.

The Romans put such a huge effort into their system of rewards and honours that it makes sense to believe that it had some real impact on people's behaviour. Certainly, triumph-hunting seems to have been a significant cause of war. Once generals could only receive *ornamenta*, the incentive for such belligerence diminished. This was especially true once Emperors had devalued the *ornamenta* by giving out too many of them. Tacitus claims that under Claudius, Germany was peaceful, 'because, prodigal awards having cheapened the honorary Triumph [*ornamenta*], our generals looked for greater glory from maintaining peace'.[95]

At the lower levels, the evidence about soldiers' attitude to honours is contradictory. Confronted by mutinous troops, Octavian at one point promised to give out additional crowns. This sparked an outburst by one of the soldiers, Ofillius, who 'called out that crowns … were toys for children, and that soldiers' rewards were land and money'. The rest of the crowd shouted out agreement.[96] The general attitude was very different. Valerius Maximus records a story in which one of the Scipio family fighting in Africa in 47 BC refused to accept a recommendation by one of his officers, Titus Labienus, that an ex-slave receive a gold armband, after which Labienus gave the man a handful of gold in consolation.

> 'All you have there', said Scipio, 'is a present from a rich man.' At these words the soldier, confused, lowered his eyes and threw the gold at Labienus' feet. But when he heard Scipio say 'The general gives you silver *armillae*', he was filled with joy.[97]

The soldier's rejection of the gold, and his joy at receiving the armband indicate that what mattered was the symbolic nature of the decoration. Anybody could have money, but an armband was proof of valour.

An excellent summary of the importance of decorations is given by Polybius. In his eyes, they were the source of Roman success:

> The men who receive these trophies not only enjoy great prestige in the army and soon afterwards in their homes, but they are also singled out for precedence in religious processions when they return. On these occasions nobody is allowed to wear decorations save those who have been awarded them by the consuls, and it is the custom to hang up the trophies they have won in the most conspicuous places in their houses, and to regard them as proofs and visible symbols of their valour. So when we consider this people's almost obsessive concern with military rewards and punishments, and the immense importance which they attach to both, it is not surprising that they emerge with brilliant success from every war in which they engage.[98]

Death and honour

Whereas the Greeks seem to have regarded death as simply preferable to dishonour, some Romans seem to have actually regarded it as almost a positive good. Josephus thus cites Titus as saying to his troops, 'it is a splendid thing to die with honour.' 'If it is fated that all men must die', Titus continued, 'how contemptible it would be not to give to the service of our country what we must yield up to fate.'[99]

This attitude led to a predilection for suicide in the face of defeat, especially in civil war. The alternative was to be at the mercy of one's enemy, a humiliating concept for any proud Roman. Men such as Cato the Younger therefore killed themselves rather than be captured after defeat. This behaviour spread down from officers to ordinary soldiers. During the assault on the temple in Jerusalem during the Jewish revolt, for instance, one Roman soldier, Longus, found himself trapped in the temple's colonnade. Asked to surrender by the Jews, Longus refused. Instead, believing that surrender 'would tarnish his own name and disgrace the Roman army, he killed himself'.[100]

Compared with the effort they put into honouring the living, the Romans gave little thought to the dead. Certainly, there is nothing to compare with the Athenians' efforts to ensure that every soldier received some memorial. A good number of ordinary soldiers' tombstones have survived to this day, but these were erected by the families. The state, possibly because of its hierarchical character, and possibly because of the sheer scale of its armies compared with those of the Greeks, does not appear to have been particularly interested in the fates of individuals.

Romans originally brought their dead back to Rome. As armies got larger and fought farther afield, this became impractical, although the practice seems to have continued for the officer class. Appian claims that a change occurred during the Social War fought from 91 to 88 BC between Rome and its Latin allies. After the defeat of a Roman army under the consul P. Rutilius Lupus, so many dead bodies returned to Rome that the Senate feared for the city's morale. It therefore decreed that henceforth 'war casualties were to be buried where they died, so that the rest of the population should not be deterred from military service by what they saw.'[101]

This remained the practice thereafter. The Romans buried their dead in mass graves where they fell, though occasionally especially meritorious individuals might be given a separate burial. After the battle of Pharsalus, for instance, Caesar gave posthumous decorations to one of his centurions, Crassinius, and ordered that he be buried 'in a special tomb near the mass grave'.[102]

In another instance, when Germanicus reoccupied the territory on which the Germans had massacred the armies of Varus in 9 AD, he went to some effort to collect what remained of the bodies and bury them. He also built a burial mound and an altar to commemorate them.[103] Similarly, Corbulo arranged the burial of the fallen soldiers of the army of L. Caesennius Paetus when he recaptured the site of Paetus' defeat one year later.[104] The dead were not completely forgotten.

Honour and the conduct of war

Most Romans favoured vigorous action in war. The most famous exception was Fabius Maximus, who earned the title 'Cunctator' (Delayer) for his policy of avoiding combat with Hannibal, thus also giving his name to 'Fabian' strategies. Vespasian too warned against recklessness, telling his troops that, 'to win success by biding your time is a sounder policy than courting disaster by plunging into battle.'[105] Despite this, Roman generals often preferred action over caution, and combat over stratagem.

Polybius wrote that many Romans imagined that:

> They fought their wars in a straightforward and chivalrous fashion: they did not resort to night attacks or to ambuscades, they scorned any advantage that might be gained by deceit or fraud, and they regarded open and face to face fighting as the only form of combat which was worthy of their character.[106]

In line with this, Plutarch reports a story that in the war against Pyrrhus, the Greek king's doctor sent a letter to the Roman Gaius Fabricius offering to poison him. Fabricius, Plutarch claims, turned the letter over to Pyrrhus, saying that he did so in order that nobody could 'say of us that we brought this war to an end by treachery because we could not do so by our own valour.'[107]

In practice one can find many examples of Roman generals resorting to deceit or subterfuge. Fabius, for instance, captured Tarentum from the Carthaginians with the help of a traitor within the city. Quintus Caecilius Metellus tried unsuccessfully to capture Jugurtha by arranging for some of his close colleagues to betray him. Sertorius, leading his rebellion in Spain, resorted to hit-and-run guerrilla-style tactics. Nevertheless, the Romans' self-image as straight dealers did have an impact. When combined with the desire for glory, and the predilection for action, it prompted many of them to seek battle in circumstances when the interests of strategy dictated otherwise.

Hannibal benefited greatly from Roman recklessness. When he arrived in Italy, the two Roman generals facing him disagreed on what to do. One wanted to avoid battle, while the other, Tiberius Sempronius Longus, wanted to fight. The reason was that Longus' term as consul would soon run out, and 'he had no desire that the fighting should be put off until new consuls were in control, and he himself … should lose the chance of gaining the glory.'[108] Sempronius confronted Hannibal at the river Trebia, and suffered a crushing defeat.

After this success, Hannibal moved south and began ravaging the Roman countryside. The new Roman commander, Flaminius, 'exploded into a fury of rage, imagining that the enemy were treating him with contempt'. He refused to listen to those of his officers who advised caution, but 'asked them to imagine what would be said in Rome if the army were to remain in its encampment in the rear of the enemy, while the whole Italian countryside was ravaged'.[109] Led by this concern for his reputation, Flaminius marched after Hannibal, and fell into the trap the latter had prepared at Lake Trasimene, losing his own life along with those of 15,000 of his men.

When Fabius then embarked on his famous delaying strategy, it brought him only contempt. According to Plutarch, 'the soldiers mocked at Fabius and contemptuously called him Hannibal's governess.'[110] Fabius eventually had to hand over half of his command to his deputy Marcus Minucius Rufus after the latter denounced Fabius' timidity, asking the troops if they were not ashamed to see the

Carthaginians marching freely over Roman land.[111] Minucius led his half of the army against Hannibal, only to suffer yet another defeat.

Fabius had responded to his critics by saying that 'the man who allows himself to be frightened by the opinions of others or by their slanders or abuse proves that he is unworthy of such a high office.'[112] Even very great Romans were, however, unable to follow this sage advice. Pompey, for instance, cared so deeply about what the members of the senatorial class thought of him that he became putty in the hands of those whose applause he wanted. When he had Caesar's army cut off from its supply base in Greece, he understood that his best bet was a strategy of attrition. But his friends, eager for the glory of a quick victory, begged him to attack Caesar immediately, and accused of him of prolonging the war simply in order to maintain his status as commander. Stung by this insult, Pompey engaged Caesar at Pharsalus and suffered a decisive defeat.[113]

To be successful, the honour-seeking general had to temper his boldness with a certain degree of strategy. It was also not the general's job to endanger himself recklessly, and so Romans did not lead from the front like Greeks. They were more like the generals of modern armies, who keep to the rear and oversee the conduct of operations. Thus, when Jewish forces attacked the Romans outside Jerusalem, Titus' officers reminded him of his duty to stay in safety, asking him to 'bear in mind his unique position and not play the part of a private soldier when he was commander-in-chief of the army.'[114]

Another reason for the commander to take a place in the rear of the army was that such a position inspired the troops. This may seem odd, since it is generally thought that men are better heartened by seeing their commander ahead of them. But, as we have seen, Roman soldiers cared greatly for honours and rewards. To get these, they had to be seen excelling in combat, and for that, somebody in command had to be behind them watching. For this reason, when attacking a stronghold in Dalmatia, Tiberius 'seated himself on a platform in full view of both sides', both so that he could know when to throw in his reserves, and because his watching would, as Cassius Dio says, 'encourage his men to fight with more spirit'. The strategy succeeded, and the Romans captured the stronghold.[115]

Honour and the enemy

Livy wrote that, 'War has its laws as peace has, and we have learned to wage war with decency no less than courage. We have drawn the sword not against children, even in the sack of cities, but against men, armed like ourselves.'[116] Livy was too idealistic. The Romans often disobeyed the laws of war, and were sometimes quite prepared to kill children. His idealism did, however, have some basis. Romans also often obeyed the law, punished those of their soldiers who broke it, and tempered their brutality with clemency.

The laws of war stated that if a town failed to surrender before the first battering ram struck its walls, all those within it forfeited their right to life. Massacre was then perfectly legal, and the Romans exploited this fact to terrorize all those who might challenge Rome. When ordering the assault on New Carthage, for instance, Scipio gave instructions to his troops 'to exterminate every form of life they encountered, sparing none'. Polybius stated that, 'this practice is adopted to inspire terror, and so when cities are taken by the Romans you may often see not only the corpses of human beings but dogs cut in half and the dismembered limbs of other animals.'[117]

The aim of these terror tactics was to deter future resistance. Deterrence cannot work unless those planning to fight believe that resistance will result in destruction. But there is a reverse side to the equation. To be deterred, those contemplating resistance must also believe that if they refrain from action, or desist once they have started, they will be spared. Otherwise, they might as well fight on to the end. Brutality and clemency thus go hand in hand.

Clemency was an important aspect of Roman honour. Caesar, in particular, praised himself for it in his memoirs.[118] He spared many of his enemies during the civil war and even promoted them to senior positions in his service. Perversely, this concern for clemency meant that one could sometimes get better terms from the Romans by surrendering to them unconditionally than one could by negotiation, because if one put oneself completely at their mercy they might feel obliged to treat one well. Octavian found this out when, much to his inconvenience, he felt himself obliged to spare the lives of Lucius Antonius (the brother of Mark Antony) and his followers, when they surrendered to him at Perusia in 40 BC. As Octavian told Lucius, with, one feels, something of a sense of frustration:

> If you had wanted to negotiate terms with me, you would have found yourself dealing with a victor who was an injured party; but by surrendering yourself and your friends and your army to us unconditionally, you rob me not only of all the expression of my anger but also of the power you would necessarily have given me in making terms. For the question of what you deserve to suffer is bound up with the propriety of the action it is right for me to take. It is the latter consideration I shall honour.[119]

One could not show mercy all the time, or people would take advantage of a perceived weakness. To be effective, clemency had to be accompanied by occasional brutality. It could even encourage massacres, because sometimes it was better not to let the enemy surrender, lest one have to spare them. When besieging the town of Uspe in the Crimea in 49 AD, the Romans refused the surrender of the town because they had no means of providing guards for the 10,000 slaves there, but felt that, 'it was barbarous to slaughter men who had surrendered … better that they should die in normal warfare. So the soldiers, who had scaled the defences on ladders, were given orders to kill; and the inhabitants were exterminated.'[120]

Killing the enemy was one thing, breaking one's promises to him was another. Romans felt that the former was acceptable, but not the latter. 'An oath sworn to an enemy must be honoured',[121] said Cicero, praising the example of the consul Marcus Regulus, who fell into the hands of the Carthaginians in the First Punic War. Regulus' captors decided to take advantage of what chance had thrown in their laps, and asked him to return to Rome carrying an offer of a prisoner exchange. The sole condition was that he give a solemn oath that he would return to Carthage. Regulus did as he was asked, went to Rome, and delivered the offer as promised. But then he did something more. He urged the Senate to reject the offer, because it was not in Rome's interests. When the Senate accepted his advice, his friends and family urged him not to return to Carthage, where he would receive certain punishment for his hostile action. But Regulus ignored their entreaties. He had given his word. He went back to Carthage, where he suffered a slow and painful death.[122]

The Senate took very seriously any breaches of Rome's honour. During the war with Hannibal, the Carthaginian leader sent to Rome ten of the Romans he had captured at Cannae, to discuss with the Senate the ransom and release of the remaining prisoners. The ten had sworn an oath that they would return, but one of them resorted to trickery by immediately returning very briefly to the Carthaginian camp, claiming to have forgotten something. When their time in Rome was over, the other nine returned to Hannibal, but this one tried not to, saying that he had already fulfilled his oath by returning to the camp. The Senate did not take kindly to this. According to Polybius, 'they put him in chains and sent him back to the enemy.'[123]

Honour and the ending of wars

Romans tended to demand unconditional surrender from their enemies. Even when commanders did negotiate treaties, those treaties were subject to ratification by the Senate, and if the terms were considered dishonourable, they would be rejected. As a result, short of outright victory, it was quite difficult for Romans to bring their wars to a close. This was why clemency was so important, for without it the Romans had difficulty in persuading their opponents to surrender.

Glory-seeking contributed to the difficulty of ending wars. Because consuls held office only for one year, they were tempted to secure peace while still in office, so as to gain the glory entirely for themselves. Their political rivals back in Rome, meanwhile, would want to prolong the war in order to get a chance to take command. This was the situation at the end of the Second Punic War when Scipio Africanus was advancing on Carthage. Scipio wanted to capture the city, but was aware that this would take a long time. He offered Carthage terms which were more generous than might have been expected in the circumstances (although still harsh). The consul for the coming year, Gnaeus Cornelius Lentulus, tried to sabotage the peace by vetoing it in the Senate, hoping that the war would continue and he could capture Carthage himself. Scipio's supporters bypassed him by appealing to the assembly of the people, which ratified the treaty, and the war finally came to an end.[124]

A different result transpired when T. Quinctius Flamininus took command of the Roman armies fighting King Philip V of Macedon in 198 BC. The military situation was one of stalemate, and Philip, who had achieved quite good peace terms with Rome in a previous war, felt that he might do equally well again. He therefore offered to negotiate with Flamininus. This did not suit the Roman, because the military situation was not good enough for him to sign a treaty which would bring him glory. When he met Philip, he went out of his way to humiliate him, demanding that he withdraw entirely from Greece. Philip broke off negotiations, and the war continued.

This was as Flamininus had hoped. The continuation of war gave him the opportunity to win a victory and the glory he desired. By the end of the year the military situation had turned in Rome's favour. Now, though, Flamininus had a new problem – his term of office was coming to an end. A new consul might come out and take over, exploit the improved situation and win for himself the honours which belonged to Flamininus. It was necessary to make peace.

In consequence, Flamininus invited Philip to new negotiations, and this time treated him with the utmost respect and deference, finally agreeing to a peace treaty which gave Philip more than the treaty which Flamininus had rejected previously, even though in the meantime Philip's position had deteriorated.

The Senate then voted to let Flamininus stay in control of operations in Greece. At this point, his treaty with Philip no longer suited him, so his supporters in Rome sabotaged it, and the war continued. Flamininus finally got the glory he wanted in a decisive victory over the Macedonians at Cynoscephalae in 196 BC.[125] The honour of one man had dictated the waging and ending of an entire war.

Women and honour

Just as in Greece, women played little role in the conduct of war. Roman honour was decidedly masculine, the word 'virtue' itself being derived from 'vir', the word for man. One of the few stories which concerns the other sex is that of the Sabine women. According to legend, having been abducted by the Romans as intended wives, they placed themselves between the Roman and Sabine armies and shamed the two sides into making peace.

According to another legend, when the rebel general Coriolanus marched on Rome, his mother visited him and persuaded him to desist. This reflected Romans' expectations of filial devotion. Nonetheless, allowing women to dictate one's actions was not normally considered honourable. Rather it was a sign of softness and effeminacy. According to historian Sarah Pomeroy, women's 'interference in politics aroused resentment'.[126] Thus, Aeneas showed his manliness in Virgil's *Aeneid* by abandoning his lover Dido, and replacing the pleasures of life with her with the harshness of a life in pursuit of duty.

Octavian's great rival, Mark Antony, was condemned for his dependency on women. His first wife, Fulvia, managed his interests in Italy while he campaigned overseas, and pushed his brother Lucius into an unsuccessful rebellion against Octavian. Antony meanwhile divorced Fulvia, and married Octavian's sister, Octavia. But he then fell in love with Cleopatra, divorced Octavia, and married the Egyptian queen. Antony's self-subordination to Cleopatra undermined his position and convinced many of his unsuitability to govern. The insult of divorcing Octavia also gave Octavian the excuse he needed to declare war on Antony, a war which ended in Antony and Cleopatra's defeat at Actium and their eventual suicide.

In theory, Romans did not target women in war because killing a woman was no proof of valour. Thus in Virgil's depiction of the sack of Troy, Aeneas considers murdering Helen, who has brought disaster upon the city, but refrains from doing so, noting that, 'There may be no great honour in killing a woman; such a victory brings no fame.'[127] In reality, Romans did massacre women in very large numbers. Respect for the safety of non-combatants was something which would come much later, with the mediaeval concept of chivalry.

Conclusion

Roman honour emphasized martial discipline, stoical fortitude, and patriotic duty. The collapse of the Roman Empire in the fifth century AD brought an end to the professional armies of the Empire, and also to the strong central state that the Romans had developed. Until the later Middle Ages, an era of relative anarchy followed throughout Europe and warriors reverted to a model which owed more to the heroic individual honour of Classical Greece than to the disciplined collective honour of Ancient Rome. It was not until the flowering of the Renaissance, and the expansionist Elizabethan era, examined in Chapter 5, that Europe was to rediscover many of the traits of Rome. In the meantime, the knight on horseback and his code of Christian chivalry ruled the battlefield.

Notes

1 Sallust, *The Jugurthine War/The Conspiracy of Catiline*, trans. S.A. Handford, London: Penguin, 1963, p. 175.
2 Rosenstein, Nathan, *Imperatores Victi: Military Defeat and Aristocratic Competition in the Middle and Late Republic*, Berkeley: University of California Press, 1990, p. 1.
3 Marcus Aurelius, *Meditations*, trans. Maxwell Staniforth, London: Penguin, 1964, 2.11, p. 48.
4 Juvenal, Satire 13, lines 2–4, in *The Sixteen Satires*, trans. Peter Green, London: Penguin, 1974, p. 249.
5 Juvenal, Satire 10, lines 363–4, p. 217.
6 Cicero, 'The Dream of Scipio', in *On the Good Life*, trans. Michael Grant, Harmondsworth: Penguin, 1971, pp. 349–52.
7 Barton, Carlin A., *Roman Honor: The Fire in the Bones*, Berkeley: University of California Press, 2001, p. 12. See also, Santosuosso, Antonio, *Storming the Heavens: Soldiers, Emperors and Civilians in the Roman Empire*, London: Pimlico, 2004, pp. 22–4.
8 Plutarch, 'Coriolanus', in *Makers of Rome*, trans. Ian Scott-Kilvert, London: Penguin, 1965, p. 16.
9 Goldsworthy, Adrian, *Roman Warfare*, London: Cassell, 2002, pp. 114–15.
10 Appian, *The Civil Wars*, trans. John Carter, London: Penguin, 1996, p. 186.
11 Josephus, *The Jewish War*, trans. G.A. Williamson, revised E. Mary Smallwood, London: Penguin, 1981, pp. 180–1.
12 Polybius, *The Rise of the Roman Empire*, trans. Ian Scott-Kilvert, London: Penguin, 1979, p. 82.
13 Plutarch, 'Cato the Elder', in *Makers of Rome*, pp. 140–1.
14 Lucan, *Civil War*, trans. Susan H. Braund, Oxford: Oxford University Press, 1992, 2.382–3 and 390–1, p. 32.
15 Livy, *The Early History of Rome*, trans. Aubrey de Sélincourt, London: Penguin, 2002, pp. 226–30.

16 Virgil, *The Aeneid*, trans. W.F. Jackson Knight, Harmondsworth: Penguin, 1956, p. 53.
17 Livy, *The War with Hannibal*, trans. Aubrey de Sélincourt, London: Penguin, 1972, 21.4, p. 26.
18 Ibid, 22.6, p. 101.
19 Sallust, *The Jugurthine War*, trans. S.A. Handford, London: Penguin, 1963, pp. 70–1.
20 Livy, *The War with Hannibal*, 24.36, p. 276.
21 Barton, *Roman Honor*, p. 142.
22 Marcus Aurelius, *Meditations*, 2.1, p. 45.
23 Ibid, 4.7, p. 65.
24 Cicero, *On Moral Obligation*, trans. John Higginbotham, London: Faber & Faber, 1967, pp. 165, 167 and 178. Sallust states a similar opinion: *The Jugurthine War*, p. 79.
25 Cicero, cited in Barton, *Roman Honor*, pp. 126–7.
26 Josephus, *The Jewish War*, p. 233.
27 Ibid, pp. 140–1.
28 Stephen Oakley, 'The Roman Conquest of Italy', in Rich, John and Shipley, Graham (eds), *War and Society in the Roman World*, London and New York: Routledge, 1995, p. 16; and Jiminez, Ramon L., *Caesar against the Celts*, Edison, NJ: Castle Books, 1996, p. 224.
29 William V. Harris, 'Current Directions in the Study of Roman Imperialism', in Harris, William V. (ed.), *The Imperialism of Mid-Republican Rome*, Rome: American Academy in Rome, 1984, p. 17. See also Harris, William V., *War and Imperialism in Republican Rome, 327–70 BC*, Oxford: Clarendon Press, 1979, pp. 56–93.
30 Erich S. Gruen, 'Material Rewards and the Drive for Empire', in Harris (ed.), *The Imperialism of Mid-Republican Rome*, pp. 59–82.
31 Badian, E., *Roman Imperialism in the Late Republic*, Ithaca: Cornell University Press, 1968, p. 19.
32 Ibid, pp. 60–76. Even Harris, who argues that the profit motive was an important element of Roman imperialism, accepts that mercantile interests were not a significant factor: Harris, *War and Imperialism*, p. 60.
33 Jerzy Linderski, 'Si vis pacem, para bellum: Concepts of Defensive Imperialism', in Harris (ed.), *The Imperialism of Mid-Republican Rome*, p. 136.
34 Livy, *The Early History of Rome*, pp. 69–71.
35 See Harris, *War and Imperialism*, pp. 169–71.
36 Sherwin-White, A.N., 'Rome the Aggressor?', *The Journal of Roman Studies*, 1980, vol. 70, 177.
37 Polybius, *The Rise of the Roman Empire*, p. 48.
38 Payne, Robert, *Rome Triumphant: How the Empire Celebrated its Victories*, New York: Barnes & Noble, 1993, p. 80.
39 Kern, Paul Bentley, *Ancient Siege Warfare*, Bloomington and Indianapolis: Indiana University Press, 1999, p. 329.
40 See Eckstein, Arthur M., *Senate and General: Individual Decision-Making and Roman Foreign Policy (264–194 BC)*, Berkeley: University of California Press, 1987, for a detailed analysis of this phenomenon.
41 See, for instance, Sherwin-White, A.N., *Roman Foreign Policy in the East, 168 BC to AD 1*, London: Duckworth, 1984, pp. 12–13.
42 Caesar, *The Conquest of Gaul*, trans. S.A. Handford, London: Penguin, 1982, pp. 31–3.
43 Ibid, p. 45.
44 Ibid, p. 97.
45 Plutarch, 'Crassus', in *Makers of Rome*, p. 130.
46 See Plutarch, 'Caesar', in *Fall of the Roman Republic*, trans. Rex Warner, London: Penguin, 1972, p. 288.
47 Lucan, *Civil War*, p. 6.
48 Caesar, *The Civil War*, trans. Jane F. Gardner, London: Penguin, 1967, p. 37.
49 Ibid, p. 39.

50 Ibid, p. 78.
51 Plutarch, 'Marius', in *Fall of the Roman Republic*, p. 22.
52 See Holland, Tom, *Rubicon: The Triumph and Tragedy of the Roman Republic*, London: Little Brown, 2003, pp. 64–7, for a brief summary of these events.
53 Tacitus, *The Annals of Imperial Rome*, trans. Michael Grant, revised edition, London: Penguin, 1989, p. 327.
54 Suetonius, 'Claudius', 24, in *The Twelve Caesars*, trans. Robert Graves, revised Michael Grant, London: Penguin, 1989, p. 201.
55 Cicero, cited in Barton, *Roman Honor*, p. 74.
56 Polybius, *The Rise of the Roman Empire*, p. 119.
57 Mattern, Susan, *Rome and the Enemy: Imperial Strategy in the Principate*, Berkeley: University of California Press, 2002, p. xii. See also pp. 171–2 for a detailed exposition of this thesis.
58 Polybius, *The Rise of the Roman Empire*, pp. 50–1.
59 Livy, *The War with Hannibal*, 24.43, p. 283.
60 Polybius, *The Rise of the Roman Empire*, p. 51.
61 Caesar, *The Civil War*, p. 69.
62 Polybius, *The Rise of the Roman Empire*, pp. 346–7.
63 Plutarch, 'Marcellus', in *Makers of Rome*, p. 90.
64 Plutarch, 'Sertorius', in *Makers of Rome*, p. 205.
65 Josephus, *The Jewish War*, pp. 312–13.
66 Ibid, p. 313.
67 Plutarch, 'Fabius Maximus', in *Makers of Rome*, p. 64.
68 Appian, *The Civil Wars*, p. 101.
69 Ibid, p. 32.
70 Livy, *The Early History of Rome*, p. 281.
71 Plutarch, 'Sertorius', in *Makers of Rome*, p. 219.
72 Juvenal, *The Sixteen Satires*, p. 210.
73 Livy, *The Early History of Rome*, pp. 43 and 311–12.
74 There is no corroborative evidence for the *spolia opima* of either Romulus or Cossus, so in fact only Marcellus can be said with certainty to have won the honour. Flower, Harriet I., 'The Tradition of the *Spolia Opima*: M. Claudius Marcellus and Augustus', *Classical Antiquity*, 2000, vol. 19, no. 1, 46.
75 Suetonius, 'Claudius', 1, in *The Twelve Caesars*, p. 186.
76 Cassius Dio, *The Roman History: The Reign of Augustus*, trans. Ian Scott-Kilvert, London: Penguin, 1987, p. 85.
77 Payne, *Rome Triumphant*, p. 14.
78 Caesar, *The Conquest of Gaul*, p. 73.
79 Livy, *The War with Hannibal*, 30.44, p. 676.
80 Appian, *The Civil Wars*, p. 92.
81 Tacitus, *Annals*, p. 155.
82 Mattern, *Rome and the Enemy*, p. 9.
83 Payne, *Rome Triumphant*, p. 149.
84 Maxfield, Valerie A., *The Military Decorations of the Roman Army*, London: B.T. Batsford, 1981, p. 108.
85 Rosenstein, *Imperatores Victi*, p. 7.
86 Ibid, p. 6.
87 Polybius, *The Rise of the Roman Empire*, p. 302.
88 Plutarch, 'Tiberius Gracchus', in *Makers of Rome*, pp. 157–9.
89 Livy, *The War with Hannibal*, 22.60, p. 165.
90 Rosenstein, *Imperatores Victi*, p. 114.
91 Plutarch, 'Marcellus', p. 97, and Livy, 25.6, *The War with Hannibal*, pp. 299–302.
92 For the information in this section, see Maxfield, *Military Decorations*, and Watson, G.R., *The Roman Soldier*, Ithaca: Cornell University Press, 1969, pp. 114–21.

93 Maxfield, *Military Decorations*, pp. 86 and 90.
94 Ibid, p. 233.
95 Tacitus, *Annals*, p. 309.
96 Maxfield, *Military Decorations*, p. 57.
97 Appian, *The Civil Wars*, p. 343.
98 Polybius, *The Rise of the Roman Empire*, p. 335.
99 Josephus, *The Jewish War*, pp. 339 and 341.
100 Ibid, p. 352.
101 Appian, *The Civil Wars*, p. 25.
102 Ibid, p. 113.
103 Tacitus, *Annals*, pp. 67–8, and Suetonius, 'Gaius', 3, in *The Twelve Caesars*, p. 155.
104 Tacitus, *Annals*, p. 358.
105 Josephus, *The Jewish War*, p. 264.
106 Polybius, *The Rise of the Roman Empire*, p. 536.
107 Plutarch, 'Pyrrhus', in *The Age of Alexander: Nine Greek Lives*, trans. Ian Scott-Kilvert, London: Penguin, 1973, p. 408.
108 Livy, *The War with Hannibal*, p. 79.
109 Polybius, *The Rise of the Roman Empire*, pp. 248–9.
110 Plutarch, 'Fabius Maximus', p. 59.
111 Livy, *The War with Hannibal*, p. 109.
112 Plutarch, 'Fabius Maximus', pp. 59–60.
113 Appian, *The Civil Wars*, p. 104.
114 Josephus, *The Jewish War*, p. 294.
115 Cassius Dio, *The Roman History*, 56.13, p. 232.
116 Livy, *The Early History of Rome*, p. 401.
117 Polybius, *The Rise of the Roman Empire*, p. 415.
118 Caesar, *The Conquest of Gaul*, p. 221.
119 Appian, *The Civil Wars*, p. 301.
120 Tacitus, *Annals*, p. 259.
121 Cicero, *On Moral Obligations*, p. 177.
122 Ibid, p. 53.
123 Polybius, *The Rise of the Roman Empire*, p. 352.
124 Ibid, p. 669.
125 Eckstein, *Senate and General*, pp. 272–85.
126 Pomeroy, Sarah B., *Goddesses, Whores, Wives & Slaves: Women in Classical Antiquity*, London: Pimlico, 1994, p. 189.
127 Virgil, *Aeneid*, p. 68.

4 Mediaeval chivalry

Background

Chivalry, says historian Malcolm Vale, was 'the sentiment of honour in its medieval guise'.[1] It was, more precisely, the code of conduct of knights – the heavily armed and armoured mounted warriors who dominated the military landscape between the eleventh and fifteenth centuries AD. Various factors had led to their dominance. Among other things, the introduction of the stirrup into Europe in the eighth century had given horsemen greater stability, while later advances in metallurgy also improved both weapons and armour, giving knights a hitherto unattainable level of protection.[2] A group of knights acting in concert constituted a formidable fighting force.

At first the term 'knight' simply referred to any soldier who was suitably equipped. Many early knights came from humble backgrounds, and served a lord who provided them with the necessary equipment.[3] With time, knighthood became more and more associated with hereditary nobility. Knights developed a caste mentality, and came to feel some sense of moral obligation towards each other. This sense did not extend to ordinary people, who were often treated with the utmost barbarity.[4]

Much of the code of chivalry was French in origin, although it rapidly spread to other countries, most notably England (whose nobility was in many cases French and often held lands in France). It is on the France and England of the twelfth to fifteenth centuries that this chapter therefore concentrates.

Honour and virtue in the middle ages

For mediaeval knights the attainment of honour was the second greatest good, after the salvation of the soul. As one of the most famous French knights of the fourteenth century, Geoffroi de Charny, put it: 'In this vocation one should cast one's heart and mind on winning honour, which endures for ever, rather than on winning profit and booty, which one can lose with one single hour.'[5] Similarly, Ramon Lull wrote, 'honour is worth more than gold or sylver without any comparyson … it is more grete deffaulte for to stele or take away chivalry than for to stele money.'[6]

The pursuit of renown was entirely respectable, as long as one demanded only such glory as one was entitled to. Mediaeval writers stressed that, as Thomas Aquinas wrote, 'only virtue entitles a person to honour.'[7] Defining chivalric virtue was not easy. Chivalry was not the product of a single philosophy, but an amalgam of several, often opposed, ones. It blended traditional warrior values – the pursuit of glory, the display of prowess, and so on – with those of Christian morality – service of God, devotion to the poor and weak, mercy, and forgiveness – and with those of court fashion – courtesy, gentility, and largesse.[8] Inevitably this created tensions within the system.

Mediaeval chivalry was first and foremost a code of fighting men. Its primary values were those which contributed to success in war. In consequence, prowess was the highest virtue.[9] Grotesque ferocity was admired. Raoul de Cambrai, in the poem bearing his name, is called 'a splendid warrior … a man of extraordinary strength.'[10] 'Anyone who could have seen him handling his shield', says the poem, 'and going up the enemy ranks to right and left with his sword would indeed have remembered him as a fearless knight.'[11] In a similar fashion, the *Chanson de Roland* praises Roland's colleague Oliver, stating, 'Anyone having seen him dismember Saracens, piling one corpse on top of another, would remember him a true knight.'[12]

The main measure of a knight was his deadliness. Gerald of Wales wrote with admiration: 'He who had seen how John de Courcy wielded his sword, with one stroke lopping off heads and with another arms, must needs have commended him for a most valiant soldier.'[13] At Crécy, according to the chronicle of Geoffrey le Baker, Edward Prince of Wales (the Black Prince), 'displayed marvellous courage … running through horses, felling knights, crushing helmets, cutting lances apart … nor did he rest from his labours until the enemy retreated leaving behind a heap of dead bodies.'[14] This made him, according to the chronicler Froissart, 'the flower of the world's knighthood … this most gallant and chivalrous prince'.[15]

If prowess was the paramount virtue, second in significance was loyalty. In the Middle Ages this held particular importance because of the system of feudalism, which depended upon vassals swearing oaths of loyalty to their lords, in return for which they received certain benefits, such as land. When loyalty was absent, defeat in war rapidly followed. As a result, those in power sought to instil the idea that breaking one's word was disgraceful. Thus, perjury was one of the three main reasons for excluding knights from participation in tournaments (the other two being usury and marriage beneath one's station).[16]

Admittedly, there was room for deception and betrayal within the honour system. Much mediaeval warfare consisted of struggles between vassals and lords, a fact which hardly seems compatible with the emphasis on loyalty and truthfulness. The explanation is that loyalty was reciprocal in nature. A man owed his word to his lord only as long as he considered that the lord was keeping his promises. Once he felt that this was no longer the case, he was conveniently released from his obligations.

Despite this loophole, a knight's life was, in idealistic theory at least, one of loyal service. A knight served God, his lord, his lady, and supposedly also the common people. The allegiance to God elevated knighthood to a position of particular honour. Knights were supposed to serve God on earth by bringing justice and defending the faith against infidels. In terms of earthly service, the focus of loyalty shifted somewhat over time. At first, the lord was a great noble of any sort, but by the later Middle Ages, the idea was increasingly prevalent that service should be to a king.

Service of ladies was an innovation of the twelfth century, and developed with the spread of courtly culture. As the threat from outside invasion (by Vikings, Saracens, and others) receded at the end of the Dark Ages, and prosperity and some sort of stability returned to Western Europe, refined manners and culture re-emerged. Those who served a lord or prince now had to shine at home as well as at the wars. They needed to display fine manners and be able to converse not just with fellow knights but also with women. Romantic love became fashionable. Fighting became, at least in literature, increasingly a matter of contending for a lady's favour. In contrast to Greece and Rome, honour became increasingly mixed up with relationships with the other sex.

Courtesy demanded that as well as a warrior, a knight should be 'a gentleman, a scholar, perhaps a poet, certainly a lover'. Valour was to be 'blended with delicacy'.[17] In time, the values learnt at court made their way on to the battlefield. Trained to be polite, knights felt it appropriate to extend politeness or at least some basic consideration to fellow knights, even those on the other side. This could range from granting mercy to those in one's power to handicapping oneself by eschewing any 'unfair' advantages in battle.

Another influence on knights was the Christian Church, which did what it could to instil ideas of mercy, restraint, and charity into them. A major milestone was the Peace of God movement which began in the 980s. The Peace of God tried to provide protection to certain categories of persons, such as clergymen and agricultural labourers, by prohibiting attacks on them. The later Truce of God movement tried to further limit the scope of fighting by forbidding combat on certain days of the week.

The Church did not attempt to outlaw war, but to control it by diverting fighting men away from looting, pillaging, and other selfish acts into endeavours which served the public good. Knights were no longer meant to pursue their own personal profit. Instead they were to serve their lord and God, fight injustice, right wrongs, and establish order. Those who fought for gain would be damned, but those who fought to serve and protect others would win both salvation and earthly honour.

The Church built on this by Christianizing some of the rituals which surrounded knighthood. In its simplest form, the act of knighting consisted solely of another knight girding a sword and belt onto the new knight. Eventually, a whole religious ceremony developed, designed to give a holy gloss to knighthood, and thereby, it was hoped, persuade knights of their religious obligations. In its most elaborate form, the initiation rite required the initiate to purify himself in a bath, confess his sins, go to church, stay up all night praying, and then attend mass in the morning. Finally, he would kneel before the altar, where a knight would gird him and complete the ceremony.[18]

On top of this, the Church sought to displace knights' activities away from Europe by encouraging them to go on Crusade. This last move brought a change in the Church's attitude towards warfare and knighthood in general, for with the advent of crusading, knights became the spearhead of the Church, and thus unquestionably God's servants on earth. The problem was that the sacralization of knighthood gave honour to knights in general, and not just to the good ones. As a result, a plan to limit war did the opposite. As Peter of Blois complained:

> Once soldiers bound themselves by oath that they would stand up for the state, that they would not flee from the battle-line and that they would give up their lives for the public interest. Now the young knights receive their swords from the altar and thereby they profess that they are sons of the Church and that they have taken up the sword for the honour of the priesthood, the protection of the poor, for the punishment of malefactors, and for the liberation of the homeland. But matters are very different; for immediately they have been girt with the belt of knighthood they at once rise up against the anointed of the Lord and rage violently against the patrimony of the Crucified. They despoil and rob the subject poor of Christ, and miserably oppress the wretched without mercy.[19]

Honour and the causes of war

Although mediaeval theorists claimed that the sole legitimate authority to wage war belonged to sovereign princes, in reality wars between rulers constituted only a small percentage of all wars in this period. Many conflicts were either rebellions by vassals against their lords, or private wars fought between powerful individuals with their personal armies. Questions of honour often played an important role in these private wars. An injury suffered by one party demanded revenge, which in turn demanded counter-revenge, and so on, in a cycle of violence which it could be hard to end. Feuds could extend over several generations. The regular practice of revenge made it a habit which became internalized in the consciences of knights. Some even considered revenge to be a good in itself. Thus Ramon Lull praised it, writing: 'gretely is he the frende of Chyvalrye when he taketh vengeaunce of suche enemyes that wold take from hym and plucke away the wele and honoure of chyvalrye and corrupte his noble courage.'[20] As central authority increased, private wars declined somewhat in importance, but in France they continued even into the late fourteenth century. The long-standing conflict between the families of the Counts of Armagnac and Foix in southern France was perhaps the most notable example.

Given the relative lawlessness of the era, there was good reason for responding violently to insult. Kings who failed to establish a powerful military reputation very often found themselves beset by enemies not only from without but also from within their kingdoms. According to the Anglo-Saxon Chronicles, 'When the traitors realised that [King] Stephen was a mild man, gentle and good, and imposed no penalty, they committed every enormity. They had done him homage and sworn oaths, but they held to no pledge.'[21] Sensitivity to insult acted as a deterrent against attack.

Consequently, concern with loss of face played a major role in starting wars. In 1388, for instance, the French attacked the Duchy of Guelders, a small German territory between the Meuse and the Rhine. The Duke of Guelders, perhaps at the instigation of the English, had sent a message to King Charles of France, addressed simply to 'Charles de Valois' (thus implying that he was not the rightful king). In his message the Duke had announced his allegiance to King Richard II of England. Many of Charles' advisors suggested that he ignore this insult as beneath him, but others disagreed. One of the leading French noblemen, Enguerrand de Coucy, told the King that if he 'suffered such insults to pass unrequited, foreign countries would hold the nobles of France very cheap'. This convinced Charles, who ordered an expedition to march against Guelders. An additional consideration in this case may have been Charles's desire to restore his honour after a planned invasion of England was cancelled two years in a row despite huge efforts and investment. He did not succeed, as the Guelders expedition bogged down in rain and failed to achieve anything.[22]

By this stage early forms of English and French patriotism had come into being. English kings still waged war for their own personal benefit rather than that of the 'nation' as a whole, but their ability to continue fighting depended to some extent on public opinion, which increasingly viewed England's wars through patriotic lenses. The victories of the Scots against Edward II, the humiliating peace with Scotland signed in 1328, and the image of Edward III having to pay homage to the King of France for the Duchy of Aquitaine in 1325 and 1329, 'outraged public opinion' and created 'a sense of humiliation', which encouraged people to support Edward III's subsequent wars against France.[23] As the Hundred Years War went on, a similar national awakening in France played a parallel role in mobilizing popular support for war.

Elsewhere in Europe, the focus of honour was still far more local, but the dynamic was similar. The War of the Oaken Bucket lasted off and on for 12 years from 1325 to 1337, and began when some soldiers from the city of Modena in Italy took a well bucket from the territory of neighbouring Bologna. When Bologna demanded the return of the bucket, Modena refused, and the more Bologna demanded its return, the more important it became to continue to refuse. For Modena, the retention of the bucket became an issue of civic pride, proof of the city's will and refusal to be browbeaten. Eventually, the dispute turned into war, which Modena won. Nowadays the bucket is on display in Modena town hall, where it serves as a perpetual reminder of the city's defence of its honour.

Land lay at the heart of many wars in the Middle Ages, for it was the primary source of wealth. Even in the modern era, there are frequent news reports of neighbours' fights over hedges. It is not at all surprising that land disputes were endemic in the Middle Ages, and, given that there were few other ways of settling these quarrels, it is equally unsurprising that they repeatedly turned violent. We should not, however, assume that men fought for land just because of its material value. Land gave wealth, but wealth gave honour. It is no coincidence that a lord's collection of lands was known in England as an 'honour'. Land provided men with status and the ability to display their generosity and largesse. This was extremely important. Largesse, claimed Chrétien de Troyes, 'is the queen and lady who brightens all virtues. ... largesse, wherever it appears, surpasses all other virtues.'[24]

One can see the relative importance of land versus honour in the decision by King Louis IX of France to make peace with Henry III of England, in a deal whereby Henry was able to keep his lands in the Duchy of Aquitaine, but in return agreed to pay homage to Louis. Joinville, a close colleague of the French king, records that Louis' councillors spoke out against the agreement, accusing him of 'needlessly throwing away the land you are giving to the King of England'. But Louis rejected their advice, telling them: 'I gain increased honour for myself through the peace I have made with the King of England, for he is now my vassal, which he has never been before.'[25] Clearly, for Louis land for honour represented a good exchange.

Feudal disputes caused many wars as well. The Hundred Years War, for instance, was essentially a feudal dispute on a large scale. On the surface, it was a dynastic struggle for the French crown, which Edward III of England claimed as his own (with some good reason, as he was the closest living male relative of the previous French king). To some extent, however, Edward only claimed the French crown as a tool to gain a more achievable goal – the establishment of full sovereignty over the Duchy of Aquitaine. The Kings of England had long held this duchy in southern France, but, as mentioned above, in 1259 Henry III had agreed to pay homage to the French crown for it. This had put him and his successors in a very difficult position since it made them vassals of the King of France, and allowed their own vassals within Aquitaine to appeal decisions to Paris.[26] Edward felt that by exerting authority over Aquitaine, the King of France was denying him his rights. As Edward made clear, this denial was an insult to his honour. It was, he wrote, a 'grete wrong' and 'injurious'. For the English monarchs, their position as vassals of France was an offence to their honour, and their war with France was aimed at removing that offence as much as at seizing control of France itself.

War was the preferred option in this case because diplomacy was unlikely to help Edward achieve his aims. There was, however, another reason why people chose so often to resolve their differences by war, and that was that chivalry idealized war and covered it with a shroud of glory. Chivalry's worship of prowess made it necessary for knights to seek and even provoke war in order to display their skills.

It was often the case that in deliberations over whether to go to war, the younger knights, who had yet to establish their reputations, were the keenest to fight. This at least was the situation described by Jordan Fantosme, when older advisors of William the Lion, King of Scotland, urged peace with England in 1173, while the young knights urged war.[27] Some knights' desire for glory led them to seek wars wherever they could find them. This made peacemaking extremely difficult, since when two states made peace they then had to find employment for hundreds of heavily armed men. The frequent solution was to start another war somewhere else. Thus, after the Treaty of Brétigny brought peace between France and England in 1360, numerous French knights, eager for glory, went off to serve in Spain on behalf of the pretender to the throne of Castile, Enrique the Bastard. Similarly, after the Anglo-French truce of 1375, Charles V of France helped Enguerrand de Coucy to wage a private war against the Duke of Austria in order to keep busy numerous knights keen 'to advance themselves in honor'.[28] Glory-seeking meant that reaching peace in one place simply created war in another.

Honour as a motivation for fighting

Feudal obligations on freemen to serve their lord may have left some men with little choice in the matter, but in general only a small portion of royal armies were recruited through feudal levies, and in any case vassals were only obliged to serve their lord under arms for 40 days at a time.[29] For the most part, royal armies depended on paid soldiers, recruiting them through captains by a system of indentures. Even knights generally received pay for their service. One may conclude from this that money was a major incentive for people to fight.

War also offered the opportunity to enrich oneself through booty. The enormous amounts of booty taken by English soldiers in France after battles such as Crécy and Poitiers explains the enduring popularity of the Hundred Years War in England.[30] Once word got around that fortunes could be made, volunteers for active service were readily found. Geoffrey de Villehardouin described a sergeant on a boat returning from a crusade who jumped from his ship on to that of Comte Baudoin de Flandre sailing the other way towards Constantinople, saying, 'I'm going with these people, for it certainly seems to me they'll win some land for themselves.'[31] On another crusade, Joinville discovered that the men he had brought with him would continue serving only if paid.[32]

Knights could enrich themselves by plunder or by capturing other knights and ransoming them; these were honourable ways to generate wealth. One could lose as well as gain in war, however, making it a very risky business for those who already possessed wealth. Furthermore, in some instances knights willingly incurred great expenses in order to wage war without any realistic expectation of material rewards. The crusades are a case in point. Many men mortgaged everything they owned in order to take part,[33] and few ever made a profit out of the experience. A recent study of the First Crusade concludes that religious feelings dominated when knights chose to take the cross.[34] As Honoré Bonet wrote: 'if a soldier die in battle in a just war ... he ... will be saved in Paradise.'[35]

Not every soldier, or even every crusader, had such lofty religious ideals. Some of those who crusaded had no choice about it, having been sent to fight as penance for serious crimes.[36] Criminals frequently found their way into military service. English kings gave pardons to outlaws who served in their armies in France in the fourteenth century. At least 850 letters of pardon were handed out in 1339 and 1340 alone, and perhaps as much as 12 per cent of the manpower of English armies of this period consisted of outlaws.[37]

Criminals of this sort filled up the ranks of the infantry. Knights were far more often simply in search of glory. Jean de Bueil commented that 'all worldly honour is gained by conquering and fighting.'[38] According to Geoffrey le Baker, when the Dauphin attacked the English at Poitiers, 'it could not strike fear into the hearts of our men, eager for honour and for revenge.'[39] And the Herald of Sir John Chandos described the battle of Najera fought by the Black Prince in 1367, writing, 'The English, eager to win honour, now dismounted. The prince spoke to them … "Let us do such deeds today that we may depart with honour".'[40]

The pursuit of glory could lead to some strange behaviour in war. When Louis, Duke of Bourbon, was besieging the castle of Verteuil during the Hundred Years War, he dug a mine under the castle, and then challenged any defending knight to fight one of the besieging knights in the tunnel. The castle's commander, a squire by the name of Bartholomew de Montprivat, accepted the challenge, but when he learnt that he was fighting the Duke himself, he immediately surrendered and offered to surrender the castle as well if the Duke would make him a knight. The glory he would acquire from having fought a Duke and having been knighted by him more than outweighed any glory he would lose from surrendering the castle. The Duke agreed to the proposition, de Montprivat handed over the keys to the castle, and the Duke knighted him. The pair then decided to postpone the surrender for a day so that their colleagues could enjoy themselves fighting in the mine as well.[41] Except in terms of the joy of fighting and love of renown, this episode has no obvious explanation.

Honours and rewards

Land and money were two of the most important rewards for excellence in war. In a typical case, in 1349 Edward III gave 100 marks to John de Potenhale as a reward for capturing Geoffroi de Charny at Calais.[42] Further up the scale, the Black Prince promised Sir James Audley £400 a year for life for his conspicuous valour at Poitiers.[43] King Henry V of England made 358 grants of land in Normandy during his campaigns in France. This handily gave those who received the land a second reason for continuing the struggle against the French.[44]

Rewards were not only material. Chroniclers and minstrels took care to write and sing of those who had excelled. The Herald of Sir John Chandos, for instance, listed the names of all those whom he felt had fought bravely at the battle of Poitiers, and also those who had fought on the Black Prince's expedition to Spain.[45] In the same way, Jordan Fantosme's Chronicle lists those who stayed loyal to King Henry II during the revolt of his son, the Young King. Chivalric orders such as the Order of the Star kept written records of the exploits of their members.[46]

Determining who merited such honours was in part the job of heralds. These officials enjoyed a special status in mediaeval warfare. They carried messages between the warring parties, enjoyed immunity from attack, and recorded the names of those who had performed well in battle. They were also the experts in coats of arms, which had originally come into being as a means of recognizing knights on the battlefield, but soon became closely associated with the honour of a knight and his family.[47] Granting somebody the right to a coat of arms in effect ennobled him, and was often a reward for meritorious service. Those who already had noble status gained further honour from the addition of special devices and symbols to their arms. Such devices had a somewhat similar role to modern medals.[48] Chivalric orders also issued insignia which had the same purpose, and election to an order was another reward which granted great honour.

The first of the great orders of knights in Western Europe was the Order of the Garter, established by Edward III in 1349. The members were the king himself and 25 other knights selected for their distinction. In emulation, King John the Good of France founded the Order of the Star in 1351. The grandest order was probably the Order of the Golden Fleece, established by Philip the Good, Duke of Burgundy, in 1430. The charter of the Golden Fleece laid out clearly the purpose of such orders, which was a) to encourage honourable behaviour in war, and b) to reward it. A third, unstated, purpose was to bind the order's members to its leader, in this case the Duke of Burgundy.[49]

Orders took their charter to promote honourable behaviour seriously. Not only did they keep records of their members' valour in war, they also punished those members who behaved dishonourably. For instance, Sir John Falstolf was expelled from the Order of the Garter for alleged cowardice at Patay in 1429. The Order of the Golden Fleece also expelled members for offences such as cowardice and sorcery.

Membership of the great orders was only open to a few. Others could hope to win honorific titles. 'Knight' itself, originally simply a word which applied to any heavily armed soldier, had gradually became one such title. Lords often rewarded distinguished conduct in battle by knighting. Those already knighted could be further promoted to the rank of 'banneret'. Whereas ordinary knights merely flew triangular or swallow-tailed pennons in battle, bannerets had the right to fly rectangular banners. The bannerets helped to organize the cavalry during battle, and had authority to issue orders to other knights. In return they were expected to bring a troop of knights into combat with them, and for this reason, some knights refused promotion.

Similarly, some soldiers refused to be knighted. In England, knights had administrative responsibilities in local government, and many preferred to remain unknighted rather than have to endure this burden. In addition, the status of knighthood demanded an expensive lifestyle. It became necessary for lords to give those they promoted the financial means appropriate for their higher status. When the poor squire Henry Eam was knighted after the crossing of the Scheldt in September 1339, he received lands worth £200 a year to support him in his new position.[50] Similarly, on his promotion to banneret after capturing King David of Scotland at Neville's Cross in 1347, John de Coupland received a grant of £500 a year to maintain him in his new rank. In the same year Edward III gave William Fitzwarin two manors to keep him as a banneret after his promotion.[51] Money and land underpinned titular honours.

Honour and death

Chivalric writers affirmed that death was better than dishonour. 'Men of worth', wrote Geoffroi de Charny, 'teach you that it is better to die than to live basely.' 'If you want to be strong and of good courage', he continued, 'be sure that you care less about death than about shame.'[52] But deliberate martyrdom was not part of the knightly code. Suicide was contrary to Christian teaching, so there is no equivalent in chivalric history of Roman generals' habit of falling on their swords.

Equally, knights fought to win, but losing was not necessarily disgraceful. As long as one had fought gallantly for an honourable length of time, surrender was perfectly respectable. Bertrand du Guesclin, for instance, managed to get himself captured no fewer than four times, but remained the most admired knight of his era in France. Since so little dishonour attached to capture, dying to avoid it was not a reasonable trade.

Armies went to some effort to recover their dead and ensure that they received a Christian burial. After the Battle of Mansourah on 8 February 1250, the River Nile was said to be 'full of corpses', and King Louis hired 100 men for a week to clear the river and bury the dead. Later, says Joinville, after the Saracens destroyed the town of Saida, Louis himself 'personally supervised the burying of the bodies of all the Christians whom the Saracens had killed when they destroyed the city. He himself had carried some of the rotting, evil-smelling corpses to the trenches to be buried.'[53] Christian armies did not accord the same respect to their Muslim opponents. After Mansourah, while the crusaders buried their fellow Christians, 'They flung the bodies of the Saracens … over the further side of the bridge, and let them float down with the current.'[54]

Generally mediaeval armies buried those who had died in battle in a common pit, which they left without any marker or memorial. Joinville reported that the Christians recovered after Mansourah 'were buried in great trenches, all together'.[55] At Agincourt the English dug five grave pits after the battle and buried over 1,200 (mainly Frenchmen) in each of them.[56] The *Chanson de Roland* expressed this common practice quite well:

> All the friends whom they found dead
> They promptly carried to a common grave.
> …
> Then they buried them with full honours
> And they left them, what else could they do for them?[57]

Actually, they could do rather more, and did do so for those they considered important. Many aristocrats wished to be buried in their home country, and so when they died overseas, their bodies were boiled and the bones taken out and carried home.[58] The disparity in treatment between those deemed important and all the others is clear from the aftermath of the battle of Crécy, when Edward III sent out two knights and three heralds 'to identify the dead by their arms and two clerks to write down their names'. This was a common practice, but since the heralds were unlikely to have known every common soldier, it seems probable that the lists contained only the names of knights. Next, 'as an act of grace', wrote Froissart, 'the King caused the bodies of all the chief nobles to be taken up and buried in consecrated ground at the nearby church of Maintenay. He accorded the people of the district a three days' truce to go over the battlefield and bury the other dead.'[59] Nobility outweighed nationality; while the common English soldier received no special treatment after death, the English did honour those of high rank among the enemy. So, wrote the Herald of Sir John Chandos, after the battle of Crécy the English 'found the King of Bohemia [who had fought with the French] lying dead in a field. The King had him put in a coffin and placed on a litter covered in a cloth of gold. He sent him back to the enemy.'[60]

For knights who died at home, Church burials became more elaborate, as well as more militaristic, over time. By the fourteenth century, funeral ceremonies often included warhorses, presentations of armour and weapons, and even fully armed men.[61] Church effigies of knights began to appear in the thirteenth century,[62] and in the fourteenth century brasses of knights also came into fashion.[63] Tombs portrayed the deceased's coats of arms with epitaphs recounting his glorious deeds.[64] Heralds codified what degree of honour was appropriate for whom on military tombs, although their rules were not always obeyed. According to one treatise, a man who had merely fought in wars should appear armed, but with no coat of arms, and no helmet; a man who had fought with honour in tournaments should appear with a helmet, but with 'the visor raised, with hands clasped, and with his sword and spurs shown'; while someone who had died in combat on the winning side should have his visor closed, 'his drawn sword in his right hand with the point upward and his shield grasped in his left hand'.[65]

Honour and the conduct of war

Knights operated best in combination with other arms, such as infantry, archers, and engineers. Despite this, they retained a dominant position on the battlefield. This was not solely for reasons of class distinction. Rather, throughout the Middle Ages advances in technology continually improved the knight as a war-fighting machine. The introduction of plate armour, as well as other innovations such as the lance rest, enhanced knights' protection against projectile weapons and added to their ability to charge with extra force and 'shock'. Cavalry had the additional benefit of being able to pursue a routed enemy, a capability often required for a decisive victory.[66]

Furthermore, despite some failed efforts to ban crossbows (which knights disliked because of their ability to penetrate even plate armour), mediaeval military leaders were willing to experiment with new weapons systems, made regular use of longbows, crossbows, and firearms, and were not fixated on fighting from horseback. At both Poitiers and Agincourt, the mass of the French knights who died at the hands of the English did so fighting on foot. It is also the case that most campaigns consisted not of pitched battles fought to display prowess, but of a series of sieges and raids, as the armies ravaged the enemy countryside in a form of economic warfare.[67] Some degree of strategic planning was required, and good mediaeval generals were capable of coordinating several groups of forces over a wide area.[68]

The influence of chivalry came not so much at the higher level of grand strategy, weapons technology, and the like, but rather at the individual level, in the preferences of knights once they found themselves in a combat situation.[69] Then its influence could be very great indeed.

For a start, issues of precedence complicated the command of armies just as they had done in the armies of ancient Greece. The most honourable position was in the vanguard, because the vanguard was the first to strike the enemy. As a result, glory-seeking knights sometimes argued over this position. In one notable example, a French crusading army met its doom at Nicopolis in 1396. The crusaders had combined their forces with those of King Sigismund of Hungary who suggested that his Wallachian foot soldiers form the vanguard in order to absorb the shock of the expected Turkish attack; the French could then counter-attack. The French constable, Philippe d'Artois, Comte d'Eu, objected, saying that the French would be dishonoured if they took up the rear in accordance with this plan, and that they must lead the attack. The king reluctantly ceded. On seeing the Turkish vanguard, d'Eu led his men in a vigorous assault, and having initially routed the Turks, pursued them in the mistaken belief that they were the main enemy force. When, to their surprise, the latter then appeared, it crushed the exhausted Frenchmen. Almost the entire French force was killed or captured.[70]

The Battle of Nicopolis demonstrates the rashness often exhibited by knights in combat. The Battle of Mansourah in 1250 AD is another interesting example which combines recklessness with issues of precedence on the battlefield. Normally, the knights of the Order of the Temple formed the vanguard on crusade, but Joinville recounts that in this instance the Comte d'Artois, brother of King Louis of France, 'had no sooner got across the stream than he and all his men flung themselves on the Turks, who fled before them. The Templars let him know that he had gravely insulted them in assuming the lead when he should have followed after.' When the Count ignored them and pressed on, 'the Templars, thinking they would be shamed if they let the Comte d'Artois get in front of them … rushed headlong in pursuit of the Turks … right through the town of Mansourah and on into the fields beyond.' When the crusaders then tried to return, the Turks in Mansourah attacked them, throwing rocks and beams on them as passed through the narrow streets. In the ensuing chaos, the Comte d'Artois and about 300 knights perished.[71]

Such chivalric rashness also led to catastrophe for the French at Crécy. On sighting the English, King Philip of France ordered his troops to halt their advance, so as to be fresh for an assault the next day. But although the forward units obeyed this instruction, those behind them did not, whereupon the forward units began to move again. So, wrote Froissart:

> Pride and vanity took charge of events. Each wanted to outshine his companions … with disastrous consequences. … Neither the King nor his Marshals could restrain them any longer, for there were too many great lords among them, all determined to show their power.[72]

The urge to display prowess encouraged not only reckless attacks, but also various forms of single and group combat. Some knights seem to have regarded war as a type of sport, a tournament writ large. One example is the so-called 'Battle of the Thirty' in Brittany in 1351. The castle of Ploëmel was being defended by troops led by a German named Brandeburg, against forces under Sir Robert de Beaumanoir. The latter, according to Froissart, 'went up to the gate and summoned the said Brandeburg under sureties, asking whether he had not with him two or three companions who would be willing to joust with their swords against two or three of his own men for the sake of their ladies.' In reply, the German offered instead to take 30 of his men to an open space, where they could fight 30 of Sir Robert's. The combat took place the following Wednesday, and left about a dozen dead. After it was over, Sir Robert withdrew his forces back to their base.[73]

In general, once battle was joined, retreat was permissible, but only if banners had not been unfurled. The unfurling of banners indicated that high-ranking persons were present, and that others should stand and fight to defend the honour of the banners and the lords they represented. The Order of the Golden Fleece expelled the Seigneur de Montagu in 1433 because he fled from the battlefield of Anthon when banners were flying, but it dropped charges against Jean de Neufchastel, who had retreated from the French at Buxy in 1471, because, although the banner of the Duke of Burgundy had been at that battle, it had not been unfurled, and so the Duke's honour was not at stake.[74]

To encourage tenacity, the knights of the Order of the Star had to swear an oath that they would never retreat more than four acres in battle. The order's members seem to have taken this vow very seriously. Ambushed by the English at the battle of Mauron in 1352, they refused to retreat, and in consequence some 90 of them were killed.[75] The Order of the Star went out of business soon after.

Knights sometimes practised an extreme type of promise keeping, swearing preposterous vows which they were then honour-bound to keep. The more absurd and dangerous the vow, the more the honour which accrued from sticking to it. An Englishmen in the Hundred Years War wore an eye patch because he had promised to use only one eye until he carried out some great deed.[76] Joinville met a knight, named Geoffrey de Rançon, 'who, so I was told, had been greatly wronged by the Comte de la Marche. Because of this he had vowed on the Holy Gospels never to have his hair cut short, as is the custom with knights, but wear it long like a woman's until such time as he should be avenged on the count, either by his own hand or another's.' When he saw that King Louis had captured the count and his family, and the count 'was kneeling before the king and crying for mercy, he … had his hair trimmed there and then, in the presence of the king.'[77]

Keeping all forms of sworn words was as vital as it had been in earlier eras. King John of France, captured at Poitiers, went so far as to surrender himself to the English a second time after his release on parole, because one of his sons, who was being held hostage by the English as a guarantee for the King's ransom, had escaped from captivity, and John felt that the terms of his own parole had thereby been breached. To uphold his honour, he returned, entirely without prompting, to captivity.

There was room for pragmatism within this system. As previously mentioned, mediaeval loyalty was always reciprocal in nature. While besieged troops were honour-bound to hold out while there was still hope of relief, once it became clear that they had put up a reasonable resistance and that their lord had abandoned them, they were released from their obligation and could surrender with honour. This led to the custom of the 'conditional respite'. This involved the besieging forces agreeing to refrain from operations against the besieged for a set period, which could vary from a few days to a few months, and to allow the besieged to send a messenger to their lord requesting assistance. In return, the besieged gave their word that, if by the end of the stipulated period their lord had not come to their relief, they would surrender. Conditional respites benefited both sides. They spared the attackers the costs of a long siege and the risks of an assault, and allowed the defenders to escape from their predicament with honour.[78]

If a besieging force could not persuade a garrison to surrender, it could attempt to defeat it by guile, which was acceptable in a way which breach of word was not. Chivalric treatises urged the use of stratagem and surprise, and mediaeval knights, like fighters in all ages, wanted to win. Jordan Fantosme tells how Lord Richard of Lucy arranged a truce with William the Lion so that he could march south to deal with a new threat in the south of England from the Earl of Leicester. William would not have agreed to the deal if he had known of Leicester's landing in England, but Lucy hid this from him, and for this act of cunning won acclaim.[79] On another occasion, at the Battle of Evesham, the royal forces deceived Simon de Montfort into believing that reinforcements were approaching by using captured banners.[80]

Stratagems which involved any breach of word crossed the line, however, and were dishonourable. Thus Honoré Bonet wrote, 'I may conquer my enemy by craft or fraud without sin', but also stated that, 'the laws say that once a pledge is given to one's enemy it must be kept.' This meant that ambushes were acceptable, but breaking truces, seizing people during parleys, and so forth, were not.[81]

The idea of fighting fair seems not to have held much sway in the West in earlier eras. It began to come into its own in the Middle Ages. Chivalric literature preached that true men of prowess gave their enemy an even chance. For instance, in Thomas Malory's 'Morte Darthur', Sir Gareth refuses to delay a challenge to the Red Knight of the Red Laund until noon, even though he knows the latter will be weaker then, and explains his decision by saying, 'either I will win worship worshipfully, or die knightly in the field.'[82]

This line of thinking did have some influence on the behaviour of real knights. During his rebellion against his father Henry II, an unarmed Richard Lionheart found himself face-to-face with Henry's loyal servant William Marshal. The future crusader king told the Marshal: 'By God, Marshal, do not kill me. That would not be right for I am unarmed'. 'No, let the devil kill you', replied William, 'for I shall not', and then thrust his lance into Richard's horse, leaving the man unharmed.[83] Still, instances such as this were exceptional. Ninety-nine times out of a hundred, knights were quite prepared to exploit whatever advantages they had. Nonetheless, the idea of fair play had begun to sprout.

Honour and the enemy

Much of mediaeval war consisted of ravaging and pillaging the enemy's country. Innocent civilians were the main victims. 'You could have seen Flemings tying up peasants and leading them roped together like heathens', wrote Jordan Fantosme of the war in England in 1174; 'Women flee to the church only to be snatched away naked.'[84] On campaign with the English army in France in 1346, Michael Northburgh wrote home: 'Every day the men of arms spread out for fifteen or twenty miles, robbing and destroying … they burnt everything along the sea coast from Roche Masse to Ouistreham on the Caen estuary, a distance of 120 miles.'[85] 'War without fire', said Henry V, 'is like sausages without mustard.'[86]

Chivalric theorists persistently protested against brutality of this sort, but most knights did not consider it dishonourable. Ravaging served a useful military purpose, depriving one's enemy of the resources he needed to fight. 'This is the way to begin to fight', says Count Philip of Flanders in Jordan Fantosme's Chronicle; 'first lay waste the land, then destroy one's enemies.'[87] Besides, the caste nature of knighthood meant that the sufferings of ordinary people counted for little.

Respect for enemy knights was another matter. Among Christian knights, certain rules of honourable conduct were meant to apply. The sack of Limoges by the Black Prince exemplifies well the different treatments meted out to civilians and knights. Furious that Limoges had betrayed him by going over to the French, the prince determined to make the city pay for its disloyalty. When the English stormed the city, there were, according to Froissart,

> Pitiful scenes. Men, women and children flung themselves on their knees before the Prince, saying 'Have mercy on us, gentle sir!' But he was so inflamed with anger that he would not listen. Neither man nor woman was heeded, but all who could be found were put to the sword … More than three thousand persons, men, women and children, were dragged out to have their throats cut.

But, when the three knights commanding the French garrison surrendered to him and pleaded for their lives, after 'a masterful display of skilful fighting', the Black Prince wavered. He spared them, and called an end to the general slaughter.[88] No amount of appeal by women and children could sway him, but a request by three valiant knights did.

Massacres such as that at Limoges were not uncommon. The rules of war were similar to those in ancient Rome. A fortress which surrendered in good time could expect mercy, but one which fell to assault could expect slaughter. As historian Maurice Keen points out, matters of honour played a part in this. Once a commander had begun a siege he was honour-bound to see it through. Efforts to resist him offended his prestige, and those responsible lost their right to mercy.[89]

In pitched battle, knights more often aimed to capture than to kill each other. The act of capture in effect established a contract between the captor knight and the captive. The former agreed to spare the life of the latter, in return for which the captive agreed to be his prisoner. Killing prisoners was a breach of this contract, and so dishonourable.

Honour was not, of course, the only reason why knights were reluctant to kill their prisoners. Captives were a valuable source of income, as they had to pay ransom in order to gain their freedom. The code of chivalry stated that the level of a ransom should not be so high as to bankrupt the captive.[90] Knights did not always abide by this rule, and they did their best to set ransoms at the maximum level they thought their prisoners could pay. German knights had an unwholesome reputation for holding their prisoners in foul conditions in order to encourage them to agree to the highest possible ransom and pay with the greatest rapidity.[91] In England and France this sort of behaviour was frowned upon, although it sometimes occurred. A lot depended on the personal whim of the captor.[92]

To enable the captive knight to organize his ransom, his captor might release him if he gave his word (his 'parole') not to fight against the captor again until it was paid, and to return into captivity if he failed to raise the required sum. Escape was not considered honourable. 'If he is a gentleman', wrote Christine de Pizan, he 'should do what is expected of him, which is to say, keep his word to his captor … he should know that prison is not a place of entitlement … [and] endure the punishment gently and patiently.'[93] The one exception was if a prisoner was mistreated, which voided the contract between prisoner and captor and permitted the former to run away.

Inevitably, disputes arose when prisoners felt that they had been abused, or when they failed to fulfil the terms of their parole. To resolve these, the English and French established courts of honour to which injured knights could appeal. This was a rather problematic system, as in order to gain redress of grievance one had to appeal to the court which had authority over the other party, in other words to the court of the enemy, and such courts were obviously more likely to be sympathetic to knights of their own side. Nevertheless, they were on occasion willing to judge in favour of enemy knights and order their own knights to make redress.

In England matters of this sort often came before two hereditary military officers, the Earl Marshal and the Lord High Constable. In due course, their court of honour acquired the title of the Court of Chivalry.[94] Courts of honour could also be more informal collections of respected knights, well versed in the codes of chivalry and specially assembled for the occasion. An example of the latter was a court of 12 knights which met to try the Marshal d'Audreham after his capture by the army of the Black Prince at Najera. D'Audreham had fallen into the Prince's hands before, at Poitiers, and the terms of his parole were that he would not fight against him again. It seemed that he had broken his word. The Frenchman's defence was that at Najera the Black Prince had been fighting not as Prince of England but as a private individual in the pay of King Pedro of Castile. D'Audreham claimed that he had not been fighting against the Prince but against Pedro. The court accepted this defence and released him.[95]

Although knights might resort to litigation against one another, a more effective method often proved to be public shaming, for instance by displaying the arms of one's enemy reversed. In his study of mediaeval laws of war, Maurice Keen concludes that frequent employment of such methods of dishonouring opponents, shows 'how very seriously soldiers of the later middle ages regarded any matter which technically affected their honour'.[96]

Honour and the ending of wars

Matters of honour played as important a role in making peace as in making war. It was, for instance, considered dishonourable to seize somebody in the midst of a parley. Parleys could be very formal affairs, in which each side tried to impress the other by the size of their retinues and the luxuriousness of their dress. Care had to be taken to avoid giving offence by slips in etiquette. During a parley at Amiens in 1392, the French forbade anyone to insult or provoke any of the English, even in a tavern, 'on pain of death'. Instructions were given that the English were to be entertained free of charge and treated with the 'greatest honours' and courtesy.[97] The talks failed anyway because elements in the English camp still wanted war, but the fact that the French felt it necessary to issue such draconian instructions indicates how sensitive to questions of honour men at parleys often were.

Because it was so difficult to make peace, the warring parties might simply agree to a truce. It all too often proved impossible to abide even by that. During pauses in fighting, armies demobilized most of their soldiers. These then had a horrible tendency to ravage the countryside, often in large and well-organized groups such as the 'free companies' which rampaged through France during lulls in the Hundred Years War. In addition, once war between sovereign princes stopped, private wars might pick up again. In either case, one side or the other might accuse its opponent of being in some way responsible for the continued combat, and declare the truce null and void.

Relying on one's enemy's sense of honour to respect the terms of peace was generally insufficient. As a result, belligerents would sometimes demand hostages as guarantees. The Treaty of Brétigny between England and France in 1360, for instance, specified that 40 French hostages would go to England, including two of the king's sons and his brother, the Duc d'Orleans. They were to be released in small groups as the king's ransom was paid and the other terms of the treaty were fulfilled.[98] It was after one of these hostages, Louis Duc d'Anjou, absconded while on parole in Calais, that King John decided to return to captivity himself. That even a king's son would so irresponsibly jeopardize a peace treaty demonstrates the difficulty rulers had in making peace.

Another way of trying to maintain peace was through the use of a 'conservator', a sort of mediaeval judge whose job was to adjudicate complaints about breaches of truces. Sometimes tribunals of several people chosen by each side played the same role.[99] Again, the use of such interlocutors suggests that lack of trust was a major problem in peacemaking in this era. The conditioning which made knights keep ridiculous vows did not always extend to respecting the terms of promises between states.

Of course, occasions arose when one side won so convincingly that it was in a position to simply dictate terms. The victor then had to strike a delicate balance between showing strength to deter future aggression or rebellion, and imposing such harsh terms that he humiliated his opponent and built up future resentment. The ability of feuds to last over several generations suggests that such resentment was easily created. Being merciful increased the victor's honour by showing his generosity, and also helped to prevent potential future conflict. After the Battle of Najera, the Black Prince advised Pedro of Castile that: 'if you want to be king of Castile, you should send word everywhere that you have granted one thing: pardon to all your enemies. And if by bad advice and ill will anyone has supported King Enrique, pardon them at once.'[100] Unfortunately, Pedro proved so incompetent that the Spanish soon rose up against him, and Enrique once again swept him off the throne, this time for good.

Internal enemies were often given better terms than foreign foes. Until the mid-fourteenth century, when central power had become somewhat stronger, the Kings of England treated rebels with remarkable generosity, at least if they were men of high status. For two hundred years after the Norman conquest, they spared the lives of nearly every aristocratic rebel whom they defeated.[101] Non-noble rebels were not always so fortunate, but good rulers recognized that the subordinates of rebel lords had obligations of loyalty towards that lord, and did not necessarily hold them responsible for their deeds. Indeed, they might admire the loyalty shown. So, even though William Marshal stayed loyal to Henry II in that king's final, inglorious campaign against his son Richard Lionheart, Richard chose not to punish William after Henry died and he became king. Rather, he took him into his own service.[102] He gained himself a loyal servant, who might otherwise have become a dangerous enemy.

Women and honour

Chivalry brought in the wholly new idea that the role of a soldier was to serve a lady. By displaying prowess he won honour for her; by failing to do so, he disgraced her. This romantic image, once created, proved to be remarkably resilient.

In *Raoul de Cambrai*, Raoul tells a nun: 'you are a deceiving woman. I have no dealings with a slag of a chambermaid who's been a tart and a whore, a common slut for all takers.'[103] If one compares this language with that of the later Arthurian romances, in which the Knights of the Round Table wander around England helping damsels in distress, the difference in tone is exceedingly striking. The later fiction idealizes love between man and woman, and teaches that a man's greatest duty is to serve his lady and win honour for her. 'He is no lover who does not unhesitatingly do whatever pleases his lady', wrote Chrétien de Troyes.[104]

Even the hardest knights seem to have taken courtly love seriously. The great French knight Marshal Boucicaut created the Order of the White Lady, whose members pledged to defend damsels in distress wherever they found them. Geoffroi de Charny, one of the foremost knights of his era, advised:

> Love a lady truly and honourably, for it is the right position to be in for those who desire to achieve honor. … guard the honor of your lady above all else … one should protect one's own honor for the honor of one's lady and for the love she shows to oneself. That means that by your manners, your behavior, and your personal bearing you should so present yourself that your renown may be so good, so noble, and so honorable that you and your great deeds are held in high esteem in your quarters and on the field.[105]

A knight should be aware, Charny warned, that the honour of a lady depends on that of her man. Greater honour will come to a lady who is known to love a great man, but 'what honor do they confer on their ladies when it could be said that each one of these loves a miserable wretch?'[106] 'He who fails to honour ladies', agreed Chrétien de Troyes, 'finds his own honour dead inside him. Serve ladies and maidens and you will be honoured everywhere.'[107]

As well as honour, the favour of a lady was said to confer strength and courage on men. After pausing in a long fight with a hostile knight, de Troyes' hero Erec sees his love Enide, and 'As soon as he saw her, his strength was renewed; because of her love and her beauty he regained his great courage', thus enabling him to vanquish his opponent.[108] Smitten by La Belle Isode, Sir Palomides in Malory's *Morte Darthur* fights at a tournament, and 'began to double his strength … ever he cast his eye unto La Belle Isode. And when he saw her make such cheer he fared like a lion, that there might no man withstand him.'[109] Real knights echoed this literary conceit. Ladies 'inspire men to great achievements', wrote de Charny:

> It is thanks to such ladies that men become good knights and men-at-arms. Hence all good men-at-arms are rightly bound to protect and defend the honor of all ladies against all those who would threaten it by word or deed.[110]

Tournaments were the garden in which such ideas took root. Ladies gave tokens to the jousting knights to wear as they fought, and this reinforced the idea that the purpose of combat was to win the favour of one's love. This conditioning carried over into real fighting.

Examples abound. On the body of an English knight at Douglas Castle, Scottish soldiers found a letter from his lady telling him that he must hold the castle for a year to win her love.[111] The mistress of William Marmion, a Lincolnshire knight, gave him a helmet of gold and told him to make it famous 'wherever glory was most difficult to attain'. Having determined that this was Norham Castle, Marmion joined its defence, and when 160 Scots arrived, charged straight into them, eventually being rescued by the garrison.[112] Similarly, Walter Mauny sortied from Hennebaut in Brittany in 1342 to destroy a siege engine, and when French cavalry approached, charged into them, shouting, 'May I never be embraced by my mistress and dear friend, if I enter the castle or fortress before I have unhorsed one of these gallopers.' He succeeded in fulfilling his pledge, and upon returning to the castle, received his kiss.[113]

Even the highest-ranking men were not immune from the appeal of the fair sex. When King Stephen had his rival for the English throne, the Empress Matilda, surrounded in 1139, he gave her free passage to escape.[114] In so doing, he let slip the opportunity to end a prolonged civil war, but proved his chivalry. In another instance, when Queen Isabella left her husband Edward II of England and appealed for help against him, John of Hainault persuaded his fellow knights to go to England to fight for her, telling them: 'Every knight must do his best to help women and maidens in distress.'[115]

This deference to women brought about an unprecedented expansion of the warriors' honour group. Previously, the upholders of a fighting man's honour were other fighting men, and in the case of chivalry the honour group of a knight consisted of other knights. Now warriors could be called to account by those who did not fight. This was an innovation which would bear lasting fruit.

Conclusion

Chivalry as a whole simultaneously idealized war and sought to humanize it. It succeeded rather better at the former than the latter. Nowadays, the term 'chivalrous' tends to evoke positive images of courtesy and valour. The reality of chivalry was rather more brutal. Still, the humanizing element did at least establish the principle that soldiers had obligations to spare the innocent and to treat prisoners decently. In this way, chivalry arguably set precedents which eventually widened into the universally applicable laws of war of the modern era.

Advances in military technology and tactics eventually rendered knights obsolete, but a romanticized memory of the better aspects of the chivalric code carried over into subsequent eras. During the Middle Ages, Christianity and courtly love had somewhat tempered a form of warfare which in its individualistic recklessness resembled that of the Greeks. In the Renaissance, classical learning would add to that a revival of the prudence and discipline of the Romans.

Notes

1 Vale, Malcolm, *War and Chivalry: Warfare and Aristocratic Culture in England, France and Burgundy at the End of the Middle Ages*, London: Duckworth, 1981, p. 1.

2 Keen, Maurice, *Chivalry*, New Haven and London: Yale University Press, 1984, p. 23, and Bouchard, Constance Brittain, *'Strong of Body, Brave and Noble': Chivalry and Society in Medieval France*, Ithaca and London: Cornell University Press, 1998, p. 14.

3 See Bumke, Joachim, *The Concept of Knighthood in the Middle Ages*, New York: AMS Press, 1982, pp. 24–9 and 51–4; Coss, Peter, *The Knight in Medieval England, 1000–1400*, Stroud: Alan Sutton, 1995, pp. 6–11; and Strickland, Matthew, *War and Chivalry: The Conduct and Perception of War in England and Normandy, 1066–1217*, Cambridge: Cambridge University Press, 1996, p. 289.

4 Kaeuper, Richard, *Chivalry and Violence in Medieval Europe*, Oxford: Oxford University Press, 1999, p. 185; and Gillingham, John, '1066 and the Introduction of Chivalry into England', in Garnett, George and Hudson, John (eds), *Law and*

Government in Medieval England and Normandy, Cambridge: Cambridge University Press, 1994, p. 32.
5 de Charny, Geoffroi, 'The Book of Chivalry', in Kaeuper, Richard and Kennedy, Elspeth (eds), *The Book of Chivalry of Geoffroi de Charny: Text, Context, and Translation*, Philadelphia: University of Pennsylvania Press, 1996, p. 99.
6 Lull, Ramon, *The Book of the Ordre of Chyvalry*, trans William Caxton, ed. Alfred T.P. Byles, London: Oxford University Press, 1926, p. 50.
7 Aquinas, Thomas, *Summa Theologiae*, New York: Blackfriars, 1972, 2a2ae, 63, 3, vol. 38, p. 13.
8 Keen, *Chivalry*, p. 16; Bouchard, *Strong of Body*, p. 111.
9 For comments to this effect, see Kaeuper, *Chivalry and Violence*, p. 135, and Painter, Sidney, *French Chivalry: Chivalric Ideas and Practice in Mediaeval France*, Baltimore: Johns Hopkins Press, 1940, p. 29.
10 *Raoul de Cambrai*, ed. and trans. Sarah Kay, Oxford: Clarendon Press, 1992, I, p. 3.
11 *Raoul de Cambrai*, CXXXIII, p. 167.
12 *The Song of Roland*, trans. Gerard J. Brault, University Park: Pennsylvania State University Press, 1981, lines 1970–2.
13 Gerald of Wales, cited in Kaeuper, *Chivalry and Violence*, p. 140.
14 Baker, Geoffrey le, 'Chronicle', in Barber, Richard (ed.), *The Life and Campaigns of the Black Prince*, Woodbridge: The Boydell Press, 1979, p. 44.
15 Froissart, *Chronicles*, trans. Geoffrey Brereton, London: Penguin, 1978, p. 193.
16 Barber, Richard, *The Knight and Chivalry*, 2nd edition. Ipswich: The Boydell Press, 1974, p. 44.
17 Foss, Michael, *Chivalry*, London: Michael Joseph, 1975, p. 68.
18 Lull, *The Book of the Ordre of Chyvalry*, pp. 66–74.
19 Peter of Blois, cited in Strickland, *War and Chivalry*, p. 55.
20 Lull, *The Book of the Ordre of Chyvalry*, p. 35.
21 *The Anglo-Saxon Chronicles*, trans. and ed. Michael Swanton, London: Phoenix, 2000, p. 263.
22 Tuchman, Barbara, *A Distant Mirror: The Calamitous 14th Century*, New York: Ballantine, 1978, pp. 435–40.
23 Barnie, John, *War in Medieval Society: Social Values and the Hundred Years War, 1337–99*, London: Weidenfeld and Nicolson, 1974, pp. 2–4.
24 de Troyes, Chrétien, 'Cligés', in *Arthurian Romances*, trans. William W. Kibler, London: Penguin, 1991, p. 125.
25 Joinville, Jean de, 'The Life of Saint Louis', in Joinville and G. Villehardouin, *Chronicles of the Crusades*, trans. Margaret Shaw, London: Penguin, 1963, p. 178.
26 Allmand, Christopher, *The Hundred Years War: England and France at War, c. 1300 – c. 1450*, Cambridge: Cambridge University Press, 1988, pp. 7–11.
27 *Jordan Fantosme's Chronicle*, ed. R.C. Johnston, Oxford: Clarendon Press, 1981, 33, p. 29.
28 Tuchman, *A Distant Mirror*, pp. 268–70.
29 Prestwich, Michael, *Armies and Warfare in the Middle Ages: The English Experience*, New Haven and London: Yale University Press, 1996, pp. 66–73.
30 Barnie, *War in Medieval Society*, pp. 34–6.
31 Villehardouin, Geoffrey de, 'The Conquest of Constantinople', in Joinville and Villehardouin, *Chronicles of the Crusades*, p. 57.
32 Joinville, 'The Life of Saint Louis', p. 198.
33 Ibid, p. 77. Joinville reported that he 'mortgaged the greater part of my land' to take part in the 4th crusade in 1248 AD: ibid, p. 192.
34 Asbridge, Thomas, *The First Crusade: A New History*, London: The Free Press, 2004, p. 70.
35 Bonet, Honoré, *The Tree of Battles*, with introduction by G.W. Coopland, Liverpool: University Press of Liverpool, 1949, LII, p. 156.

36 Seward, Desmond *The Monks of War: The Military Religious Orders*, London: Penguin, 1995, pp. 29–30.
37 Contamine, Philippe, *War in the Middle Ages*, Oxford: Basil Blackwell, 1984, p. 239.
38 Ibid, p. 254.
39 Baker, Geoffrey le, 'Chronicle', p. 77.
40 Herald, Chandos, 'The Life of the Black Prince', in Barber, Richard (ed.), *The Life and Campaigns of the Black Prince*, p. 125.
41 Painter, *French Chivalry*, pp. 56–7.
42 Kaeuper and Kennedy, *The Book of Chivalry of Geoffroi de Charny*, p. 12.
43 Prestwich, *Armies and Warfare*, p. 101.
44 Ibid, pp. 100–1.
45 Herald, Chandos, 'The Life of the Black Prince', pp. 101–2 and 113–14.
46 Vale, *War and Chivalry*, p. 54.
47 Ibid, pp. 125–32.
48 Ibid, pp. 164–6.
49 Barber, *The Knight and Chivalry*, p. 307.
50 Ibid, p. 41.
51 Prestwich, *Armies and Warfare*, p. 14.
52 Charny, 'The Book of Chivalry', pp. 129 and 131.
53 Joinville, 'The Life of Saint Louis', pp. 236–7 and 310.
54 Ibid, p. 237.
55 Ibid.
56 Prestwich, *Armies and Warfare*, p. 322.
57 *The Song of Roland*, lines 2953–4, and 2959–60.
58 Huizinga, Johan, *The Waning of the Middle Ages*, Harmondsworth: Penguin, 1972, p. 139.
59 Froissart, *Chronicles*, p. 95.
60 Herald, Chandos, 'The Life of the Black Prince', p. 89.
61 Vale, *War and Chivalry*, pp. 88–92.
62 Bouchard, *Strong of Body*, p. 25.
63 Coss, *The Knight in Medieval England*, pp. 72 and 92.
64 Contamine, *War in the Middle Ages*, p. 302.
65 Keen, *Chivalry*, p. 169.
66 The reasons for the continued dominance of knights are well described in Vale, *War and Chivalry*, passim.
67 France, John, *Western Warfare in the Age of the Crusades, 1000–1300*, London and New York: Routledge, 1999, p. 12. Gillingham, John, 'War and Chivalry in the History of William the Marshal', in Cross, P.R. and Lloyd, S.D. (eds), *Thirteenth Century England II: Proceedings of the Newcastle Upon Tyne Conference, 1987*, Woodbridge: The Boydell Press, 1988, p. 6.
68 Prestwich, *Armies and Warfare*, pp. 187–8. Contamine, *War in the Middle Ages*, p. 227.
69 Vale, *War and Chivalry*, p. 32.
70 Tuchman, *A Distant Mirror*, pp. 558–61. Foss, *Chivalry*, p. 195.
71 Joinville, 'The Life of Saint Louis', pp. 218–19.
72 Froissart, *Chronicles*, p. 86.
73 Allmand, Christopher, (ed.), *Society at War: The Experience of England and France During the Hundred Years War*, Woodbridge: The Boydell Press, 1998, pp. 125–6.
74 Keen, Maurice, *The Laws of War in the Late Middle Ages*, Aldershot: Gregg Revivals, 1993, p. 108.
75 Huizinga, *The Waning of the Middle Ages*, p. 95.
76 Ibid, pp. 88–9. Foss, *Chivalry*, p. 194.
77 Joinville, 'The Life of Saint Louis', p. 189.
78 Strickland, *War and Chivalry*, pp. 209-12.

79 *Jordan Fantosme's Chronicle*, 82 and 87, pp. 57 and 61.
80 Prestwich, *Armies and Warfare*, pp. 236–7.
81 Bonet, *The Tree of Battles*, XLIX, pp. 154–5.
82 Malory, Sir Thomas, *Le Morte Darthur*, ed. Helen Cooper, Oxford: Oxford University Press, 1998, p. 142.
83 Painter, Sidney, *William Marshal: Knight-Errant, Baron, and Regent of England*, Baltimore: Johns Hopkins Press, 1933, p. 70.
84 *Jordan Fantosme's Chronicle*, 118, p. 87.
85 'Campaign Letters', in Barber, Richard (ed.), *The Life and Campaigns of the Black Prince*, pp. 15–16.
86 Kaeuper, *Chivalry and Violence*, p. 176.
87 *Jordan Fantosme's Chronicle*, 42, p. 34.
88 Froissart, *Chronicles*, p. 178.
89 Keen, *The Laws of War*, pp. 123–32.
90 de Pizan, Christine, *The Book of Deeds of Arms and Chivalry*, trans. Sumner Willard, University Park: Pennsylvania State University Press, 1999, 3.17, p. 170.
91 Froissart, *Chronicles*, p. 345.
92 Strickland, *War and Chivalry*, p. 196.
93 de Pizan, *The Book of Deeds*, 3.23, pp. 180–1. Keen, *The Laws of War*, p. 177.
94 Squibb, G.D., *The High Court of Chivalry: A Study of the Civil Law in England*, Oxford: Clarendon Press, 1959, pp. 14–20.
95 Keen, *The Laws of War*, pp. 51–2.
96 Ibid, p. 174.
97 Ibid, pp. 491–2.
98 Ibid, p. 190.
99 Ibid, p. 37.
100 Herald, Chandos, 'Life of the Black Prince', p. 130.
101 Gillingham, '1066', pp. 31–55.
102 Painter, *William Marshal*, p. 73.
103 *Raoul de Cambrai*, LXV, p. 85.
104 de Troyes, 'Erec and Enide', in *Arthurian Romances*, p. 111.
105 Charny, 'The Book of Chivalry', p. 119.
106 Ibid, p. 121.
107 de Troyes, 'The Story of the Grail', in *Arthurian Romances*, p. 387.
108 de Troyes, 'Erec and Enide', p. 48.
109 Malory, *Morte Darthur*, p. 261.
110 Charny, 'The Book of Chivalry', p. 95.
111 Kaeuper, *Chivalry and Violence*, p. 212.
112 Barnie, *War in Medieval Society*, pp. 93–4. Prestwich, *Armies and Warfare*, p. 219.
113 Prestwich, *Armies and Warfare*, p. 233.
114 Ibid, p. 231, and Gillingham, '1066', p. 31.
115 Shears, F.S., 'The Chivalry of France', in Prestage, Edgar (ed.), *Chivalry*, London: Kegan Paul, Trench, Trubner & Co., 1928, p. 69.

5 Elizabethan England

Introduction

By the time Queen Elizabeth I of England ascended her throne in 1558, the knight was no longer the dominant force on the battlefield. Disciplined infantry, fighting in close formation with pikes and firearms, had reduced the heavily armed cavalry to a secondary position. Meanwhile, Western European states were undergoing important political and social changes, which undermined the independence of the old nobility, brought new classes to the fore, and concentrated power increasingly in the hands of central governments. The Renaissance brought a revival of classical learning, while the Reformation brought bitter religious division. This was a period of transition between the mediaeval state and mediaeval forms of warfare and the modern state and modern ways of war.

After brief wars in France and Scotland at the start of Elizabeth's reign, England enjoyed two decades of formal peace. During this time, England's foreign policy underwent a great shift. France, the traditional enemy, ceased to hold this position, and collapsed into civil war between Protestant Huguenots and their Catholic enemies. Spain, long an ally against France, became the new adversary, and by 1585 England and Spain were at war in all but name.

In 1588 the Spanish attempted to invade England (with the famous Spanish Armada). The English in turn raided Spain, Portugal, and Spanish possessions in the Americas. English armies also took to the field in France and the Netherlands (a Spanish possession which revolted against the rule of King Philip II of Spain in 1568), and English ships attempted unsuccessfully to intercept the annual fleet which brought treasure to Spain from the Americas. Throughout this period, the English were also engaged in almost continual operations in Ireland against a succession of Irish rebellions. These reached a peak at the end of Elizabeth's reign with the revolt of Hugh O'Neill, Earl of Tyrone. By 1600, war in Ireland had replaced the wars on the continent as the major drain on English military and financial resources.

Honour in this period was the product of a great variety of influences, including a romanticized form of chivalry which was largely Burgundian in origin,[1] Italian Humanism, and Protestantism. The Reformation brought a renewed religious fervour, while the Renaissance added a belief in reason and a renewed knowledge of Classical literature (hence the examples cited in Elizabethan treatises on military honour are overwhelmingly taken from Roman histories). This mix of influences on Elizabethans often pulled them in very strange directions.[2]

Honour and virtue in Elizabethan England

'Honour', wrote the Elizabethan herald Sir William Segar, 'ought to be valued above all earthly wealth and is more precious than silver or gold.'[3] Similarly, in an unpublished manuscript entitled 'Of Honour', Robert Ashley commented that 'there ys nothing amongst men more excellent then honour.'[4] Many Elizabethans would have agreed with them and with Mowbray in William Shakespeare's play *Richard II*:

> Mine honour is my life: both grow in one;
> Take honour from me, and my life is done.[5]

Elizabethans of this view agreed with the ancient Greeks that love of honour was the engine that drove a successful society. In his *Inquisition upon Fame and Honour*, Fulke Greville noted that:

> … neer any State
> Could rise, or stand, without this thirst of *Glory*
> …
> For else, what Governour would spend his dayes,
> In enuious travell, for the publike good?
> Who would in Bookes, search after dead mens wayes?
> Or in the Warre, what Souldier lose his blood?
> Liv'd not this *Fame* in clouds, kept as crowne;
> Both for the Sword, the Scepter, and the Gowne.[6]

Some Elizabethans, however, were sceptical about honour. Greville, for instance, while noting the public benefits of honour, regarded the pursuit of it as vain godlessness. 'Who worship *Fame*, commit Idolatry', he wrote, 'Make Men their God, *Fortune* and *Time* their worth.'[7] Shakespeare's plays are replete with negative comments on the subject. Most famously, in *Henry IV Part I*, Falstaff says:

> Honour pricks me on. Yea, but how if honour prick me off when I come on? How then? Can honour set to a leg? no: or an arm? no: or take away the grief of a wound? no. Honour hath no skill in surgery, then? no. What is honour? a word. What is in that word, honour? What is that honour? air. A trim reckoning! Who hath it? he that died o'Wednesday. Doth he feel it? no. Doth he hear it? no. Is it insensible, then? Yea, to the dead. But will it not live with the living? no. Why? detraction will not suffer it: – therefore I'll none of it: honour is a mere scutcheon.[8]

Despite such comments, honour was rarely denounced in its entirety. The ideal was generally seen in Aristotelian terms as the mean between ambition and pusillanimity (see Chapter 2). As Sir Thomas Elyot wrote, ambition was 'pernicious to a publike weale', but so too was insufficient love of honour.[9] Ashley explained: 'Lett us then ... desire neither more nor lesse honour than reason alloweth.'[10]

By this date, the growth of state power meant that public honour increasingly depended on service of, and rewards granted by, the state.[11] Elizabethans were in two minds about this. Segar wrote that, 'The power and authority to bestow honour resteth only in the Prince'[12], but also that, 'My prince can make me at his pleasure rich or poor, but to make me good or bad is not in his power, for that apperteineth onlie to Gods grace and mine owne endeavour.'[13] And the Earl of Essex, smarting after Queen Elizabeth boxed his ears in a Council meeting, complained to Sir Francis Knollys:

> I owe her Majesty the duty of an earl and lord marshal. I have been content to do her Majesty the service of a clerk; but never can serve as a villein or slave. ... Cannot princes err? Cannot subjects receive wrong? Is earthly power or authority infinite? Pardon me, pardon me, my good Lord; I can never subscribe to these principles.[14]

Nevertheless, great advantages accrued from serving the monarch, not least the patronage and financial rewards she bestowed. Such service was not only of a military kind. Fulke Greville began his adulthood seeking military glory, but eventually wrote that:

> Clearly discerning action and honour to fly with more wings than one, and that it was sufficient for the plant to grow where his sovereign's hand had placed it, I ... bound my prospect within the safe limits of duty in such home services as were acceptable to my sovereign.[15]

Furthermore, a gentleman could now gain a reputation for himself purely by his manners and demeanour. 'How can Honour be sooner gotten', wrote Ashley, 'then by being kind, affable, gentle, and courtuous unto all.'[16] 'A man by nothing is so well bewrayd', claimed Edmund Spenser, 'As by his manners.'[17]

While the Italian author Castiglione stated that, 'The principall and true profession of a Courtyer ought to be in feate of armes',[18] in general English books on the ideal gentleman made little or no reference to arms, although a gentleman was still expected to fight if called upon.[19] This led to complaints that soldiering was no longer valued. As Barnabe Rich wrote:

> Because as the warre of itself is an evil, and that so loathsomely detested: even so, to be professours, followers, and ministers in the same, is esteemed a thing more fite for ruffians, roysters, blasphemers, and people of the vylest condicion, rather then as exercise for honest men.[20]

Paradoxically, the declining interest in martial affairs coincided with the rise in popularity of the duel. The practice of duelling arrived in England, probably from Italy, in the late sixteenth century.[21] Honour increasingly demanded that every insult be met by a challenge. 'Everie injurious action not repulsed', wrote Segar, 'is by common consent of all Martiall mindes holden a thing dishonorable, infamous, and reproachfull.'[22] The duel acted as a 'guarantor of civility', deterring impolite behaviour through the threat of violence.[23]

Some Elizabethans condemned duelling. 'The best revenge and most honorable victorie, which a man can have against his enemie', wrote John Norden, 'is to surpasse him in patience.'[24] Among the warrior gentlemen of Elizabethan England such views were unusual. Many of the great heroes of this era fought duels or brawls. Sir Richard Grenville killed someone in a street brawl; Walter Raleigh was imprisoned twice for duelling in 1580;[25] and Essex was wounded in a duel against Charles Blount, later Lord Mountjoy. Essex also challenged Raleigh, but the Queen forbade the fight.[26]

Disagreements over duelling reflected similar disagreements regarding the role of birth in honour. On the one hand, one treatise entitled *The Institucion of a Gentleman* stated clearly that, 'Honour falleth to no man by discent, no man can intayle honour to hys heyres male.'[27] On the other hand, many Elizabethans felt that the low-born were unlikely to be virtuous. As Edmund Spenser wrote:

> For seldome seene, a trotting Stalion get
> An ambling Colt, that is his proper owne:
> So seldom seene, that one in basenesse set
> Doth noble courage shew, with curteous manners met.
>
> But evermore contrary hath bene tryde,
> That gentle bloud with gentle manners breed.[28]

At any rate, it all came down to virtue. 'No man becometh gentle without vertue', said the *Institucion of a Gentleman*;[29] 'honor is in nothing more gained, than by noble vertues', claimed John Norden;[30] 'Fame but Virtue's shadow is', said Fulke Greville.[31] But defining virtue had become more difficult, as new values challenged those of martial prowess.

In the late sixteenth century, the gentleman replaced the knight 'as a term to describe the ideal type of man', as the new gentry class replaced the old aristocracy.[32] High society regarded a number of professions other than warrior as honourable and worthy of this new title.[33] The gentleman, said *The Institucion of a Gentleman*,

> Ought to be learned, to have knowledge in tongues, and to be apte in the feates of armes, for the defence of his cuntrey … It behoveth also that such a gentleman to have in him courtlye behavoure, to know how to treate and to interteyne men of all degrees, and to be ignoraunt of howe he hymselfe ought to be used othres. To such a Gentilman also sume knowledge in Musik, or to know the use of musicall Instrumentes is muche commendable.[34]

Prowess for the first time had lost some of its importance. A new virtue was competing with it – learning. To serve the crown properly one had to be learned, and so the aristocracy turned to education to secure its hold on power. In due course, learning then acquired an importance as an end in itself. 'Al thinke', said *The Institucion of a Gentleman*, 'no reasonable person wil denye but that corporal gifts are not to be compared with giftes of the mind.'[35]

Many leading soldiers had attended Oxford or Cambridge universities and took up the pen to write poetry, literature, memoirs, or military treatises. Their books insisted on the need for soldiers to study their profession. 'Neither are the commendable vertues of the minde so necessarye for any occupatione, as they are for them that professe and exercise arms', wrote Geffrey Gates.[36] And similarly George Whetstone said: 'He that is studious, and occupieth his leasurable times, in working out of advauntages, is likely to hurt ye enemie more by his devices in ye campe, then by fighting in the field.'[37]

Associated with learning was the virtue of 'prudence'. While Elizabethans continued to maintain that cowardice is 'the most deadly enemie to militarie proceedings',[38] like the Romans they recognized that imprudent courage was also detrimental, that:

> ... to attempt hie dangers evident
> Without constraint or neede, is infamie,
> And honor turnes to rashnes in th'event;
> And who so darrs, not caring how he darrs,
> Sells vertues name, to purchase foolish stars.[39]

'*Fortitude* accompanied with *Prudence*', wrote Segar, 'is the much more commendable, seeing he that unwiselie or inconsideratlie adventureth himself, is not to be reputed valiant but furious: neither is he accompted valiant, that without counsell or cause, delighteth in dangers.'[40] At the same time, a passion for gambling rather compromised the practice of prudence. Skill in cards, dice and other games of hazard was often listed as a desirable characteristic for gentlemen, and Elizabeth and her courtiers gambled heavily.[41] Gentlemen carried this risk-taking habit with them into war.

The virtue of 'magnanimity' was related to prudence and fortitude. 'Magnanimitie', wrote Sir Thomas Elyot, 'is an excellencie of mynde concernynge thynges of great importaunce or estimation, doing all thynge that is vertuous for the achievynge of honour.' This, he said, was more easily rendered as 'good courage'. This makes one seek an appropriate level of glory, do what is hard and dangerous, and endure sufferings in order to obtain it.[42] 'A Gentleman should alwaies be armed with fortitude or strength of the mynde, called otherwise Magnanimitie', said *The Institucion of a Gentleman*.[43]

In line with such thinking, Elizabethan authors put great stress on discipline and obedience. 'Courage without discipline is nearer beastliness than manhood', declared Sir Philip Sidney.[44] 'He that will come soonest to the perfection of a souldier', wrote John Norden, 'must yeeld most to discipline, and settle himself to sustaine all travailes, to adventure all perils, and to be resolute rather and dye in flight.'[45] 'Obedience is specially required of a well governed Souldier', agreed

Whetstone.[46] '*Obedience* is the mother of all vertues', chorused Norden.[47] The story of the Roman consul Manlius Torquatus, who beheaded his son for disobeying orders (see Chapter 3), was a favourite in Elizabethan military treatises.

The warrior-gentleman was meant to be honest. 'True honor', said *The Institucion of a Gentleman*, 'take his first beginning of honestie, which is the fruyt of vertue and wel doing: and no other thing is honour than the sound or Trumpet of honestie, which bloweth forth into the eares of others the fame and report of him whyche is honeste.'[48] A soldier, claimed John Norden, should 'be resolute in maintaining his honor, by the effects of true fidelitie, which is to lose his life rather than to be touched with cowardly untruth and perjury.'[49]

He also had to be pious. 'True glorie', wrote Norden, 'is never gotten in the warres without Religion and virtue.' 'Every man that longeth for honour ... must foster religion', he continued,[50] although in fact he recognized that soldiers themselves did not consider pious colleagues particularly honourable: 'Some in an armie may perchance have an inclination to serve the Lord ... But they bee not graced of their fellow souldiers, nor of their Leaders, as they ought, they rather be scorned than fostered or followed.'[51]

The military commander also had to practise 'liberality', which meant sharing the spoils of war, and rewarding those who deserved it. 'Among many other parts of commendation required in a soveraigne commander,' wrote Segar, 'there is not any more to bee honoured than liberalitie.'[52] 'Men of warre ought to be more open hearted, more liberall, and more affable, than any other profession', wrote Sir Roger Williams, 'and liberall to confess good deserts as well as with their purses.'[53]

The ordinary soldier, meanwhile, was expected to show 'loyaltie to his soveraigne', carry out his 'duetie to his commander', and display 'love and concord towardes his fellow souldiers'.[54]

Military writers were often naive in their demands of the honourable soldier. Norden wrote reproachfully that, 'It is too generall that our Generals for the most part have fought more for a multitude of men than for godly and religious men, and a swaggering ruffian is yet often preferred in warres, before a modest discreet man fearing God.'[55] 'I speake this for Captaines in generall', agreed Sir Roger Williams, 'but there are honest, vertuous, & just, yet so few that the number must be imbraced, els the multitude of the enemies would bee too manie for the fewe friends.'[56] Neither was exaggerating. As Geffrey Gates lamented:

> The common sort of our Countrie men that go to warre, of purpose more to spoyle than to serve: and under colour of pursuite of Armes, they put themselves to the libertie and use of swearing, dronkenes, shameles fornication, dicing, and Theevery. ... that they seeme rather to come from hel, then from the exercise of warlike armes, or from the regiment of military discipline.[57]

Honour and the causes of war

In February 1589, Sir Christopher Hatton opened the new session of the English Parliament with an emotional appeal to his colleagues to support their country's war effort. If the Spanish had succeeded in invading and conquering England, men like Hatton would have lost a great deal more than their honour. But it was not to such mundane matters of personal security that Hatton appealed. 'Shall we now suffer ourselves with all dishonour to be conquered?' he asked. 'England hath been accounted hitherto the most renowned kingdom for valour and manhood in all Christendom, and shall we now lose our reputation? If we should, it had been better for England we had never been born.'[58]

Many shared Hatton's views, but not all. 'Make love, not war' was the message of the poet John Donne (who participated in the 1596 raid on Cadiz) in his poem *Love's War*:

> Long voyages are long consumptions,
> And ships are carts for executions.
> …
> Here lett mee warr: in these armes lett me lye:
> Here lett mee parle, batter, bleede, and dye.
> Thyne armes imprison me, and myne armes thee.
> …
> Other men war that they their rest may gayne:
> But we will rest that wee may fight agayne.
> Those warrs the ignorant, these th'experience'd love,
> There wee are alwayes under, here above.
> …
> There men kill men, we'll make one by and by.[59]

The Queen also disliked war, but many of her courtiers favoured it. As Herbert Languet told Sir Philip Sidney: 'You and your fellows, I mean men of noble birth, consider that nothing brings you more honour than wholesale slaughter.'[60] While overall interest in martial honour was declining, there were some Elizabethans who felt that too much peace was bad for the nation, and that it led to degeneracy. As Barnabe Riche wrote:

> Peace is the nourisher of vices, the roote of evils the proppe of pride, and to be short, it is the mother of al mischiefes … in peace men growe to be slouthful, ydle, proude, covetouse, dissolute, incontinent, vicious, folowing al maner of vanities, given to al delights, to inordinate lust, gluttonie, swearing, & to be short, to al maner of filthines.[61]

Those of this persuasion had no domestic outlet for their martial energy. By now, on land at least, private war had almost entirely disappeared. In addition, rebellion against the Crown appeared increasingly dishonourable. Outside Ireland, there were only two revolts of note during Elizabeth's reign – that of the northern Earls in 1569 and that of Robert Devereux, second Earl of Essex, in 1601. Both were almost completely bloodless.

Essex's rebellion is especially illuminating. According to historian Mervyn James, 'the revolt was motivated by, and arose out of … the cult of honour and its code'; it was 'the last honour revolt'.[62] Essex was obsessed with martial glory, and won the Queen's favour, becoming one of the most powerful men in the land. Gradually, though, he began to feel that he was the victim of a political conspiracy. His paranoia grew after he returned without permission from Ireland, where he had been leading the fight against the Earl of Tyrone. Disgraced both by his failure to defeat Tyrone and by his disobedient return, Essex lost the Queen's favour and the financial patronage that went with it. He and his retainers faced ruin. Essex decided to restore his honour through a coup d'etat which would force the Queen to dismiss his opponent, Robert Cecil, and his supporters, 'base upstarts' who had deprived noble warriors of their rightful place of precedence.

Matters of honour thus led Essex and his followers into revolt. They also ensured his defeat. Essex had considered launching an invasion of England with his army in Ireland. His followers, however, considered such an act treasonable and dishonourable. An invasion, said Charles Blount, would be 'a matter most foul ... an irrecoverable blot'.[63] Essex instead chose to make a show of force in the City of London. The citizens of London, despite their admiration for him, refused to rise on his behalf. Within hours, Essex had to withdraw and surrender himself to the authorities. Shortly afterwards, he was executed.

The most dangerous revolts against the Crown were not in England, but in Ireland, where in the 1590s English rule came under serious threat. English monarchs had held notional suzerainty over Ireland since the Norman conquest, but outside the Pale the rule of the Crown had always been weak and dependent on the good will of the Irish nobility. In the sixteenth century, on the verge of the age of empire, Englishmen began to look on Ireland as a backward and chaotic country, which required modern, English, systems of governance.

The English introduced into Ireland the English system of shires, confiscating the land held by clan chieftains on behalf of their clans, and then giving them back the land as their private property. This way, the chieftains became English-style gentry, with the benefit of actually owning their land, but they also lost the status and sovereignty of chieftainship. Done with due care, as in the 'Composition of Connaught', this 'surrender and regrant' could pass off peacefully. But some chieftains could not be convinced, feeling that the new system of government undermined their autonomy and honour.[64] Any system of land reform invariably creates losers as well as winners, and in Ireland the natural response of the losers was to rebel. The fact that Ireland remained resolutely Catholic added to the problem.

On the English side, the 'New English', would-be colonial landowners such as Humphrey Gilbert and Walter Raleigh, saw Ireland as a place where they could build themselves a landed fortune, and so acquire status and honour unavailable to them in England. The normal attitude of the Crown towards Ireland was to leave it alone as much as possible. However, the fame and fortune-seeking ambitions of the poorer gentry endlessly pushed the Crown into further conflict.[65] Their private pursuit of honour incited resistance among the Irish, which in turn engaged the honour of the English state. War resulted.

A very similar process worked to generate war between England and Spain. At the start of Elizabeth's reign, Anglo-Spanish relations were good, despite religious differences between Protestant England and Catholic Spain. An important factor in worsening relations was the behaviour of English pirates such as John Hawkins and Francis Drake. The same drive that led Englishmen to seek honour and fortune in Ireland also impelled them to hunt these on the high seas at the expense of the Spanish empire in the Americas.

Between 1562 and 1568, Hawkins led three expeditions to sell slaves to Spanish America. The Spanish forbade their colonies to trade with foreigners, so Hawkins forced them to do so, bombarding Spanish possessions which refused his trade. In 1568 he entered the port of San Juan de Ulua, after the local authorities promised not to attack his ships. As soon as his guard was lowered, they did just that, and only three English ships escaped. This treacherous act marked the beginning of the collapse of Anglo-Spanish relations, and was never forgiven by many English sailors.[66]

One of those who escaped from San Juan was Francis Drake. Some accused him of cowardice in fleeing. Consequently Drake loathed the Spaniards for showing him in a poor light.[67] He determined to regain face by launching a private war against them. Over the next few years Drake undertook a succession of piratical raids on Spanish America. Near the end of his life he told his biographer Philip Nichols that it was righteous 'indignation engrafted in the bosom of all that are wronged' that had turned him into a pirate.[68]

Drake also sought financial gain, but not solely as an end in itself. The profits from seized Spanish property were the route to social status and honour. According to Robert Mansell, who knew him, 'In Sir Francis was an insatiable desire of honour indeed beyond reason.'[69]

Drake very rapidly became a scourge of the Spanish, capturing huge amounts of plunder and gaining both fame and fortune. Piracy was not a dishonourable activity among the English of this era. Indeed, the state sanctioned it by issuing letters of marque and reprisal, allowing those who claimed to have lost property from foreign countries to 'reclaim' it by seizing ships belonging to citizens of those countries. Those operating under letters of reprisal were 'privateers' rather than 'pirates', but as time went on it became easier and easier to get the necessary letters, and those seeking them ceased to have to prove that they had suffered losses. As long as they paid the Lord Admiral's fee, they received the letters and with them in effect a licence to rob on the high seas. Hundreds of Englishmen took up the practice.[70]

Unsurprisingly, this undermined the Anglo-Spanish relationship. Worse was to come. In retaliation for English piratical practices, in 1575 the Spanish seized a ship belonging to the Englishman Sir Thomas Osbourne. After this, Elizabeth met Drake and told him that she would 'gladly be revenged on the King of Spain' for the 'divers injuries' that she had received.[71] She invested in his voyage to circumnavigate the world, during which he attacked numerous Spanish ships and made a new fortune in plunder. The final act in the naval tit-for-tat came in 1585 when the Spanish government seized English ships which had travelled to Spain to sell corn. In response, Elizabeth sent out a fleet under Drake, which attacked the town of Vigo in North West Spain, and then raided the Caribbean.[72] Although England

and Spain never formally declared war, from this point on, matters had gone beyond individual acts of piracy.

This is, of course, not the whole story. Questions of religion and national security also played an important part in pushing England into war against Spain. In particular, many in England feared that if the Spanish army crushed the Dutch revolt and managed to destroy the Protestant forces in France, England might be its next target. Military intervention on the continent was necessary to ensure that the Spanish did not become so powerful that they would be in a position to attack England. This meant supporting the Dutch and Huguenots in their armed struggles.

For this reason, Elizabeth permitted volunteers to form unofficial military units which travelled overseas to help both the Huguenots and the Dutch. Eventually, the patience of King Philip of Spain grew thin. He supported plots to assassinate Elizabeth and install Mary Queen of Scots on the throne of England, offered help to Irish rebels, and began to consider plans to invade England. This provoked Elizabeth into further resistance to Philip, and in 1585 she agreed to openly send 4,000 infantry and 1,000 cavalry to the Low Countries to assist the Dutch rebels. Following the assassination of King Henry III of France in 1589, she also sent several thousand troops to assist the Protestant Henry IV to secure his throne against the Spanish-backed Catholic League. With these decisions, Elizabeth committed England to war on the continent on two fronts.

Although it is a simplification, it is possible to view the Queen's council prior to 1585 as being divided into two factions – a more cautious one led by Lord Burghley, and what one might call the 'war party', led by the Earl of Leicester and Sir Francis Walsingham.[73] The motives of the war party were complex. They included militant Protestantism, a desire to combat Spanish 'tyranny', a predilection for chivalry, and an ambition for martial glory. Members of this party included many of the younger members of the court who harboured military ambitions, professional soldiers, and others likely to win honour and glory through war.[74]

The proponents of war were forceful and persistent. They pushed the Queen in a direction she did not want to go, and the security arguments for war appear in retrospect rather weak. After all, if the object of military intervention in the Netherlands was to prevent a Spanish invasion, it had the opposite effect, provoking the Armada of 1588. Historians insist that the Queen sought to avoid war, but she allowed her honour-seeking subjects free rein to keep provoking the mightiest state in Europe, and in this way she made war inevitable.

Honour as a motivation for fighting

'Duty, honor & welth, makes men follow the wars', wrote Sir Roger Williams.[75] The pursuit of honour was largely the preserve of a limited group of aristocratic warriors and professional soldiers, such as Williams himself. The ordinary soldier and sailor in Elizabeth's forces was for the most part a reluctant conscript, drawn from the lowest stratum of English society. Those who could, avoided military service. Recruiters had to resort to conscripting convicts, debtors, and men so impoverished that they either could find no way to avoid service or were desperate enough to take their chances in the army and fleet.[76] Muster commissioners in Bristol complained in 1602 that, 'There was never men beheld such strange creatures brought to any muster. They are most of them either old, lame, diseased, boys or common rogues.'[77]

If such men fought for anything, it was their pay. Since this was often not forthcoming, desertions and mutinies were common. In 1592, 600 of the 1,300 men recruited for Sir John Norris's campaign in Brittany deserted even before they left England.[78] 'I see wee shall starve on everie side', wrote the Earl of Leicester from the Netherlands in 1586, 'it is no marvell our men runn fast awaye.'[79]

If the rank and file were reluctant warriors, their officers were not. Many motives fed their martial fervour. Patriotism and religious belief were important to some. The former was loosely tied to honour in this era. Roger Williams, for instance, refused offers to join the Spanish army, because to betray his Queen and country in this way would be dishonourable. 'It is well known the Spanish sought to debauch me of late', he wrote to Francis Walsingham, 'no misery nor particular ingratitude shall force me to dishonour myself, nor seek bread of any others till England does refuse me.'[80]

For professional soldiers, money was an important consideration. The importance of money-making in war can be seen in the manner in which the English fought the Armada in 1588. Leading admirals focused their attention on capturing valuable prizes for themselves; Drake abandoned his station leading the fleet in order to sail back to seize the beleaguered Spanish vessel, the *Rosario*, while later the Lord Admiral, Charles Howard, missed much of the fighting at Gravelines as he concentrated instead on looting a stricken enemy warship.[81] This helped many other Spanish ships escape.[82]

Honour mattered too, and was, indeed, inseparable from profit. Men had to spend lavishly and display wealth in order to be honoured at court.[83] As Thomas Fuller wrote of the privateering expedition of his contemporary, George Clifford, Earl of Cumberland: 'his fleet may be said to be bound for no other harbour but the port of honour, though touching at the port of profit thereunto.'[84]

Some men's craving for martial glory was such that it overrode even their sense of obedience to their ruler. Essex disobeyed Elizabeth's orders and stowed away on the ship *Swiftsure* to join Drake's fleet on an expedition to Portugal in 1589; and Philip Sidney and Fulke Greville tried to sneak onto Drake's 1585 expedition to the Caribbean without the Queen knowing, but had to return to court when Elizabeth discovered their plans and ordered them off their ships.[85]

Many hardened military professionals shared the desire for glory. 'The most great Captaines cannot denie', wrote Sir Roger Williams, 'but their profession overreacheth themselves, more than any other, because al their speeches, deedes, and mindes consists in ambition for honour.'[86] Even ordinary soldiers were not entirely immune from the pull of honour once in arms. As John Norden wrote:

> A souldier thinketh it a great grace that can obtaine the place to leade the *Vangard* of a battell, the *Forlorne hope*, which is to betake him into the greatest danger for a little glory among men, and priseth life of little value, in regarde of the reputation of being desperate in the field.[87]

Thomas Churchyard concluded that:

> As the duetie to a mannes countrey, and the wages that he taketh, bindes him to doe the uttermoste he maie: so were there not an other cause, that forceth further matter. Full coldly some would feight, and full slowly some would march to the battaill, albeit the Princes quarrell and wages received, commaundeth much, and is a thyng stoutly and wisely to be looked at. But I tell you, fame and reputation is the marke that men shoote at, and the greedinesse of glorie and ambition, pricketh the mynde so fast forward, that neither the man lookes upon the multitude of enemies: Nor regardes the daunger of death, so he maie be eternified, and live in the good opinion of the Prince and people.[88]

Honours and rewards

Having risked his life, the Elizabethan soldier expected appropriate recognition. 'The Captaine that liberally rewardeth his souldiers', wrote George Whetstone, 'shall have his souldiers resolute in execution.'[89] 'There is no other safe way or meane to preserve an armie from tumult, sedition, and daungerous mutinies', echoed John Norden, 'than to reward the well doer, and punish the offender.'[90]

For all the fanfare with which military writers proclaimed this principle, in practice the ordinary soldier received very little in the way of rewards and honours. Often he did not even receive his basic pay, which the government withheld for as long as possible in order to cut costs. Captains also often misappropriated the pay of their subordinates. The sailors who helped to defeat the Armada had to wait months for their discharge pay, during which time Charles Howard noted that:

> Sickness and mortality begins wonderfully to grow amongst us; and it is a most pitiful sight to see, here at Margate, how the men … die in the streets. … It would grieve any man's heart to see them that have served so valiantly to die so miserably.[91]

By contrast, the rewards for higher ranking personnel could be very great. This was particularly true for the privateers. Francis Drake returned from his voyage around the world with plunder equivalent to several years of royal revenue. This he surrendered to the Queen, who permitted him to keep the substantial sum of £10,000.[92] As a mark of favour, Elizabeth subsequently also gave Drake jewels, property, and land.[93]

Elizabeth was notoriously tight-fisted in dispensing honours. By keeping them rare, she kept their value high. As Fulke Greville noted, 'she made merit precious, honour dainty and her grants passing rare; keeping them … to set an edge upon the industry of men, and yet … sparingly reserved within the circuit of her throne.'[94] For instance, Elizabeth granted few knighthoods, and the number of knights in the Kingdom fell substantially during the first half of her reign, from about 600 in 1558 to about 300 in 1580.[95] Thereafter the numbers rose as England's armies once again sailed overseas to fight. Commanders in the field still could, and sometimes did, grant knighthoods to those who distinguished themselves in battle. Leicester, for instance, knighted two men who captured Spanish battle flags at Zutphen in September 1586.[96] Similarly, Essex knighted 24 men during a fruitless expedition against Rouen in 1591, and Charles Howard knighted John Hawkins, Martin Frobisher, and several others for their contributions to the defeat of the Armada. After their forces captured Cadiz in 1596, Essex created 33 knights and Howard 27.[97]

Such profligacy enraged Elizabeth. Despite this, and despite strict instructions from the Queen to exercise more restraint,[98] in 1599 Essex knighted almost 100 men in Ireland, even though his army had not fought any major engagements.[99] Essex's behaviour had important political consequences. Through his generosity he created a clientele of young warriors who felt indebted more to him than to the crown. Many of those knighted by Essex then joined him in his failed revolt in 1601.[100] His example illustrates clearly why the Tudor monarchy sought to limit and monopolize the distribution of honours.

Honour and death

Essex's revolt ended in his death. He was beheaded in the Tower of London. This was fitting, as beheading was the most honourable form of execution for Elizabethan gentlemen. On his circumnavigation of the world, Francis Drake sentenced his colleague Sir Thomas Doughty to death for supposed sabotage of the voyage. Drake offered to shoot Doughty, so that he might die 'at the hands of a gentleman', but Doughty refused, and chose to be beheaded. Drake in his turn, when dying, asked his servant to dress him in his armour, so that 'he might dy like [a] soldier.'[101]

According to Fulke Greville, after Sir Philip Sidney was mortally wounded at Zutphen,

> He called for a drink, which was presently brought him; but as he was putting the bottle to his mouth he saw a poor soldier carried along, who had eaten his last at the same feast, ghastly casting his eyes at the bottle; which Sir Philip perceiving, took it from his head before he drank, and delivered it to the poor man with these words: 'Thy necessity is yet greater than mine.'[102]

The story is possibly apocryphal, but it passed into English legend as a glorious example of honour in death. Other glorious deaths include that of Sir Humphrey Gilbert who perished at sea in a terrible storm, during which he sat calmly on deck reading his Bible;[103] and that of Sir Richard Grenville, who died of wounds received after single-handedly attacking the entire Spanish fleet with his ship the *Revenge*. Grenville tried to blow up his ship rather than surrender it to the enemy, but was prevented from doing so by the few remaining members of his crew.

Elizabethans extolled the gloriousness of death in war. 'Wounds and death … gotten in the field in the face of the enemie, bring immortall fame to the valiant', wrote John Norden.[104] Sir Roger Williams, a veteran of many battles, took the logic one step further: 'There can bee no brave encounter without men slaine on both sides', he wrote, 'True it is, the fewer the better conduct; but the more dyes, the more honour to the fight.'[105]

Dead, the ordinary soldier received little or no acknowledgement of his sacrifice. In keeping with past practice, his body was buried in a mass grave and forgotten. Honour in death belonged only to more senior personnel. Roger Williams, for instance, 'was buried in St Paul's Cathedral with full military honours' after his death in 1595.[106] The most spectacular funeral was for Sidney, including a procession of 700 people through the City of London to St Paul's, where an impressive service was held.[107] Elegies were published in his honour, the composer William Byrd wrote three laments for him, and many Londoners wore mourning clothes for months.[108]

The Heralds' office laid down protocols for funerals such as Sidney's, ensuring that the honour received was appropriate to the rank of the departed soul. Funeral organizers might suffer fines if discovered to be breaking the rules.[109] Thus, William Segar specified that at funerals, 'no man of greater title than the defunct should be permitted to mourne, so as the chiefe mourner may ever be *in pare dignitate* with the defunct.' So, 'at the funerall of a Knight, onely Knights, Esquires, Gentlemen and their inferiors' should be mourners,[110] although this does not seem to have meant that superiors could not attend in a capacity other than that of official mourner. Several noblemen attended Sidney's funeral, and the Earl of Essex attended that of Sir Roger Williams.

Similar rules also applied to monuments, though they were regularly broken. Coats of arms, for instance, often appeared upon the tombs of men who were not entitled to them. In the Elizabethan era, it was common for the bodies of gentry who died overseas to be brought back home for burial. The number of monuments also increased throughout this period. Often, these were built while those to whom they were dedicated were still alive.[111] Heraldic imagery was commonplace, as were depictions of armour to attest to the deceased's supposed martial virtue. This was the case even when the dead man was a civilian with no military experience.[112] There was clear 'correlation between armour, effigies and honour'.[113] Even *arriviste* gentry with no military background liked to portray themselves as knights.

Honour and the conduct of war

Strategems were commonplace in late sixteenth century war. Those which fell short of direct breach of word were not dishonourable. Rather they were signs of prudence. By the later period of Elizabeth's reign, professional soldiers had replaced aristocratic amateurs as commanders of many of her armies. Generals such as Sir Roger Williams and Sir Francis Vere represented the model of the learned, prudent officer, willing to use whatever ruse was necessary for victory. Vere, nicknamed 'The Fox' on account of his cunning, described the ruse by which he retook Zutphen in 1591:

> I chose a good number of lusty and hardy young soldiers, the most of which I apparalled like the country women of those parts, the rest like the men, gave to some baskets, to others packs, with such burthens as the people usually come to market, with pistols and short swords and daggers.[114]

Pretending to go to market, the men sat around near the town gates until such time as they opened, whereupon they rushed into the town, and seized it.

In another example, the English garrison of Bergen-op-Zoom in 1588 played on Spanish successes in taking cities by treachery. An English ensign, William Grimston, contacted the Spanish commander, the Duke of Parma, with an offer to open the gates of the north fort, claiming to be a disaffected Catholic. The Duke took the bait, and allowed Grimston to lead his men into a trap on the night of 10 October 1588. The waiting English then killed between 400 and 800 Spaniards, and captured 14 captains and gentlemen.[115]

Such tactics contained none of the chivalric preference for ‘fair play’ or a straight fight. For this reason, some historians like to contrast the growing professionalism of Elizabethan generals with the supposedly outmoded chivalric pretensions of aristocratic commanders like the Earl of Essex. Essex had a habit of challenging his opponents to single combat. When the English army invaded Portugal in 1589, it marched up to the walls of Lisbon but found itself too weak to assault the city. Frustrated at being denied the possibility of glorious combat, Essex rode up to the city gates, drove a pike into them, and challenged anybody in the town to fight him (nobody took up the offer).[116] In a similar fashion, in Ireland in 1580, Walter Raleigh sent a formal challenge to the rebel John Fitzedmund Fitzgerald, Seneschal of Imokellie, but Fitzgerald did not reply.[117]

Such behaviour undoubtedly seems rather futile and in contrast to the studied prudence and professionalism of men like Vere and Williams. In fact these professional officers were not exempt from the chivalric desire for martial glory and some of its preference for recklessness. Sir Roger Williams, for instance, shared Essex’s passion for single combat. In 1581, a Welshman fighting in the Spanish army in the Netherlands challenged Sir John Norris to single combat. Williams took up the challenge as Norris’s champion, and the two Welshmen fought each other in sight of the two armies. Having struck each other some heavy blows, they ceased fighting, and drank each other’s health.[118]

Williams and others were exhibitionists who occasionally took needless risks to display their valour. The Earl of Leicester wrote from the Netherlands in September 1586:

> Roger Williams hath gott a blow thorow the arme, one evil fire. I warned him of it, being in trench with me, and would need run upp and downe so oft out of the trench, with a great plume of feathers in his gylt morion, as so many shott coming at him he could hardlie escape with soe little hurt.[119]

Flamboyant uniforms were popular. When Walter Raleigh led English troops assaulting the island of Fayal in the Azores, he personally went on a reconnaissance of the High Fort, with his cousin Arthur Gorges. Both were wounded, and Raleigh suggested to Gorges that he remove the prominent red scarf he was wearing. Gorges pointed out that he was merely following Sir Walter's example, since the latter was wearing an even more obvious white scarf around his neck.[120] The two cousins completed the reconnaissance dressed as they were. In the same fashion, the Earl of Leicester described the heroism of Edward Stanley during the assault on the fort of Zutphen, commenting: 'I ... saw it besides, [he] being all in yellow save his curass.'[121] Exhibitionism was not entirely irrational. Certainly, it brought added danger, but it also got one noticed.

Land warfare offered the most opportunity for such ostentatious displays of courage, but some managed to extend the principle to the war at sea. In September 1591, a small English fleet lay in wait off the Azores hoping to catch the Spanish treasure fleet as it passed by on its way from America. The English were, however, surprised by a separate Spanish war fleet from the east, and fled. The *Revenge*, commanded by Sir Richard Grenville, was slow in getting going. By the time it was well underway, the Spanish had arrived, advancing in two parallel columns. At this point, Grenville could have ordered his ship to turn around and flee. Instead, he sailed the *Revenge* straight between the two lines of the Spanish fleet, and succeeded in sinking two of the enemy before surrendering to overwhelming force. The *Revenge* was the only English ship captured by the Spanish during the entire war.

Grenville's act was foolhardy in the extreme. The only logical explanation of it was that provided by Raleigh who wrote in his account of the action, that:

> Sir Richard utterly refused to turne from the enimie, alledging he would rather chose to dye, then to dishonour him selfe, his countrie, and her Maiesties shippe, perswading his companie that he would pass through the two Squadrons, in despight of them.[122]

This and other examples lead one to conjecture that courtiers took their passion for gambling games with them onto the battlefield. In another example, on 21 September 1586, the Earl of Leicester ordered 200 cavalrymen and 300 infantry to intercept a Spanish supply convoy headed towards Zutphen, expecting to overwhelm it easily. On meeting the convoy, the English discovered that it had an escort of 3,000 Spanish infantry and 1,500 cavalry. Nevertheless, the 200 English cavalrymen charged, lances couched in mediaeval fashion, not just once, but three times, and routed the enemy. The Earl of Essex gained the title of Knight Banneret for his part in this victory.[123] Sir Philip Sidney, less fortunate, died of a wound in the thigh. He had removed his thigh armour. Possibly this was in order to lighten the load in combat, but according to legend, it was because he noticed that the English commander, Sir William Pelham, was unable to wear his due to a previous wound; Sidney's courtesy was thus held to have led to his death.[124]

The pursuit of honour affected grand strategy as well as low-level military tactics. Some in the government of England favoured a purely defensive strategy, sending troops to help the Dutch and to help Henry IV in France, but no more.

But others insisted that such a strategy could never bring Spain to its knees and create the conditions for a victorious peace. They argued for a more aggressive stance, taking the war to Spain itself, by invading its territory, sinking its ships, and seizing its treasure. There was little glory to be won on the defensive. By contrast, expeditions which captured Spanish towns and brought home great plunder would reap honour for those who joined them. So it was that men like Drake and Essex were fervent proponents of this option, and won the Queen's support for adventures such as the 1589 expedition to Spain and Portugal, and the 1596 attack on Cadiz.[125]

The former was a complete failure. The English Queen had very limited financial resources. As a result, many of her military ventures were what nowadays we would call 'public-private partnerships'. That is to say that the Crown paid part of the costs of the venture, but private investors paid the rest, and they expected to make a profit in return – mainly in financial terms, but also in terms of honour gained. This meant that those leading military expeditions often followed strategies entirely at cross-purposes to those demanded by the Queen. So, in 1589 Elizabeth gave Sir Francis Drake and Sir John Norris, who commanded the expedition, the prime task of destroying the remnants of the Spanish Armada, which had taken refuge in the northern Spanish ports of Santander and San Sebastian. After doing that, they were to sail to Portugal, seize Lisbon, and restore the pretender Don Antonio to the throne. As a final mission, they were to sail to the Azores to capture the Spanish treasure fleet. From the Queen's point of view, and from the perspective of national security, the first objective was by far the most important one. But Drake and Norris made no effort to achieve it. They did not even bother to sail to Santander, but instead attacked Corunna, and then sailed onto Lisbon. The reason was obvious. There was no profit or glory to be had in sinking ships in Northern Spain, but Don Antonio would be extremely generous in rewarding those who put him on the throne. In the event, the attack on Lisbon failed, and storms prevented the English from sailing to the Azores. The expedition returned to England with little to show for its efforts except a few ships captured off the Spanish coast. The Queen was furious. Drake and Norris, she complained, 'went to places more for profit than for service'.[126]

In this case, glory-seeking brought failure. But it could also bring success, as it did at Cadiz, where it drove the English commanders to compete with one another in a frenzy to prove themselves pre-eminent. The Earl of Essex and Charles Howard were joint commanders of this expedition. Under them were four English squadrons, and one Dutch, the English squadrons being commanded by Essex, Howard, Raleigh, and Lord Thomas Howard. There were also 6,000 soldiers under Sir Francis Vere. From the start, all five English commanders quarrelled over precedence, Essex and Charles Howard eventually settling a dispute between Raleigh and Vere by giving Raleigh 'precedence at sea and Vere precedence on land'.[127] Essex and Howard, however, also quarrelled. Essex deliberately signed a joint report right at the top of the page, so high that Howard would be forced to sign below. Howard responded by cutting out Essex's signature.[128]

When they arrived off Cadiz, Raleigh asked for the honour of leading the attack the next day. Charles Howard and Essex assented. Lord Thomas Howard then complained that his rank was superior and he deserved precedence, so the commanders changed their minds and granted him the right to lead the assault. This did not deter Raleigh. The next morning, he weighed anchor early, and set off ahead of the rest of the English fleet. Seeing him, the others followed, including Essex, who was supposed to be waiting in reserve, but who now joined the battle lest others win it without him. Wishing to overtake Raleigh, Vere fastened a rope to Raleigh's ship and began hauling his vessel up to it. Raleigh then cut the rope.[129] The English fleet sank four of the most powerful galleons of the Spanish navy, and cleared the way for the soldiers to land. They rapidly seized the city, Essex at their head, and the battle was a tremendous victory.

Honour and the enemy

A notable feature of the capture of Cadiz was the courteous behaviour of the English towards the defeated Spaniards. The Dutch who accompanied the expedition were keen to exact revenge on their Spanish enemies, but Essex stepped in to prevent them from massacring the population of the city. He gave orders that women and clergymen were not to be mistreated, and organized the evacuation of 1,500 people. Walter Raleigh also claimed some credit for himself and Charles Howard, writing that: 'ourselves spared the lives of all after the victory; but the Flemings, who did little or nothing in the fight, used merciless slaughter, till they were by myself and afterward by my Lord Admiral beaten off.'[130]

Cadiz was not the only occasion on which Essex intervened to prevent slaughter. Ten years earlier, after English and Dutch forces stormed Duesburg, the Earl of Leicester reported that, 'the usual horrors pursued ... till the Earl of Essex and divers other gentlemen came downe the breach, and by smiting the souldiers made them leave off.'[131] Essex's career indicates that a chivalric passion for martial glory could go hand in hand with great generosity of spirit.

Similarly, Francis Drake was well known as a courteous pirate. Attacking Vera Cruz in 1573, for instance, he told his men that they 'should never hurt a woman', nor any man that 'had not weapon in hand'. Discovering that there were three gentlewomen in the town who had recently given birth, he personally visited them to give his assurance that they would not be harmed.[132] On seizing Spanish or Portuguese ships, his habit was to spare all those captured, entertain the enemy captain, and lend him his cabin, before releasing him with a small present as a token of his regard (the present inevitably having a mere fraction of the value of what Drake had just stolen from him!).[133]

Crews of Armada vessels who fell into English hands received less generous, but not unreasonable, treatment. At one point the Privy Council ordered that the crew of the *San Pedro Mayor*, which was shipwrecked after circumnavigating Britain, be executed, but this order was subsequently rescinded. All Armada crews who landed in mainland England were spared. The Council put the prisoners in the care of private individuals, and provided a small stipend for their maintenance. It also ordered that the gentlemen and officers be separated from the rest, with the intention of extracting ransom for them. The government was slow in providing the necessary stipends, and this caused some unnecessary suffering, but as the government was also not paying its own sailors at this time, this was more the result of parsimony than deliberate neglect of the prisoners. Most of the rank and file were ransomed in late 1589 after protracted negotiations with representatives of the Duke of Parma. Release of the officers and gentlemen took rather longer, but in 1593 the last to be released, Don Pedro de Valdez, was exchanged for an Englishman in Spanish hands, along with a ransom of £3,500.[134]

The sparing of the Armada prisoners, along with the occasional courtesies extended to Spaniards in general, suggest that the English regarded the Spaniards as a more or less honourable enemy.[135] The English had a particular regard for the Spanish commander in the Netherlands, the Duke of Parma. After the surrender of English forces in Sluys in 1587, Parma asked Sir Roger Williams to show him Sir Thomas Baskerville, and when Williams did so, he 'imbraced him, turning towards his Nobilitie, he said, there serves no Prince in Europe a braver man'.[136] Behaviour of this sort meant that the English generally regarded Parma highly for his humanity and courtesy.[137]

The laws of war still prevailed, though. During sieges this meant, as in times past, that troops which surrendered in good time would be spared, while those who succumbed to assault lost the right to life. At Corunna in 1589, the English slaughtered some 500 Spanish troops, sparing only a few officers for ransom,[138] and when English and French forces captured the Spanish-held fort of Crozon in Brittany in 1594, they spared the lives of only a handful of the 300-strong garrison.[139]

Different – and worse – rules applied in Ireland. There the English were merciless, and felt no need to honour their enemies or treat them with respect. This applied also to foreign troops who came to Ireland. Thus, whereas Armada crews who landed in England were spared, those who landed in Ireland were massacred. When 600 Spanish and Italian mercenaries sent by the Pope surrendered in October 1580, the English commander Lord Grey de Wilton ordered his captains (one of whom was Walter Raleigh) to slay them all.[140] When Scottish mercenaries supporting Irish rebels surrendered on the island of Rathlin in 1574, the English accepted the surrender and then massacred them along with their families, ruthlessly hunting down all those who had hidden, men, women and children, some 500 in total.[141] And after Lord Mountjoy seized Duboy Castle, all who surrendered were killed, an act not excusable by the frenzy of assault, as the killing took place the day after the surrender.[142]

To the English, the Irish were not just traitors; they were barbaric and uncivilized, barely human. Barnabe Riche stated that the Irish were 'more uncivill, more uncleanly, more barbarous and more brutish in their customs and demeanures, then in any other part of the world that is known'.[143] The Irish, according to Riche, acted with 'treason … treacherie … fraude … deceipt … There is no hope of their promise, no holde of their worde, no credite in their othe, nor no trueth in their dealings.' Riche urged that they receive the harshest possible treatment:

> The greatest cause of all those endlesse warres, that are holden in Ireland, do only proceede of the mercie & lenitie that is bred amongst them: and that the

> onely means to bring the people soonest to conformitie, and the countrie to quietnesse, is without compassion to punishe the offenders, and without either grace or mercie to execute the rebelles.[144]

This was certainly the attitude of many English commanders in Ireland. Perhaps the most notorious was Sir Humphrey Gilbert. Tasked to put down a rebellion in Munster in 1568, he would give all those he confronted just one chance to surrender. Those who failed to do so received no mercy, regardless of subsequent events. According to Thomas Churchyard, whenever Gilbert 'made any osting, or inrode, into the enemies Countrey, he killed manne, woman, and child, and spoiled, wasted, and burned, by the grounde all that he might.'[145] Furthermore, Churchyard wrote:

> His maner was that the heddes of all those (of what sort soever thei were) which were killed in the daie, should be cutte of from their bodies, and brought to the place where he incamped at night: and should there bee laied on the ground, by eche side of the waie leadyng to his own Tente: so that none should come into his Tente for any cause, but commonly he muste passe through a lane of heddes, which he used *ad terrorem*, the dedde fealying nothing the more paines thereby: and yet did it bryng great terrour to the people, when thei sawe the heddes of their dedde fathers, brothers, children, kinfolke, and freendes, lye on the grounde before their faces, as thei came to speak with the said Collonell. Which course of government maie by some bee thought to cruell, in excuse of which whereof it is to bee aunswered. That he did but then begune that order with them, which thei had in effect ever tofore used toward the English.[146]

To Churchyard, there was nothing dishonourable about Gilbert's actions. On the contrary, they were a product of Gilbert's sense of honour. Gilbert 'helde it dishonourable for the Prince, to practise with Rebelles to accepte her Maiesties mercie', he wrote, 'he never would parley with any Rebell', and 'by this course of governement … there was muche blood saved, and greate peace ensued in haste.'[147]

However shocking English tactics in Ireland appear to modern eyes, few if any Englishmen of the Elizabethan era saw them as unacceptable. To some extent at least, the English considered the Spanish to be honourable enemies, and treated them accordingly. They regarded the Irish in an entirely different fashion, and so killed them without mercy.

Honour and the ending of war

In one sense Gilbert's tactics in Ireland proved justified. By use of terror, he succeeded in suppressing the Munster rebellion in just six weeks. In the longer term, though, his brutality solved nothing, and possibly made matters worse. Resentment grew, and rebellion sparked up again. Bringing peace to Ireland proved to be exceptionally difficult.

The English had two options in Ireland. First, they could attempt to subjugate the Irish chieftains entirely, but this was beyond the means of the Crown, which could not afford to keep a large standing army in Ireland for a prolonged period of time. The second option was to compromise with the Irish in some way. The problem with this was that it undermined the dignity of the Crown to treat with rebels. Elizabeth was willing to compromise, but she made it clear that rebels would only receive a pardon if they submitted unconditionally, thus upholding the honour of the Crown.[148]

In effect, what mattered here was the order in which things were done. Elizabeth would not accept a negotiated settlement or a conditional surrender. The rebels would have to submit totally and fall on their knees before her. Then and only then would they receive mercy. In fact, it was to be made clear to them that if they did submit, they would be treated generously, but Royal dignity meant that this was something which had to be tacitly understood and not officially negotiated. The problem with such a process was that submission was a humiliation which Irish chieftains were often unwilling to accept. In consequence, for a long time the English did neither one thing nor the other, neither sending sufficient forces to achieve outright victory, nor accepting a compromise peace.

In the end, when peace finally came, the terms offered to the defeated Earl of Tyrone were generous. After submitting unconditionally in 1603, he received a pardon from the dying Queen, and retained possession of many of his lands, although his independence as an autonomous chieftain came to an end. What made this possible was the crushing defeat he suffered at the hands of Lord Mountjoy in 1601. This altered the situation in two ways. First, it forced Tyrone to accept the humiliation of submission. Second, it allowed the Queen to be generous. For, whereas before Mountjoy's victory she would have been seen as acting out of weakness, now she could be seen to be acting honourably from a position of strength.

Peace in Ireland came only a month before the Queen died. Peace with the Spanish had to wait until after her death. This was not for lack of trying. Elizabeth sought peace with Spain from the moment that war began. In 1588, in an attempt to avert the launching of the Armada, Elizabeth sent negotiators to the Duke of Parma, and peace talks began at the town of Bourbourg. The Spanish, though, were not negotiating in good faith. Philip II had told Parma that he would launch the Armada anyway; Parma was to drag the talks out and thereby to confuse the English about Spanish intentions. In that way, the Armada might achieve surprise.[149] When the Armada arrived, and the English realized what the Spanish had done, they were outraged. Henceforth, Elizabeth no longer trusted Spain when it came to peace negotiations.[150]

This breach of honour made it exceptionally difficult for the two sides to end their war, even though by the mid 1590s both were exhausted by it. Only in 1598 did an opportunity arise to reopen negotiations. King Philip II died, and Cardinal Archduke Albert of Austria became ruler of a notionally autonomous Netherlands. This met an essential English demand, namely that the Spanish restore to the Low Countries their traditional autonomy. As a result, many in England now proposed that the Queen should seize the opportunity to make peace. This did not convince everybody. Some of the Queen's councillors still cited the example of Bourbourg as evidence that the Spanish could not be trusted.[151] Eventually, though, Elizabeth accepted the arguments of the peace camp, and appointed commissioners to negotiate a settlement with Spain. When these received their instructions, they discovered that they were to insist on 'precedency', which meant that the commissioners were to demand 'first place in all matters of protocol' during negotiations.[152]

This demand scuppered the peace talks which finally began in Boulogne in May 1600. The King of Spain, after all, possessed a huge empire, and (except at sea) was much more powerful than the Queen of England. Besides, his representatives pointed out, the Kings of England had always ceded precedence to the Kings of France. So, if the King of Spain granted the English their wish, he would have to cede precedence to France also. That was unacceptable. As a compromise, the English proposed that both sides accept equality, taking turns to have precedence. The Spanish rejected this idea too. The talks could go no further, and did not resume for the rest of Elizabeth's life.

The fact that negotiations broke down so easily perhaps suggests that neither side was truly ready for peace. However, precedence was not a trivial issue. It touched on the dignity of both monarchs, as well as on the ability of their representatives to negotiate from a position of strength.

Peace finally came when King James VI of Scotland succeeded Elizabeth as ruler of England in 1603. As a new monarch, with no prior involvement in the war, he had much less stake in the outcome. Keen to bring the fighting to a close, James acceded to some Spanish demands, such as a stop to English privateering, and invited Spain to send commissioners to England. This they did, and in 1604, the undeclared war between England and Spain at last came to an end. On occasion a change of leader may be the only way to overcome the obstacles thrown up by a stubborn sense of honour.

Women and honour

Elizabeth was as protective of her honour as any male sovereign. Indeed, the nature of honour meant that war posed a significant political threat to the Queen.[153] It gave her male subjects the opportunity to win glory for themselves, and thereby challenge her pre-eminence. For this reason, she took care always to portray her generals as acting to defend her honour. Thus when Lord Hunsdon put down the revolt of the northern Earls, she thanked him for being the 'instrument of *my* glory'.[154] The manner in which the Earl of Essex used his martial reputation to collect a band of followers who owed loyalty primarily to himself and not to the Queen proved the dangers which successful generals could pose to a female monarch.

Men like Drake and Essex took care not to harm women during their battles. The courteous warrior was undoubtedly one who treated women well. But, although Edmund Spenser claimed that love, 'of all honour and vertue is the roote, and brings forth glorious flowers of fame',[155] in Elizabethan literature and military treatises (some exceptions notwithstanding), mention of service of ladies is markedly rare compared with the literature of chivalry. The rhetoric of the era did not encourage men to portray their acts as being driven or restrained by ordinary women's assessments of their virtue. By contrast, Elizabethans were extremely keen to present themselves as patriots and loyal servants of their sovereign.

Elizabeth exploited the mediaeval idea of the lady. At one tournament, for instance, she sent Charles Blount 'a golden queen from her set of chessmen', which Blount wore during the jousting. This infuriated the Earl of Essex, who then challenged Blount to a duel.[156] While this rivalry went rather further than the Queen perhaps intended, it is indicative of the way in which she replaced service of a private lady with service of the Queen as the chivalric ideal and encouraged her noblemen to compete for glory on her behalf.

The devotion of many Elizabethans to the queen appears to have been quite authentic. They did not regard pursuing their own glory as necessarily contradicting their service to the monarch. The two were complementary.[157] Essex prophetically wrote to Elizabeth on one occasion:

> The two windows of your privy chamber shall be the poles of my sphere, where, as long as your Majesty will please to have me, I am fixed and unmoveable. When your Majesty thinks that heaven too good for me, I will not fall like a star, but be consumed like a vapour by the same that drew me up to such a height. While your Majesty gives me leave to say I love you, my fortune is as my affection, unmatchable. If ever you deny me that liberty, you may end my life.[158]

Essex was being slightly disingenuous. As a man, he did not think that his honour could ever be dependent entirely on a mere woman, even a queen. According to Mervyn James, when Elizabeth boxed his ears in July 1598, it 'generated so much bitterness precisely because of the earl's assessment of their respective sexual roles in terms of honour. ... He told her it was "an intolerable wrong", done, he said, "against the honour of your sex".'[159]

Conclusion

What strikes one about Elizabethan war and honour is the degree to which layers of ancient and more modern ideals intermingled, often within the same personalities, and often with very contradictory consequences. The famous warriors of the age were at the same time highly educated, well versed in military science, and ruthless in pursuit of their enemies; and yet obsessed with winning martial glory, enthused with a passion for single combat and other displays of courage, and merciful and generous to defeated opponents (Irish ones excepted).

One of the lasting achievements of the Elizabethan era, although its success was not yet evident, was to be the early colonization of north America. In Virginia,

Sir Walter Raleigh and others planted the seeds which eventually grew into the United States of America. Western honour now spread across the Atlantic.

Notes

1 Kipling, Gordon, *The Triumph of Honour: Burgundian Origins of the Elizabethan Renaissance*, The Hague: Leiden University Press, 1977, pp. 116 and 127.
2 For various theories about Elizabethan honour, many of which centre around analyses of Shakespeare's plays, see the list of modern secondary sources in this chapter's bibliography.
3 Segar, William, *Honor Military and Civill*, London: Robert Baker, 1602, p. 210.
4 Ashley, Robert, *Of Honour*, edited with an introduction by Virgil B. Heltzel, San Marino: The Huntington Library, 1947, p. 28.
5 Shakespeare, William, 'Richard II', Act 1, Scene 1, in *The Complete Works*, ed. Charles Jasper Sisson, London: Odhams Press, 1953, p. 452.
6 Greville, Fulke, 'An Inquisition upon Fame and Honour', verses 6 and 7, in Bullough, Geoffrey (ed.), *The Poems and Dramas of Fulke Greville*, vol. 1, New York: Oxford University Press, 1945, p. 193.
7 Ibid, p. 213.
8 Shakespeare, 'King Henry IV, Part I', Act 5, Scene 1, in *The Complete Works*, p. 507.
9 Elyot, Sir Thomas, *The Boke Named the Governour*, London: J.M. Dent, 1907; first published: London, 1531, p. 244.
10 Ibid, p. 47.
11 James, Mervyn, 'English Politics and the Concept of Honour, 1485–1642', *Past and Present*, supplement 3, 1978, p. 62.
12 Segar, *Honor Military and Civill*, p. 210.
13 Segar, William, *The Booke of Honor and Armes*, London: Richard Jhones, 1590, p. 34.
14 Neale, J.E., *Queen Elizabeth I*, St Albans: Triad, 1979, p. 354.
15 Greville, Fulke, 'A Dedication to Sir Philip Sidney', in Gouws, John (ed.), *The Prose Works of Fulke Greville, Lord Brooke*, Oxford: Clarendon Press, 1986, p. 89.
16 Ashley, *Of Honour*, p. 58.
17 Spenser, Edmund, *The Faerie Queene*, ed. Thomas P. Roche Jr., Harmondsworth: Penguin, 1978, Book VI, Canto III, Verse 1, p. 403.
18 *The Courtyer of Count Baldessar Castilio*, trans. Thomas Hoby, London, 1561, p. 48.
19 Kelso, Ruth, 'The Doctrine of the English Gentleman in the Sixteenth Century', *University of Illinois Studies in Language and Literature*, 1929, vol. 14, February–May, no. 1–2, p. 48.
20 Riche, Barnabe, *Allarme to England*, London, 1578, p. Ai. See also Gates, Geffrey, *The Defence of Militarie Profession*, London: Henry Middleton, 1579, p. 19.
21 See for instance the comments of Castiglione: *The Courtyer of Count Baldessar Castilio*, p. 48.
22 Segar, *The Booke of Honor and Armes*, p. A2, reverse page.
23 Peltonen, Markku, *The Duel in Early Modern England: Civility, Politeness and Honour*, Cambridge: Cambridge University Press, 2003, p. 55.
24 Norden, John, *The Mirror of Honour*, London: Thomas Man, 1597, pp. 25 and 26. For a similar comment, see also Elyot, *The Boke Named the Governour*, p. 236.
25 Adamson, J.H. and Holland, H.F., *The Shepherd of the Ocean: An Account of Sir Walter Ralegh and his Times*, London: Bodley Head, 1969, p. 46.
26 Lacey, Robert, *Robert Earl of Essex: An Elizabethan Icarus*, London: Weidenfeld & Nicolson, 1971, pp. 62–3.
27 *The Institucion of a Gentleman*, London: Thomas Marshe, 1568, pages not numbered.
28 Spenser, *Faerie Queene*, Book VI, Canto III, Verses 1 and 2, p. 903.
29 *The Institucion of a Gentleman*.

30 Norden, *The Mirror of Honour*, p. 20.
31 Greville, Fulke, *The Friend of Sir Philip Sidney: Being Selections from the Works in Verse and Prose of Fulke Greville*, ed. Alexander B. Grosart, London: Elliot Stock, 1894, p. 114.
32 Shalin, Alice, *The Relationship of Renaissance Concepts of Honour to Shakespeare's Problem Plays*, Salzburg: Institut fur Englische Sprache und Literatur, 1972, p. 2.
33 James, 'English Politics', p. 65; Elias, Norbert, *The Civilizing Process: State Formation and Civilization*, Oxford: Basil Blackwell, 1982, p. 259.
34 *The Institucion of a Gentleman*. See also, *The Courtyer of Count Baldessar Castilio*, pp. 368–73.
35 *The Institucion of a Gentleman*.
36 Gates, Geffrey, *Defence of Militarie Profession*, London: Henry Middleton, 1579, p. 18.
37 Whetstone, George, *The Honorable Reputation of a Souldier*, London: Richard Jones, 1585, p. Fi.
38 Norden, *The Mirror of Honour*, p. 47.
39 Markham, Gervase, 'The Most Honourable Tragedy of Sir Richard Grenville, Kt.', in Edward Arber (ed.), *The Last Fight of the Revenge*, Westminster: A. Constable & Co., 1895, p. 59.
40 Segar, *The Booke of Honor and Armes*, p. 24.
41 Lacey, *Robert Earl of Essex*, pp. 73–4.
42 Elyot, *The Boke Named the Governour*, pp. 238–9.
43 *The Institucion of a Gentleman*.
44 Sidney, Sir Philip, *Arcadia*, Harmondsworth: Penguin, 1977, p. 525.
45 Norden, *The Mirror of Honour*, p. 42.
46 Whetstone, *The Honorable Reputation of a Souldier*, p. Diiii, reverse side.
47 Norden, *The Mirror of Honour*, p. 38.
48 *The Institucion of a Gentleman*.
49 Norden, *The Mirror of Honour*, p. 49.
50 Ibid, p. 20.
51 Ibid, p. 64.
52 Segar, *Honor Military and Civill*, p. 45.
53 Williams, Sir Roger, 'A Brief Discourse of Warre', in *The Works of Sir Roger Williams*, ed. John X. Evans, Oxford: Clarendon Press, 1972, p. 5.
54 Norden, *The Mirror of Honour*, p. 37.
55 Ibid, p. 13.
56 Williams, 'A Brief Discourse', p. 19.
57 Gates, *Defence of Militarie Profession*, p. 43.
58 Neale, *Queen Elizabeth I*, p. 307.
59 Donne, John, 'Love's War', in *The Complete English Poems*, ed. A.J. Smith, Harmondsworth: Penguin, 1971, pp. 126–7.
60 Cited in James, 'English Politics', p. 68.
61 Riche, *Allarme to England*, p. Biii, reverse side.
62 James, Mervyn, 'At a Crossroads of the Political Culture: the Essex Revolt, 1601', in *Society, Politics, and Culture: Studies in Early Modern England*, Cambridge: Cambridge University Press, 1986, p. 416.
63 Ibid, p. 442.
64 Rowse, A.L., *The Expansion of Elizabethan England*, 2nd edition, with a foreword by Michael Portillo, Basingstoke: Palgrave Macmillan, 2003, p. 146.
65 Lenman, Bruce P., *England's Colonial Wars, 1550–1688: Conflicts, Empire and National Identity*, Harlow: Longman, 2001, p. 80.
66 Rowse, *Expansion*, pp. 175–6.
67 Norman, Andrew, *Sir Francis Drake: Behind the Pirate's Mask*, Tiverton: Halsgrove, 2004, p. 26; Mattingly, Garrett, *The Defeat of the Spanish Armada*, London: Jonathan Cape, 1959, p. 87.

68 Hughes-Hallett, Lucy, 'Francis Drake', in *Heroes: Saviours, Traitors and Supermen*, London and New York: Fourth Estate, 2004, p. 236.
69 Ibid, p. 292.
70 For a history of English privateering in the later part of Elizabeth's reign, see Andrews, Kenneth R., *Elizabethan Privateering: English Privateering during the Spanish War, 1585–1603*, Cambridge: Cambridge University Press, 1964.
71 Norman, *Sir Francis Drake*, p. 37.
72 Ibid, pp. 96–100.
73 Rebholz, Ronald A., *The Life of Fulke Greville, First Lord Brooke*, Oxford: Clarendon Press, 1971, pp. 19–28.
74 Ibid, p. 70.
75 Williams, 'A Brief Discourse', p. 9.
76 MacCaffrey, Wallace T., *Elizabeth I: War and Politics, 1588–1603*, Princeton: Princeton University Press, 1992, pp. 43–7.
77 Ibid, p. 47.
78 Wernham, R.B., *The Making of Elizabethan Foreign Policy 1558–1603*, Berkeley: University of California Press, 1980, p. 92.
79 *Correspondence of Robert Dudley, Earl of Leycester, during his Government of the Low Countries*, ed. John Bruce, London: John Bowyer Nichols and Son, 1844, p. 338; Letter, Leicester to Walsingham, 8 July 1586.
80 Cited in John X. Evans, 'Introduction', in Williams, *The Works of Sir Roger Williams*, p. xxiii.
81 Hughes-Hallett, 'Francis Drake', pp. 310–11.
82 Adamson and Holland, *Shepherd of the Ocean*, p. 162.
83 Andrews, *Elizabethan Privateering*, p. 61.
84 Ibid, p. 71.
85 Greville, 'A Dedication to Sir Philip Sidney', p. 88.
86 Williams, 'A Brief Discourse', p. 19.
87 Norden, *The Mirror of Honour*, p. 64.
88 Churchyard, Thomas, 'A Generall Rehearsall of Warres', in *Churchyard's Choise*, London: Edward White, 1579, p. Mii, reverse side.
89 Whetstone, *The Honorable Reputation of a Souldier*, p. Aii, reverse side.
90 Norden, *The Mirror of Honour*, p. 19.
91 Rowse, *Expansion*, p. 279.
92 Norman, *Sir Francis Drake*, p. 86.
93 Ibid, p. 92.
94 Greville, 'A Dedication to Sir Philip Sidney', p. 112.
95 Lacey, *Robert Earl of Essex*, p. 87.
96 *Correspondence of Robert Dudley*, p. 416. Letter, Leicester to Walsingham, 28 September 1586.
97 Kenny, Robert W., *Elizabeth's Admiral: The Political Career of Charles Howard, Earl of Nottingham, 1536–1624*, Baltimore and London: Johns Hopkins Press, 1970, p. 194.
98 Lacey, *Robert Earl of Essex*, p. 87.
99 Adamson and Holland, *Shepherd of the Ocean*, p. 307.
100 James, 'At a Crossroads', p. 428.
101 Norman, *Sir Francis Drake*, p. 158.
102 Greville, 'A Dedication to Sir Philip Sidney', p. 77.
103 Adamson and Holland, *Shepherd of the Ocean*, pp. 83–4.
104 Norden, *The Mirror of Honour*, pp. 25 and 48.
105 Williams, 'The Actions of the Lowe Countries', in *The Works of Sir Roger Williams*, p. 116.
106 Lacey, *Robert Earl of Essex*, p. 128.
107 Rebholz, *The Life of Fulke Greville, First Lord Brooke*, p. 75.

108 Day, J.F.R., 'Death be Very Proud: Sidney, Subversion, and Elizabethan Heraldic Funerals', in Hoak, Dale, *Tudor Political Culture*, Cambridge: Cambridge University Press, 1995, pp. 181–2.
109 Ibid, p. 186.
110 Segar, *Honor Military and Civill*, pp. 253–4.
111 Llewellyn, Nigel, 'Honour in Life, Death and in the Memory: Funeral Monuments in Early Modern England', *Transactions of the Royal Historical Society*, sixth series, no. 6, 1996, 192.
112 Ibid, pp. 194 and 197.
113 Ibid, p. 198.
114 Rowse, *Expansion*, p. 401.
115 Wernham, R.B., *After the Armada: Elizabethan England and the Struggle for Western Europe, 1588–1595*, Oxford: Clarendon Press, 1984, pp. 41–6.
116 Lacey, *Robert Earl of Essex*, p. 68.
117 Adamson and Holland, *Shepherd of the Ocean*, p. 69.
118 Evans, 'Introduction', p. xviii.
119 *The Correspondence of Robert Dudley*, p. 407. Letter, Leicester to Walsingham, 4 September 1586.
120 Adamson and Holland, *Shepherd of the Ocean*, pp. 274–5.
121 *Correspondence of Robert Dudley*, p. 427. Letter, Leicester to Walsingham, 6 October 1586.
122 Raleigh, Walter, 'A Report of the Truth of the Fight about the Iles of the Acores', London: William Ponsonbie, 1591, in Arber, *The Last Fight of the Revenge*, p. 19.
123 Lacey, *Robert Earl of Essex*, pp. 37–8.
124 Greville, 'A Dedication to Sir Philip Sidney', pp. 76–7.
125 See, for instance, Rebholz, *The Life of Fulke Greville*, p. 95.
126 The 1589 campaign is analysed in detail in Wernham, *After the Armada*, pp. 95–114.
127 Adamson and Holland, *Shepherd of the Ocean*, p. 252.
128 Kenny, *Elizabeth's Admiral*, p. 183.
129 Adamson and Holland, *Shepherd of the Ocean*, p. 256; Lacey, *Robert Earl of Essex*, pp. 150–9; Kenny, *Elizabeth's Admiral*, pp. 183–90.
130 Cited in Rowse, *Expansion*, p. 308. See also Lacey, *Robert Earl of Essex*, p. 159.
131 *Correspondence of Robert Dudley*, p. 405, footnote.
132 Norman, *Sir Francis Drake*, p. 31.
133 Ibid, pp. 71 and 129.
134 The treatment of the Spanish Armada prisoners is discussed in detail in Martin, Paula, *Spanish Armada Prisoners*, Exeter: University of Exeter Publications, 1988.
135 MacCaffrey, *Elizabeth I*, p. 58.
136 Williams, 'A Brief Discourse', p. 48.
137 Rowse, *Expansion*, p. 373.
138 Wernham, *After the Armada*, p. 109.
139 Ibid, p. 551.
140 Rebholz, *The Life of Fulke Greville*, p. 45.
141 Norman, *Sir Francis Drake*, pp. 36–7.
142 Ibid, p. 436.
143 Canny, Nicholas P., 'The Ideology of English Colonization: From Ireland to America', *The William and Mary Quarterly*, 3rd Ser., 1973, vol. 30, no. 4, Oct, p. 588.
144 Riche, *Allarme to England*, p. Eiii.
145 Churchyard, 'A Generall Rehearsall', p. Qii.
146 Ibid, p. Qiii, reverse side.
147 Ibid, pp. Qii and Qiiii.
148 MacCaffrey, *Elizabeth I*, p. 408.
149 Mattingly, *The Defeat of the Spanish Armada*, p. 173.
150 MacCaffrey, *Elizabeth I*, p. 209.

151 Ibid, p. 222.
152 Ibid, p. 227.
153 Fraser, Antonia, 'Elizabetha Triumphans', in *The Warrior Queens*, Markham, Ontario: Penguin Canada, 1990, p. 210.
154 Ibid, p. 211.
155 Spenser, *Faerie Queene*, Book IV, Verse 2, p. 563.
156 Lacey, *Robert Earl of Essex*, pp. 62–3.
157 See, for instance, Kenny, *Elizabeth's Admiral*, p. 36.
158 Lacey, *Robert Earl of Essex*, pp. 88–9.

6 Southern honour and the American Civil War

Introduction

In nineteenth century America, political defeat was taken very personally. Frequently the loser provoked a duel with the winner or some other prominent political opponent so as to restore his pride.[1] The most famous such episode took place in 1804, when Vice President Aaron Burr lost the New York gubernatorial election. Within weeks, Burr challenged Alexander Hamilton, one of the founders of the American Republic, and killed him.

Fifty-six years later, in 1860, the slave-owning states in the southern half of the USA similarly lost an election, when the Republican Abraham Lincoln beat three Democratic candidates for the presidency. The southern states responded by seceding from the Union and engaging it in war. The American Civil War did of course spring from economic and social factors as well as affronted pride, but the role of honour was key both in causing it and in the way it was fought.

Honour had played a vital role in American politics since the War of Independence, when American revolutionaries felt that the British were denying them 'the honor due them as morally responsible adults'.[2] Thereafter, American politicians continued to act as if every setback was a personal attack on them and their honour, and were prepared to take this all the way to war.[3]

The Civil War came as the culmination of decades of divergence between North and South. The slavery-free North had industrialized and urbanized much more rapidly than the South, and the two regions bitterly disputed several issues, including slavery, expansion to the West, and tariff duties. The tariff issue had, in fact, led to South Carolina's first threat to secede, during the 'Nullification Crisis' of 1832–1833.

By 1860, slavery was the pivotal issue. As the United States expanded, it appeared that newly incorporated states might be decreed slave-free. Gradually, this would shift the balance of power in Congress, until anti-slavery elements eventually got a majority to legislate slavery's abolition. Many Southerners saw moves to restrict slavery as classifying the South as inferior. They denounced such moves as 'degrading inequality'. One indignant veteran of the Mexican war (1846–1848) declared that 'No true Southron', would submit to such 'social and sectional degradation … Death is preferable to acknowledged inferiority.'[4]

The fiercest disputes arose in Kansas. On 21 May 1856, pro-slavery militants with five cannons seized the anti-slavery town of Lawrence, Kansas, and looted it in a skirmish which could almost be considered to be the first battle of the Civil War. 'The admission of Kansas into the Union as a slave state', commented South Carolina Senator Preston Brooks, 'is now a point of honour.'[5]

The election of Lincoln four years later was the final straw. A New Orleans newspaper stated that every vote for Lincoln was 'a deliberate, cold-blooded insult and outrage'. Having threatened to secede if Lincoln won power, honour left Southerners little choice but to do so when he did.

Accordingly, in 1860 the State of South Carolina announced its secession. It was joined by six other Southern states, which together formed the Confederate States of America. Military operations began in April 1861 when Confederate cannon opened fire on Fort Sumter, a Union fortress in the harbour of Charleston, South Carolina. Four more Southern states then joined the Confederate nation and the war was underway.

Honour and virtue in the south

It is important to note that the South was not a homogenous whole. Nevertheless, the antebellum South had a distinct overall culture from the North. According to one theory, this was because Southerners originated primarily from Celtic stock, whose culture emphasized traditional ideas of honour and shame, whereas the Northern population derived more from Anglo-Saxon types, among whom such ideas were less pronounced. In addition, Southerners lived primarily in small agricultural communities, where they were more exposed to the judgements of their neighbours than urban Northerners. The ever-present fear of slave revolts also made a reputation for strength indispensable. Together, these factors caused honour to be an essential aspect of Southern culture.

The most prominent modern scholar of these matters, Bertram Wyatt-Brown, identifies two main strands of Southern honour: that which he calls 'primal honour', which was 'almost entirely external in nature' and is immediately identifiable with that of the Greeks and other groups already examined in this book; and a more modern type which he calls 'gentility', which was mostly associated with the upper ranks of Southern society and aspiring social climbers.[6]

Another modern historian, Grady McWhiney, divides civil-war era Southerners into two types: 'Crackers' (whom one may associate more with 'primal honour'), and 'Cavaliers' (whom one may associate with 'gentility'). Crackers were the sort of people who endlessly bragged of their exploits in a competitive manner, seeking in this way to win precedence over one another. Inevitably, such competition, so reminiscent of that of ancient societies, tended to result in violence. Cavaliers, by contrast, behaved with romanticized chivalry and were courteous and well-mannered. Still, they shared the Crackers' concern for personal and family honour as well as their penchant for violence.[7] Consequently, Southern 'gentlemen' often displayed the extreme touchiness associated with primal honour, while their social inferiors did what they could to present themselves as gentlemen through dress, attentiveness to ladies, and the like. The different versions of honour managed to live fairly happily side by side.

The newest development in ideas of honour was an evolution from the Elizabethan focus on service to the Crown into a wider concept of 'duty'. Honour by now had become even further detached from physical prowess and fighting ability, and there was no single focus for it. Each man had some liberty in choosing whom he wished to serve and where his duty lay. Some judged that it lay in serving their nation under arms. Others judged that it lay in serving their women and their family.

In another break with the past, honour had now evolved to be a 'total condition'. Whereas in relative concepts of honour one can go up or down in honour, mid-nineteenth century honour was an absolute – one either had it or did not.[8] In consequence, avoiding any loss of honour was far more important than winning more of it. If in the slightest doubt as to whether one had been insulted, it was best to assume that one had, and respond appropriately. A Northerner, Alexander Mackay, visiting Richmond, Virginia, in 1849, noted that:

> Their code of honour is so exceedingly strict that it requires the greatest circumspection to escape its violation. An offence which elsewhere would be regarded as one of homeopathic proportions, is very apt to assume in Richmond the gravity of colossal dimensions.[9]

The appropriate response was violence. As the mother of President Andrew Jackson reputedly told him: 'The law affords no remedy for such an outrage [as insult] that can satisfy a gentleman. Fight.'[10] This principle carried through into the sphere of politics. Most notably, in 1856, Senator Preston Brooks thrashed Senator Charles Sumner of Massachussetts with his cane in the Senate chamber after the latter insulted Brooks' home state of South Carolina. The same year, Representative Albert Rust of Arkansas struck the editor of the *New York Tribune*, Horace Greeley, on the back of the head with his cane outside the House of Representatives,[11] and a year later, Laurence Keitt from South Carolina started a melée in the House of Representatives after a quarrel with Galusha Crow of Pennsylvania.[12]

One of the most common causes of violent clashes was an accusation of lying. This was taken especially seriously. Primal honour was to a large extent about showing the 'face' that one wanted others to see.[13] This concern with appearances led to an emphasis on display. Confederate cavalry general J.E.B. Stuart, for instance, liked to dress up in the manner of a Cavalier officer from the English Civil War. Another option was ostentatious risk-taking. In peace-time this took the form of high-stakes gambling, just as in the Elizabethan age.[14] Confederate General John Bell Hood, for instance, when still a young officer, once staked the enormous sum of $2,000 in a single hand of poker on a bluff.[15] Confederates carried the same behaviour into war. Hood, above all, became an extreme practitioner of battlefield gambling, with often reckless, near-suicidal, tactics.

If primal honour required courage, gentility demanded additional virtues. A gentleman was polite, well-read and religious. The prototypical gentleman was the great Confederate general Robert E. Lee. He was handsome, undoubtedly brave, and a superb soldier, having won great acclaim for his performance in America's war against Mexico. Despite his achievements, he was modest, gentle, and kind. He spent much of his life personally caring first for an invalid mother and then for an invalid wife. Expressing sentiments entirely opposite to the ancient Greek concept of hubris, Lee once commented that, 'A true man of honor feels humbled himself when he cannot help humbling others.'[16] Lee's gentlemanly style of leadership carried tact to extremes. While working as President of Washington College in Virginia after the Civil War, he met one of his colleagues who was riding his horse across the College lawn. Lee then quietly expressed sympathy that his colleague's horse had sore feet. Only later did the man realize that this was Lee's way of reprimanding him for not riding on the road.[17] In war, extreme politeness of this sort occasionally translated into a lack of firmness, earning Lee the sobriquet 'Granny Lee', and leading ultimately to disaster at the Battle of Gettysburg, where he appears to have been altogether too well-mannered to get a grip on his unruly and somewhat insubordinate generals.

The language used about Lee often harks back to Romantic images of chivalric knights. The writings of Sir Walter Scott were particularly popular in the American South, which has been described as 'Walter Scottland'. During the Civil War a South Carolina volunteer wrote, 'I am blessing old Sir Walter Scott daily for teaching me how to rate knightly honour.' After being wounded at the First Battle of Manassas, he wrote, 'I am like a knight at a beleaguered fortress and must not pass out with the women and the sick, when the castle is to be stormed, so long as I can put on my harness and wield my blade.'[18] Departing for the war, Captain Nathaniel H.R. Dawson wrote likewise to his fiancée Elodie Todd, 'Am I not fighting for you, am I not your knight and soldier?'[19]

Southerners' passion for stories of Stuart Cavaliers and defeated Scottish clansmen has made some historians regard the Confederates as people who romanticized failure.[20] Despite this, it would be a mistake to think of them as having gone willingly to their doom in search of some Romantic notion of honour. They started the war because they expected to win. This is clear from the letters of Confederate soldiers. Captain J.Q.A. Nadenbousch, for instance, wrote to his wife on 31 July 1861: 'I know the South will gain the day.'[21] Almost three years later, Sergeant Archie Livingstone commented that, 'I grow every day in the faith of a crowning result of glorious victory.'[22] And even in January 1865, just a few months before the final defeat, George Phifer Erwin felt able to write to his sister that, 'I believe our nation will rise fortified and ennobled by this struggle, and march on to its destiny, the highest place on the roll of nations. Hope on, hope ever, is my motto.'[23]

The Civil War was not, therefore, some bizarre effort to seek a glorious end in honourable defeat. The South both expected and wanted to win the Civil War. To do so it called upon virtues associated with honour, namely duty and obedience. Robert E. Lee, for instance, wrote that 'obedience to higher authority is the foundation of manly character', and said that 'You cannot be a true man until you learn to obey.'[24] This idea is reflected in a letter by one John Hooper, who served in the Confederate Army of Tennessee. Hooper wrote on 28 May 1864:

> A soldier ... is at all times subject to orders which he is sworn to obey, and the good soldier never stops to enquire whether the order is right or wrong, but goes forward in discharge of duty ... the man or officer who receives an order from a superior and fails to execute it, if he can do so, violates the most solemn oath.[25]

This letter links obedience to duty. Elsewhere we see duty linked to honour. Thus Lee wrote in a note for his satchel: 'There is a true glory and a true honor. The glory of duty done, the honor of integrity of principle.'[26]

The letters of Confederate soldiers contain numerous appeals to duty. So too do those of Northern soldiers. Yet there is a difference between the two. James McPherson, after analysing thousands of Civil War letters and diaries, came to the conclusion that duty and honour had difference nuances in North and South: in the North they were associated with abstract ideas such as patriotism and defence of the Constitution and the Union; in the South with self-sacrifice on behalf of family and race.[27]

To many Confederates the focus of loyalty, and thus duty and honour, was the family. This was possibly because the farming family was the basic economic unit in the South.[28] Nonetheless, some Confederate soldiers did also feel a sense of duty to their nation as a whole which transcended local or family loyalties. A sergeant in the 45th Georgia Regiment wrote in early 1864:

> I want this war to end and to be at home as bad as anyone, but I do not believe I could enjoy myself at home in such times as these ... Others would be fighting for their Country and My Country and home while I would be skulking my duty, and it would render me miserable.[29]

Southern honour gained strength from religion, producing what one historian calls 'a hybrid and distinctly southern value, a holy honor that ... justified southern behavior.'[30] There was a huge religious revival during the war, and thousands of soldiers were baptized. This helped to restore morale, and so supported the Southern war effort.[31] William Samuel Woods reflected a common sentiment in a letter to his mother, writing: 'I feel it is my Duty to serve God as well as to serve my country.'[32] Race, family, country, God, and duty thus came together.

Honour as a cause of the American Civil War

Examining the causes of the Civil War solely in terms of economic interests and questions of power fails to explain why the Southerners insisted on feeling personally threatened to such a degree. In 1860 slavery was not actually under immediate threat. Lincoln was not intending to abolish it, and even if he had been, he would not have been able to. As a Virginia newspaper wrote: 'We have the Senate, the House of Representatives and the Supreme Court in our favor, either one of which would of itself be sufficient protection of our rights.'[33] In addition, the great majority of Southerners owned no slaves. It seems strange that they should have been willing to split their country and fight a war to preserve the institution of slavery.

Honour is the key. Since what made every white man, however poor, a man of honour, was the fact that he was not black and was not a slave, it did not particularly matter that most whites owned no slaves. Slavery gave status to all of them, and attacks upon it were assaults upon their own honour. Because of this, the more the Northerners attacked slavery, the more the Southerners rallied around it.

As slavery became identified with Southern honour, pride ensured that the institution came to be seen as a positive good – as 'the mightiest engine in the universe for civilization, elevation and refinement of mankind – the surest guarantee of liberty among ourselves.'[34] Whereas in the early 1800s there had been quite a few abolitionists in the South, by mid-century there were hardly any. Republicans fuelled this contrariness by using inflammatory language almost designed to ignite the fury of honour-sensitive Southerners. Their rhetoric spoke of 'arrogant planters', the South's 'bullying arrogance', 'aristocratic haughtiness', of the South as a 'backward, degraded, barbaric society built on brutality and depravity'. One Republican said that, 'the South … is the poorest, meanest, least productive and most miserable part of creation, and therefore ought to be continually teased and taunted and reproached and reviled.'[35]

In a modern democracy, harsh partisan rhetoric is not unusual, but it is taken for granted that one can attack a man's politics without attacking his personal integrity. This was not the case in large parts of the South. John C. Calhoun said that the aim of the abolitionists was 'to humble and debase us in our own estimation, and that of the world in general; to blast our reputation, while they overthrow our domestic institutions'.[36] When some Northern states passed laws protecting fugitive slaves from being handed back to Southern owners, such laws were also seen as 'an insult to Southern honor'. As Senator James Mason of Virginia commented, 'Although the loss of property is felt, the loss of honor is felt still more.'[37]

By the late 1850s, a decade of bitter disputes over slavery had created a situation in which touchy Southerners saw insults in almost every issue. The use of the language of honour was then decisive in swinging public opinion behind secession. Initially, most Southerners did not support it. To change their minds, secessionists played on their emotions, portraying those who opposed secession as weak and unmanly, as 'submissionists'.[38] In the aftermath of Lincoln's election, this ploy was extremely effective. On 3 January 1861, the *Daily Herald* newspaper of Wilmington, North Carolina, said, 'We have argued and protested against secession, but we should … dishonor the blood that flows in our veins … if we hesitated to beat back the armed aggressor.' Eventually the issue came down to a simple question: 'submission or resistance?'[39] For a culture of honour, there was only one option – resistance.

Secession was merely a first step towards war. The North, at least in theory, could have accepted Southern independence. The South gave it no option; in April 1861 it launched the war by attacking Fort Sumter. Honour again played a vital role in the course of events.

In the immediate aftermath of secession, the Confederate states had seized control of nearly all Federal property on their territory, including fortresses and arsenals. Only two forts remained in Federal hands. One of these was Fort Sumter in the harbour of Charleston, South Carolina. Lincoln had promised to hold onto all remaining federal property, and could not hand over Fort Sumter without a catastrophic loss of face. Since the fort only had enough supplies to last a few more days, he ordered the Federal Navy to resupply it. Learning of this decision, the Confederates bombed Fort Sumter into submission.

Southern leaders must have known very well that attacking Sumter meant war. The fort had practically no military value. Its garrison was small, and it could have been left alone with no great loss. But Fort Sumter became a vital Southern symbol. The presence of the Union flag on Southern territory was a denial of Southern sovereignty.[40] It became a 'point of honour' to take down the offending flag. General Pierre Gustave Toutant Beauregard, commanding Confederate forces in Charleston, ordered his artillery to open fire, and the Civil War began.

Honour as a motivation for fighting

Before General Beauregard turned his guns on Fort Sumter, some Southern states, including Virginia, had refused to secede. When Lincoln responded to the Sumter attack by recruiting an army and announcing his intent to put down the rebellion, the holdouts changed their minds and joined the Confederacy. While they were doubtful about the wisdom of secession, the idea of seeing force used to suppress their fellow Southerners was unacceptable. Virginian William Nelson Pendleton wrote down on 1 May 1861 his reasons for joining the Confederate army:

> My beloved native State abstained from all hasty action … and continued under wrongs of the most serious character, to plead for justice, equality, and peace – even indeed as long as such course seemed at all consistent with her honor and independence as a state. The astounding call by the hostile representative of the aggressive section – for a force of 75,000 men – on her immediate border, – compelled Virginia to arm for her own defence and that of her Sisters, – if she would in any measure meet her obligations for the cause of justice on earth. … no man in my judgement, whatever his calling, or his love of peace, has a right to shelter himself from the common danger behind the bravely exposed breasts of his fellow citizens. I should therefore deem it my sacred duty – in some capacity – fairly to share the peril.[41]

Pendleton's note contains many of the factors which encouraged Confederates to take up arms: basic issues of self-defence; a feeling that the South had been wronged by the North and that honour did not permit it to accept Northern insults any longer; and finally a sense of duty, which made it an obligation to fight when others did. These were fairly much the factors which determined the decision of hundreds of thousands of other Southern men.

There can be no doubt that very many Southerners initially expected a quick and glorious victory, and wanted to be part of it, or at least felt that they could not stay out of the fighting with honour. General W.D. Pender wrote to his wife, 'I sometimes feel that if it were manly and honorable I would be willing to give up all hopes of distinction and military ambition, to live quietly with my wife and children.' But as a graduate of West Point military academy, he felt, as he said, that 'anyone with a military education is in honor bound to come forth these times and defend his country.'[42] Such sentiments of personal honour lasted until the very end of the conflict.

Many Confederates cited duty as their reason for fighting. Given Campbell, who ended the war as the personal escort of Confederate president Jefferson Davis, wrote to his fiancée, Sue Bettie Woods, on 18 October 1863: 'It seems an age since I saw you, as I have been unable to get leave of absence ... It is the dictator of honor and duty which prevent me from going to see you anyhow.'[43] Captain J.Q.A. Nadenbousch wrote on 31 July 1861, 'I expect to follow the army and do my duty until this difficulty is settled', and followed this up by writing on 8 August 1861, 'This is a hard life to live but duty first.'[44] Two years later, Sergeant Archie Livingston complained of those who were not in the army: 'Are they in the field of *practicable service*, exposing their lives, fortune and honor? ... These troubles are upon our country and for me I am here and expect to do my duty.'[45] And George Phifer Erwin wrote to his mother on 8 October 1863:

> I am heartily sick of war but under the circumstances would not be out of the army for any consideration. It is a pity that a person's duty and inclination so often conflict. But the army is the place for every able bodied person and just so long as the Yankees pursue their diabolical work, just so long I intend remaining here and contributing my mite in keeping them back.[46]

Men continued to fight, as they always have done, to avoid shame. In the waning months of the war in 1865, for instance, a Private in the 11th Georgia Regiment wrote to his mother that for the past four years he had done his:

> Deuty while in the Noble Army of Northern Va [Virginia] and were I to desert and lie out of this Strugle as many are doing I could not go any where but that the Eys of man and Woman would look at me ... I would feel worse than a Sheep killing Dog.[47]

The war became a test of masculinity. Soldiers' letters contain numerous references to the writers' desire to prove their manhood. For instance, a soldier in the 8th Missouri Regiment, wrote: 'I would be less than a man if in any way I fell short of the discharge of duty at my country's call.'[48]

Men believed that their family's honour depended on their behaviour, so that if they failed to live up to the highest standards, disgrace would fall not just on them, but also on those they loved. In a masterpiece of unschooled eloquence, William Samuel Woods wrote to his sisters from a camp near Vicksburg in February 1863, explaining that many of his colleagues were deserting because of the lack of food, but that he would not be following their example:

> You must not think Sisters Mar or Par that if they was not to give any thing at all to eat that I wold desert no no no never wold I desert no never that stain that it wold throw on my Par Mar Brothers and Sisters so long as they lived on no never I wold steal something to eat first and stay with my Regiment unless I cold get a onorable leave of absence.[49]

Similarly, a private in the 20th Georgia Regiment wrote: 'I had rather dye on the battle field than to disgrace my self and the hole family',[50] and a soldier in the 24th Mississippi Regiment told his sister: 'I much reather be numbered among the slain than those that stay at home for it will be a brand upon their name as long as a southren lives.'[51]

Confederate soldiers generally served in units with men from their own community. This heightened the peer pressure, as troops may have feared that their colleagues would write home about their behaviour, and so 'reports of cowardice would quickly find their way back to the community.'[52] This provided strong incentives not just to stay in the ranks, but also to pull one's weight within the unit.

With time, however, what is known as 'primary group cohesion' (i.e. the cohesion which develops within a small group of soldiers who fear shame in others' eyes) broke down. Battle losses meant that hometown groups disintegrated as men disappeared and newcomers came in.[53] 'Secondary group cohesion' (that which comes from larger groups, such as unit, country, community, and family) was in the long term possibly more important in holding men together.[54] The military unit played a prime role in this regard. Evidence of this can be seen by soldiers' willingness to fight and die for the sake of regimental flags.

At the start of the Civil War, Confederate units had a wide variety of battle flags. These were often presented to them by the women who had sewn them, thereby making them an embodiment of the ideal of Southern womanhood which soldiers would be honour-bound to defend.[55] Eventually, the Confederates standardized their flags into the format of the famous 'Southern Cross', which first appeared at a Grand Review overseen by General Beauregard. Fond of symbols, Beauregard ensured that women were involved in such ceremonies and drew attention to them in his declarations. At the Grand Review, he read a proclamation stating that:

> Soldiers: Your mothers, your wives, and your sisters have made [this flag]. Consecrated by their hands, it must lead you to substantial victory, and the complete triumph of our cause. It can never be surrendered, save to your unspeakable dishonor, and with consequences fraught with unspeakable evil. Under its untarnished folds beat back the invader, and find nationality, everlasting immunity from an atrocious despotism, and honor and renown for yourselves, or death.[56]

The task of carrying these flags in battle was considered a very great honour. It was also exceedingly dangerous. Flag-bearers were natural targets for enemy fire, as Calvin Leach described when recording his experiences at the Battle of Sharpsburg: 'Their front line was lying by a fence and I could see the old "Stars and Stripes" waving over them. I fired as near as I could aim at the men around the flag.'[57] Nonetheless, and perhaps even because of this, there was never any shortage of volunteers. As a Northern flag-bearer, Leopold Karpelen, noted, expressing a sentiment shared by men both Northern and Southern:

> I am aware that while I'm providing a rallying point and courage for my comrades, I'm also a prime target for the enemy. I vowed to accept that risk when I assumed this obligation which I consider a privilege and an honor.[58]

Capturing an enemy flag was as honourable as saving one's own. General Hood, in particular, attached great significance to capturing flags, and sent out several messages to his troops reminding them of the importance of doing so. They were, he told his Corps Commanders in April 1864, 'the most valuable trophies of war, establishing the valor of the troops capturing them … [they constitute] a proud memorial to future generations of their heroic achievements.'[59] It sometimes appears that, to Hood, somewhat like the ancient Greeks, the sole point of war was the winning of trophies. After losing a large part of his army in a suicidal attack on Federal entrenchments at Franklin, Tennessee, he consoled himself that he had won a great triumph because his troops had captured numerous enemy flags. 'Guns and colors', he stated in an order to his army on 25 July 1864, 'are the only unerring indications of victory.'[60]

Honours and rewards

Given the importance assigned to regimental honour and flags, it is not surprising that Confederate armies adopted the habit of awarding battle honours to units who participated in important engagements.

The Confederate government authorized the use of battle honours in General Order no. 52, issued on 23 July 1862.[61] It was sufficient for a Confederate unit to have participated in a battle and not lost its flag to receive the honour. The unit then marked the name of the battle on the flag. Some additional marks also appeared on flags to record specific achievements. A unit which captured enemy cannon, for instance, was entitled to place crossed cannons on its colour.

There was no set format for the inscription of battle honours. At first they were sewn or painted in an ad hoc fashion. By 1863, General Lee's Army of Northern Virginia had standardized the issue of flags, and honours appeared horizontally in blue stencil in the red areas between the blue and white stripes of the southern cross. Units of the Army of Tennessee tended instead to inscribe their honours diagonally in the white stripes which run along the edge of the blue cross in the centre of the flag. Whatever the format, the honours provided a record of the unit's performance and helped to embody the unit's honour in the flag. This made its retention in battle even more important.

The Confederate army was rather less efficient at honouring individual soldiers. Prior to the Civil War, the US army rewarded officers with a system of 'brevet' ranks, which entitled an officer to use the title and sometimes even wear the insignia of a higher rank than that which he officially held (although pay continued to be determined by substantive rank). But brevets were a rather unsatisfactory form of award. It was possible for an officer to be breveted several ranks above his substantive rank without ever receiving a 'real' promotion. Lee, for instance, was breveted major, lieutenant colonel, and then full colonel, during the Mexican War, while theoretically remaining still a captain. During the Civil War, when the officer corps expanded rapidly, the result was a flurry of officers with high breveted ranks but low substantive ones. Until the US Army recreated the rank of Lieutenant General for Ulysses Grant in 1864, the highest substantive rank available in the US forces was Major General, with the result that commanders of armies, corps, and divisions could all have the same rank. The Confederates took a rather more sensible approach and almost immediately after the start of hostilities appointed officers to the ranks of lieutenant-general and full general, thus providing more scope for promotion.

Desire for promotion undoubtedly inspired some Confederate soldiers. Senior officers, in particular, seem to have been very sensitive to their rank and position. William Nelson Pendleton complained that despite having been to West Point he had not got a Brigadier's commission:

> I was indifferent about it. Intrinsically, I am so still. But relations change. I find men, some of whom, with all my modesty, I cannot but deem my inferiors in military qualifications and services, made Brigadiers. ... can it be other than a reproach to a man with my antecedents and surroundings to have service with them?[62]

Others were less concerned. William F. Slemons wrote to Mattie Slemons on 23 April 1862 that he had been made a First Lieutenant in his absence, and commented: 'I do not desire the position and I am not inclined to accept if I can get out.'[63] John Hooper learnt that all regimental commissaries were to lose their commissions. Expecting this to affect him, he wrote on 9 June 1863: 'I am decided what I shall do, that is, return to the ranks whence I came. I am not one of those who think it a disgrace to be in the ranks if honorably dismissed from office.'[64]

Hooper's comments reflect a dramatic change in attitudes toward service in the ranks. Previously, this was something that no gentleman would have considered honourable. Now, possibly because of the democratic nature of American society, people valued the contribution of the private soldier. 'I have never yet been a private', wrote Given Campbell on 1 July 1862, 'though I do think that it is the most honorable position.'[65]

In any case, promotion is not always an appropriate reward for bravery, because the bravest fighters may lack the aptitude for greater responsibilities or command.

Consequently, in October 1862, the Confederate Congress approved a law authorizing the President:

> To bestow medals … upon such officers of the Confederate States as shall be conspicuous for courage and good conduct on the field of battle, and also to confer a badge of distinction upon one private or non-commissioned officer of each company after every signal victory it shall have assisted to achieve.[66]

In the latter case, the privates and NCOs of each company were to vote for which of their company received the reward.

Despite this order, no badges or medals were ever issued. The Confederate government gave a contract to make them to one Julius Baumgarten, but as no machinery for making them was available in the Confederacy, which was suffering severe shortages due to a Federal naval blockade, Baumgarten had to travel to Europe to get it. His efforts to bring the necessary equipment back to America failed, and the medals were never made.

Because of this, in October 1863 the army ordered that, while waiting for the medals and badges to appear, 'the names of all those who have been, or may hereafter be, reported as worthy of this distinction, be inscribed on a Roll of Honor, to be preserved in the office of the Adjutant and Inspector General for reference in all future time.'[67] Units continued to add names to the Roll, some 2,000 in all, until the end of the war.

Punishment was another way of motivating soldiers. Shaming tactics were popular. Confederate generals who lost favour with their superiors sometimes had to ride at the rear of the column as a mark of dishonour. When Hood refused to hand over captured ambulances to Brigadier General N.G. Evans, Evans made Hood ride at the back of the army as it marched into Maryland during Lee's first invasion of the North.[68] Stonewall Jackson punished A.P. Hill in the same way after charging him with 'neglect of duty'.[69] These incidents reflected the feuding among generals which was not uncommon among honour-sensitive Confederate officers.

At a lower level, it was common also to punish deserters by shaming. As the war went on, Southern leaders became more prone to executing deserters as an example to others, but the common practice was to brand them with a 'D', or make them 'appear conspicuous or ridiculous' by 'having half or all of the head shaved', and by marching them in front of the regiment bearing a placard saying 'Deserter' or something similar.[70]

Such punishments seem to have been only slightly effective. Desertion was a considerable problem throughout the war for Confederate armies. On the whole, formal means of reward and punishment seem to have played less of a role in keeping men in the army than pressure from family and home and the soldiers' own sense of duty and honour.

Death and honour

The lack of medals may have meant that ordinary soldiers did not receive much by way of honour in life, but efforts were made to honour them in death. For the first time since ancient Athens, states started to commemorate and honour each and every fallen soldier, however humble his position.

Nineteenth-century Romanticism managed to endow death with the aspect of glory.[71] 'The warmest instincts of every man's soul', wrote Robert E. Lee, 'declare the glory of the soldier's death.'[72] The one exception to this was suicide. Strongly held Christian beliefs meant that, unlike the defeated Roman, the defeated Southerner was not meant to take his own life, and very few did. 'It is our duty to live', said Lee after his surrender, 'What will become of the women and children of the South if we are not there to protect them?'[73]

The Union government enacted a law establishing national cemeteries for fallen soldiers in 1862. The Confederacy was less organized, but did try, where possible, to give an individual burial to those of its soldiers that it could identify. Aware of this, and also wishing their relatives to know their fate, Civil War soldiers took to wearing tags which would enable burial parties to identify them if they fell in battle. Often these were no more than slips of paper pinned onto their uniforms. As a result, they did not survive long, and were of little use if the body was left for a prolonged period before receiving a proper burial. Bodies reburied after the war were rarely identifiable. Still, the introduction of the practice of self-identification showed that ordinary soldiers now expected some type of individual attention after death.

Both sides took rather better care of their own dead than of the enemy dead. After the Battle of Franklin, for instance, the Confederates laid their own soldiers out in two-man graves, covered them with blankets, and, when their names were known, placed markers at the head of the graves. By contrast, the Union dead 'were simply piled pell-mell into the ditch by the breastworks – most after being stripped of their clothes – and a foot or two of dirt shoveled on top of them.'[74]

Sometimes parties went out under flags of truce to collect the dead, so that each side could give their own men a proper burial. This led to a situation similar to that encountered in Greek warfare, where the losing side might have to request the permission of the victor, and thereby admit its defeat. After the Battle of Cold Harbor, General Grant sent a note to General Lee asking for an agreement that neither side would shoot at stretcher parties sent out for the dead and wounded. As he had no dead or wounded outside his own lines, Lee refused, and instead demanded a formal truce. He wanted Grant to admit defeat. Initially Grant refused, but after two days he relented. Unfortunately, by that time all but two of the wounded had died.[75]

Despite the desire to give every soldier an individual burial, the sheer scale of casualties often made this impossible at the time, and the dead were then buried in mass graves. After the war both sides went to considerable efforts to re-inter them. Many Civil War cemeteries date from after the war. Confederate and Federal cemeteries differ somewhat. In line with their loyalty to local community, Confederate soldiers often lie together in groups according to their state of origin. Federal troops do not. Asked if he wanted such an arrangement at the burial ground near Chatanooga, General George Thomas said no. 'I'm sick and tired of hearing about States' rights', he commented.[76]

Honour and the conduct of war

There is a temptation to take Southern ideals of chivalry at face value and assume that Confederate soldiers followed these ideals on the battlefield, making the Civil War, as one commentator puts it, 'a chivalric war'.[77] The South's defeat can then be ascribed to its adherence to outmoded means of warfare, based on ideas of 'fair play' and honour, while its industrialized opponents embarked, under the influence of Grant and Sherman, on unrestrained 'total war'.

Ideas of honour did have some restraining impact on the South, but it would be a mistake to see the Confederates as not understanding 'total war'. The commanders of Southern armies were nearly all professional soldiers whose ethos was based on a desire to win. They were quite at ease with the fact that in order to do so, they had to kill as many of the enemy as possible. Thus when one of Stonewall Jackson's subordinates, Colonel J.M. Patton, expressed regret at having killed some of the enemy who had behaved particularly courageously, Jackson reprimanded him, saying, 'No, Colonel, shoot them all. I don't want them to be brave.'[78]

At first, some officers undoubtedly did feel that certain means of warfare were unacceptable. When General Gabriel Rains of D.H. Hill's division planted landmines on the road to Richmond in 1862, Hill objected that they were not 'a proper or effective method of war'. By 1864, however, landmines had become commonplace,[79] as had other 'underhand' methods which did not require stand-up face-to-face valour, such as snipers and submarines. In September 1861, Given Campbell wrote of his horror that the Confederate government was engaging in espionage, which he described as 'one further step towards despotism'.[80] But war made acceptable what previously would not have been. As early as April 1862, General Richard Ewell wrote home to say, 'Does Lizza still have ideas of chivalry? Here they seem to be pretty generally played out.'[81]

Ruses de guerre and deception were quite acceptable. 'Strategy', said the great Virginian partisan commander, John Mosby, 'is only another name for deception and can be practised by any commander.'[82] War, he added later, was not 'a tournament or pastime, but one of the most practical of human undertakings; I learned the maxims on which I conducted it from Napoleon and not from Walter Scott.'[83] Still, he also said categorically that, 'we observed the ethics of the code of war.'[84] This was true. While fighting what nowadays would be called a guerrilla campaign in Federal-occupied northern Virginia, Mosby took care to abide by the norms of his era. 'We are soldiers, not highwaymen', he told his troops.[85]

The ethics of war particularly restrained Southern soldiers when it came to the treatment of non-combatants, above all women and children. John Hooper expressed his contempt that the Federals had taken women prisoner. In a letter to a friend, he wrote: 'What a humane enemy we have to contend with! It makes me mad to think of them. I long to get on their soil, but God forbid that I or any of our army shall ever wage war upon women and children.'[86] This attitude had some meaning in practice. Robert E. Lee issued strict instructions during his 1863 invasion of Pennsylvania that his troops were not to loot or otherwise mistreat Northern civilians, on pain of death.

This contrasts clearly with the strategy adopted in 1864 by Northern generals such as William Tecumseh Sherman and Philip Sheridan, who sought to dent Southern morale by the destruction of civilian property. Their tactics did eventually encourage some Southern generals to follow suit. In 1864, General Jubal Early extorted ransom money from several Northern cities, and in July of that year he burnt down the city of Hagerstown, Maryland. This, though, was an exceptional instance, and could be regarded as a legitimate reprisal under the rules of law of the time.[87]

The constraints imposed by ideas of honour can be very clearly seen in the attitude of Southern leaders towards guerrilla and partisan war. At the time theorists drew a clear distinction between the two. Partisans were legitimate. They were part of the armed forces of a belligerent, although they operated separately behind enemy lines. Guerrillas were not. They were defined as 'self-constituted sets of armed men ... who form no integrant part of the organized army'.[88]

As Northern armies were often operating deep inside Confederate territory, the South had the opportunity to use partisans and guerrillas to threaten Federal lines of communication, and thereby force enemy commanders to detach large numbers of men to protect their rear. With this in mind, in 1862 the Confederate Congress passed the Partisan Ranger Act, authorizing the Southern President to form bands of partisans. A number of such groups soon emerged. Guerrilla bands also came into being, most notably in Missouri, where a vicious guerrilla conflict continued throughout the whole four years of the Civil War.

In the ranks, many Confederates saw partisan warfare as rather romantic. 'I should prefer the dashing and reckless life of a partisan to any position in the regular line', wrote Given Campbell in 1862.[89] The professional commanders of the Confederate forces viewed matters rather differently. General McCulloch, who commanded Confederate forces in Northern Texas, refused to use William Clarke Quantrill's guerrilla band when it fled south to Texas after massacring the population of Lawrence, Kansas. McCulloch denounced Quantrill's mode of warfare, as:

> Little but little, if at all, removed from that of the wildest savage; so much so, that I do not for a moment believe that our Government can sanction it in one of her officers. … we cannot, as a Christian people, sanction a savage, inhuman warfare, in which men are to be shot down like dogs, after throwing down their arms and holding up their arms supplicating for mercy.[90]

Sentiments like this encouraged the Confederate Congress to repeal the Partisan Ranger Act in February 1865. This was a remarkable decision. In the face of final defeat, a resort to partisan and guerrilla war offered the only real prospect of continuing the struggle. Yet at that very moment, the Confederates turned their back on this option.

Matters of honour seem to have played a decisive role. The Confederates appear to have decided that if they were going to be defeated, it was better to lose with honour. When the Confederate Cabinet met to discuss the terms of surrender offered to the army of General Joseph Johnston by Sherman, they did consider the possibility of continuing the war by means of irregular warfare. But the Secretary of War, Major General John C. Breckinridge, warned that it they did so, they would 'be likely to lose entirely the dignity of regular warfare'.[91] Similarly, when Lee's artillery commander, E. Porter Alexander, suggested that they disperse their army to fight a guerrilla war rather than surrender it to the Federals, Lee told him that once dispersed, his men 'would be compelled to rob and steal in order to live. They would become ... bands of marauders.'[92] Alexander noted that 'He had answered my suggestion from a plane so far above it, that I was ashamed of having made it.'[93]

The Confederate preference was, therefore, for conventional battle, and almost to a man, Southern generals preferred attacking to defending, even when the odds were stacked heavily against them. As a result, casualties in Confederate units were often extremely high. Over a third of all Confederate soldiers were killed or wounded at some point in the war.[94]

From a strategic point of view, defence made more sense for the South, which did not have to conquer any territory, merely hold what it had. Tactically, it was also prudent. Increases in firepower gave an undoubted advantage to defenders, especially those in fortifications. But psychologically it appears that the Confederates were incapable of adopting a defensive posture. The one general who tried to, General Joseph Johnston during the campaign for Atlanta, was disparaged for his efforts. Thus, John Hooper, who served under Johnston in the Atlanta campaign, complained about his general's battle-avoiding manoeuvres, that, 'To move and accomplish nothing is worse than to be defeated in battle.'[95] President Davis shared his view, and replaced Johnston with the belligerent Hood, upon whom he could rely to attack.

Honour helps to explain this feature of Confederate warfare. After Hood lost nearly his entire army at the Battle of Nashville, where he chose to stand and fight against overwhelming Northern forces, he justified his actions, saying: 'It was more judicious that the men should face a decisive issue, rather than retreat – in other words, rather than renounce the honor of their cause, without having made a manful effort to lift up the sinking fortunes of the Confederacy.'[96]

This mentality led to a dislike of defensive fortifications, which supposedly unmanned soldiers and made them unsuited for offensive action. Robert E. Lee was the first Confederate general to make his troops dig in, and they mocked him for it, denouncing him as 'The King of Spades'.[97] Lee's men eventually overcame their prejudices, and became adept diggers, pulling out their spades as soon as they stopped moving. Many other troops remained hostile to the idea. Digging was 'something done by Negroes',[98] not by soldiers.

General Hood was one of those who deplored the practice of entrenching whenever troops stopped. As he said:

> A soldier cannot fight for a period of one or two months constantly behind breastworks … and then be expected to engage in pitched battle and prove as intrepid and impetuous as his brother, who had been taught to rely solely on his own valor.[99]

Hood was not entirely wrong. Experience showed that once troops stopped to fire their weapons, or to take cover from their enemy, it was extremely difficult to get them moving again. The only way an attack could succeed was if momentum was maintained. This meant instilling aggressive spirit at the expense of everything else. As Brigadier General Henry Wise stated:

> It was not the improved arm, but the improved man, which would win the day. Let brave men advance with flintlocks and old-fashioned bayonets … reckless of the slain, and he would answer for it with his life, that the Yankees would break and run.[100]

Although aggression of this sort sometimes worked, defensive firepower grew so rapidly that more often it led simply to the slaughter of the attacking forces. The nadir of Hood's gambling penchant came in his period as commander of the Army of Tennessee, when he succeeded in destroying almost his entire army. First, he launched three failed assaults against the Federal forces besieging Atlanta, and lost so many men that he had to abandon the city. Then he embarked on an offensive into Tennessee, attacked entrenched Federal forces at Franklin at enormous loss to himself, and finally lost most of what remained of his troops at the Battle of Nashville.

Because Southerners placed such value on bravery, they tended also to want to fight without putting in the dreary hard work of preparing properly. Confederate commanders all too often possessed the qualities needed of junior leaders – raw courage, aggressiveness, an urge to lead by example – but not those needed at higher levels of command. Hood, for instance, as a brigade commander was superb; as a divisional commander, good; as a corps commander, indifferent; and as an army commander, disastrous. In the latter role, he paid insufficient attention to logistics and mundane staffwork.[101] Other Confederate generals were similar.[102]

Combined with this administrative incompetence, offensive tactics wore Confederate armies down until they ran out of men. General D.H. Hill commented some years after the war that: 'It was thought to be a great thing to charge a battery of artillery or an earthwork lined with infantry … we were lavish of blood in those days.'[103] A great thing it may have been, but it cost the Confederacy the war.

Honour and the enemy

Guerrillas' behaviour was often atrocious, and Confederates often slaughtered black Federal soldiers. When fighting white men, though, Confederates tended to regard them as honourable opponents.

This can be seen in a courteous exchange of letters between Major General Samuel French of the Confederate Army of Tennessee and Brigadier John M. Corse, who was defending a Federal supply depot at Allatoona, Georgia. French's forces had surrounded those of Corse, and he wished to capture the depot without a fight. He therefore wrote to Corse suggesting that he surrender:[104]

> Around Allatoona, October 5, 1864
> Commanding Officer United States Forces, Allatoona
> I have placed the force under my command in such positions that you are surrounded, and to avoid a needless effusion of blood I call upon you to surrender your forces at once, and unconditionally.
> Five minutes will be allowed for you to decide. Should you accede to this, you will be treated in the most honorable manner as prisoners of war.
> I have the honor to be, very respectfully yours,
> S.G. French
> Major General commanding forces
> Confederate States

To which, Corse replied:

> Headquarters Fourth Division, Fifteenth Corps
> Allatoona, Georgia, 8:30 AM, October 5th, 1864
> Major General S.G. French, Confederate States etc.
> Your communication demanding surrender of my command I acknowledge receipt of, and respectfully reply that we are prepared for the 'needless effusion of blood', whenever it is agreeable to you.
> I am, very respectfully, your obedient servant,
> John M. Corse
> Brigadier General commanding forces
> United States

Faced with Corse's resistance, French decided to seek easier prey, and called off his attack.

Chivalric ideas affected more than just the language of war. In 1861, for instance, Confederate General Nicholas Pierce invited four captured Federal officers to a dinner, on condition they gave their word of honour not to escape. They did and the dinner went ahead.[105] Such behaviour was rather more common at the start of the war than the end. Mutual respect never entirely disappeared, however, and there are numerous stories of officers on both sides helping former friends who fell into their hands.

Ordinary soldiers, too, acted in this way. Fraternization was quite common, and little, if anything, seems to have been done to stop it. On occasion, soldiers even stopped to give succour to the enemy wounded. Most famously, at the Battle of Fredericksburg, Sergeant Richard Kirkland of the 2nd South Carolina Volunteers insisted on going out into the land between the two armies to give water to wounded Federal troops, repeating his journey several times over one and a half hours.[106] A statue in his honour stands on the battlefield today.

For most of the war, a system of parole and exchange existed. Prisoners were released on condition that they gave their word not to fight again until properly exchanged (that is to say, swapped for a prisoner from the other side). Interestingly, whereas in previous wars, parole was something only an officer could give, in the American Civil War all ranks were considered to be gentlemen whose word of honour was sufficient guarantee for their release.

The system of exchange collapsed in 1864, in part because Union commanders realized that the system favoured the South. The Union had almost limitless manpower at its disposal. Any men who were captured could be replaced. The South was running out of manpower, and prisoner exchanges allowed it to replenish its ranks. A more pressing reason why the system came to an end was the Confederates' refusal to exchange captured black soldiers whom they believed to be former slaves. The North refused to accept this, Secretary of War Edwin Stanton saying that to do so would be 'a shameful dishonour'.[107]

The end of exchanges placed a huge burden on the South, which was barely able to feed its own troops, let alone tens of thousands of prisoners. Many of these prisoners ended up in a prison camp at Andersonville, Georgia, which became notorious for its appalling conditions. It is easy to see Andersonville as the negation of all chivalric principles, living proof of their practical irrelevance. On the whole, though, modern historians tend to attribute the conditions there (which resulted in the deaths of thousands of men) to supply shortages and gross incompetence rather than deliberate neglect.[108]

There were occasional reports of troops killing prisoners. Many of these feature irregular forces. Mosby, for instance, executed seven Northern soldiers, after Federal troops had killed seven of his own. He justified this reprisal as an 'act of mercy' designed 'to prevent the war from degenerating into a massacre', and his action does appear to have had the desired effect, because Northern forces thereafter ceased killing those of his men that they captured.[109]

Even more notorious than Mosby was William Clarke Quantrill. In August 1863, his men attacked Lawrence, Kansas, and killed 150 of the male inhabitants in cold blood. He also on occasion shot prisoners. Still, it is interesting that at first even Quantrill seems to have had chivalric ideas, keeping promises made to the enemy, granting paroles, and ensuring that his men never harmed women.[110] But the war in Missouri was a particularly nasty one. In response to the guerrilla campaign, Union generals resorted to deporting the civil population and executing captured fighters. Guerrillas such as Quantrill became more brutal in retaliation, violence escalated, and restraints fell away.

The respect shown to women even by men such as Quantrill did not extend to blacks. As we have seen, Southern honour had a racial element, and the introduction of black troops in the Northern army was interpreted as a particularly insulting act. After all, if blacks proved to be capable soldiers, then they would be the equals of whites, and the whole basis of Southern racial honour would collapse. Consequently, the presence of black troops could drive Southern soldiers into a fury, and they were prone to massacre those who attempted to surrender. In October 1864, for instance, troops under Colonel Felix Robertson killed over 100 wounded black soldiers left behind on the battlefield after the Battle of Saltville, Virginia. General Breckinridge tried to arrest Robertson for murder, but had to contend with Jefferson Davis who wanted to promote him to Brigadier.[111] In another incident, in April 1864 troops under Nathan Bedford Forrest refused to accept the surrender of over 100 blacks at Fort Pillow on the Mississippi, and instead killed them all. A lieutenant in the 9th Alabama Regiment wrote in a letter:

> I hope there may never be another exchange ... One thing I think is very certain and that is that the army in Virginia will not take negro prisoners. Much as we would deplore such a state of affairs I say let it come rather than take the alternative. If we lose everything else, let us preserve our honor.[112]

Honour and the ending of the war

Honour led the South into war, and contributed to its defeat. On the positive side, a sense of honour helped it to come to terms with its fate and enabled the two sides to bring the war to a satisfactory conclusion. Southern generals, once they realized the complete futility of further struggle, placed the search for an honourable conclusion to the war above vain hopes of continued resistance. In their turn, Northern commanders showed a remarkable understanding of the need to honour their enemy and treat him with respect.

The first of these factors has already to some extent been discussed. When junior officers suggested that their generals disperse their armies and continue the war through irregular means, the generals refused to do so, believing that such methods of war were dishonourable. When President Davis pressed General Johnston to keep on fighting even after the surrender of Robert E. Lee's Army of Northern Virginia, Johnston refused.[113] General Breckinridge urged the government to surrender its armies in one piece, saying:

> What I propose is this that the Confederacy should not be captured in fragments, that we should not disband like banditti, but that we should surrender as a government, and we will thus maintain the dignity of our cause ... This has been a magnificent epic, in God's name let it not terminate in farce.[114]

Jefferson Davis rejected Breckinridge's plea, but his generals were no longer paying attention to him. Once they learnt of Lee's surrender, even though the Confederacy still had over 100,000 men in arms, they one by one laid down their weapons. In doing so, they appealed to duty, honour, and manhood. So, when Lieutenant General Richard Taylor, commanding Confederate forces in Alabama, told his men to disband, he instructed them that, 'We have but one course to take, and that is manfully and honorably meet our responsibilities as soldiers and citizens.' If they did so, he said, 'even our enemies will respect our manliness and consistency and do justice to our motives.'[115]

Having surrendered gracefully, Confederate leaders won further credit by urging their men to accept their defeat and reconcile themselves to life in the Union. Robert E. Lee encouraged his men to take an oath of loyalty to the United States, and set an example by doing so himself. Others made similar gestures. General Nathan Bedford Forrest told his troops on 9 May 1865:

> Civil War … naturally engenders feelings of animosity, hatred and revenge. It is our duty to divest ourselves of all such feelings. … Obey the law, preserve your honour, and the government to which you have surrendered can afford to be and will be magnanimous.[116]

Forrest's prediction was correct. The main Northern commanders, Grant and Sherman, both gave extremely generous terms of surrender, paroling the Confederates *en masse* and allowing the men and officers to go free. Little gestures also eased the way to peace. When Federal troops celebrated Lee's surrender by firing their artillery, Grant ordered them to stop: 'The Confederates were now our prisoners', he explained, 'and we did not want to exult over their downfall.'[117] More touchingly, when Lee's men marched up to the Federal army at Appomattox Court House to lay down their weapons, General Joshua Chamberlain, commanding the Federal forces, spontaneously ordered his troops to shoulder arms, honouring the Confederates in defeat. The Confederates saluted back, and regained some pride at the moment of their humiliation. Later, politicians stepped in, and began imposing harsher conditions on the South, but by honouring their opponents, the Federal generals had laid the ground for future reconciliation.

Women and honour

Many Southern men equated their honour with manhood. As they saw it, women were frail, but good; men were strong, but expendable. Men's role was to protect the women, who embodied the highest values of civilization.[118] As Nathaniel Dawson wrote to Elodie Todd: 'You tell me that you have made your mind up to be secondary to my country. You are my country, and be secondary to nothing … Without [you] I would have no country to live for and to die for.'[119]

There were few examples of Confederate soldiers mistreating women. As John Hooper noted, 'the name of woman is too sacred among southerners to treat them amiss even in war.'[120] Hooper's words were more than pure rhetoric. Rape, for instance, was very rare during the American Civil War.[121]

What were perceived as Northern assaults on Southern women particularly offended Southern honour, and helped to rally support to the cause. Especially notorious was the 'Woman Order' issued by General Benjamin Butler, commander of the occupied city of New Orleans. Fed up with Southern women's insults to his soldiers, culminating with a woman's emptying a chamber pot on the head of Admiral David Farragut, Butler ordered that any woman who insulted a Federal soldier was to be arrested as a prostitute.[122] Butler was a 'traducer of Southern women', wrote Given Campbell,[123] enunciating a sentiment which was widespread.

Because Southern men defined their honour in terms of defending women, it was possible for women to use this to shame would-be shirkers into fighting. Mary Chestnut, asked in 1865 whether she would be happier if all the men in the family were killed, replied, 'Yes, if their life disgraced them. There are worse things than death.'[124] When William Mason Smith was granted a 60-day furlough in April 1864, his mother wrote to him:

> You are bound by the duties of your position, and can only be 'free' when you conscientiously perform them. ... Your time belongs to your Country and not to your pleasures. ... I hope you will not need the whole 60 days.[125]

In Autumn 1864, Jefferson Davis urged young ladies to 'marry none but a soldier', and throughout the war many women seem to have shared the idea that they should only accept the advances of those in uniform. 'I could not love you', wrote Elodie Todd to Nathaniel Dawson, 'if you had stayed at home content to remain inactive at such a moment.'[126] Martha Virginia Stevens, whose husband served in the Confederate army, summed up the feeling with a little poem of advice to Southern men:

> I think I hear the ladies say,
> 'Young men you'll have to go away,
> You would not go and fight for me,
> Therefore you'll have to let me be.'[127]

Women not only encouraged men to enlist, but also discouraged desertion. Confederate authorities sought to exploit this habit. In an address of early 1865, the Confederate Congress instructed communities to shun deserters: 'Let the reproachful glance of our women between whose honor and the brutal foe our noble army stands as a flaming sword, drive him back to the field.' In March 1865, a large meeting of women in Mobile, Alabama, pledged:

1 To recognize no man socially who is either a deserter, a loafer from his post, or a skulker from service.
2 To hold all such persons marked as of leprous soul and as unworthy the respect of woman, whom they have not the manhood to defend.[128]

Asked many years later why he and his colleagues had fought for so long, an old Confederate veteran replied that 'We were afraid to stop.' 'Afraid of what?', he was asked; 'Afraid of the women at home', was the answer, 'They would have been ashamed of us.'[129] During the war itself, Captain David Pope expressed the sentiments of many when he wrote to his wife in Spring 1864:

> When I think of the undying patriotism of the women, me thinks I can hear you in my imagination say, I would rather know that my husband died at his post than for him to be a coward and remain with me.[130]

Having sent their men off to war, the women discovered as time went on that they had difficulty surviving without them. This was especially true for those who came from small farming families, in which the man had previously done an essential share of the manual labour. Consequently, letters from wives reminding men of their duties at home were not uncommon in the later stages of the war. Two examples serve to illustrate the tone of such letters:

> I don't want you to stop fighting the Yankees … but try to get off and come home and fix us all up some and then you can go back … my dear, if you put off a-coming, 'twont be no use to come, for we'll all hands of us be out there in the garden in the old graveyard with your ma and pa.

And:

> I would not have you do anything wrong for the world, but before God, Edward, unless you come home, we must die. … And Lucy, Edward, your darling Lucy, is growing thinner every day. And before God, Edward, unless you come home we must die.[131]

Men who received such letters were torn between two opposing poles of duty: towards their country, and towards their homes. Since many of them defined honour first in terms of duty to home and family, it is not surprising that they deserted. An example was Edward Cooper, the recipient of the second letter above. Desertion became a serious problem for the Confederate army. Eight per cent of the Army of Northern Virginia deserted between 15 February and 18 March 1865 alone.

Some historians go so far as to attribute the South's demise to loss of faith in the cause among Southern women. Others maintain that the role women played in shaming men to stay in the ranks was always stronger than that which they played in encouraging them to desert. Edward Cooper, when he arrived home after deserting his unit, found a wife who, despite her letter, was far from pleased to see him. As he explained at his court-martial, when his wife saw him, she exclaimed in horror: 'O Edward, Edward, go back! Go back! Let me and the children go to the grave but save the honor of your name.'[132] Cooper dutifully handed himself over to the Confederate authorities. A court-martial sentenced him to death for desertion, but Robert E. Lee commuted the sentence and spared his life.

In other cases, soldiers proved able to resist their women's blandishments to come home. 'I want you all to stop writing about deserting', wrote Private Daniel Gilley to his sister on 2 January 1865, 'It won't do any good. I am a man of my own head.'[133] And in a similar tone, an officer on the staff of Stonewall Jackson wrote to his wife:

> Would you have me return there [home] the subject of such conversation as had been freely lavished on those who remained behind? … My manhood is involved in a faithful and fearless sticking to the job until it is finished, or it finishes me.[134]

Conclusion

Depending on which examples one chooses, one can either argue that honour kept Southerners fighting to the end, or that it persuaded many of them to quit; either that it helped their war effort, or that it hindered it. At every juncture, the impact of honour depended on how each man interpreted his duties. What one can say, however, is that honour mattered. When it came to choosing whether to fight and risk death, or to desert to help one's family and risk arrest and execution, questions of honour often played a decisive role. And this was true with respect to all the other aspects of the Civil War covered in this chapter. Honour brought the Confederacy into being. It also kept its armies in the field, directed the way they fought, and finally contributed to their defeat.

Notes

1 Freeman, Joanna, *Affairs of Honor: National Politics in the New Republic*, New Haven: Yale University Press, 2002, pp. 183–4.
2 Wyatt-Brown, Bertram, *The Shaping of Southern Culture: Honor, Grace, and War, 1760s to 1880s*, Chapel Hill: University of North Carolina Press, 2001, p. 34. Honour also played a vital role in persuading Americans to embark on the War of 1812. See Perkins, Bradford (ed.), *The Causes of the War of 1812: National Honor or National Interest*, New York: Holt, Rinehart & Winston, 1962, and Risjord, Norman K., '1812: Conservatives, War Hawks and the Nation's Honor', *William and Mary Quarterly*, 1961, vol. 18, no. 2, 196–210.
3 For analysis of the importance of honour in the politics of the early Republic, see Freeman, *Affairs of Honor*, passim.
4 McPherson, James M., *Battle Cry of Freedom: The Civil War Era*, New York and Oxford: Oxford University Press, 1988, pp. 56–7.
5 Ibid, p. 148.
6 Wyatt-Brown, Bertram, *Southern Honor: Ethics and Behavior in the Old South*, New York and Oxford: Oxford University Press, 1982, pp. 33–4.
7 McWhiney, Grady, *Confederate Crackers and Cavaliers*, Alexis: McWhiney Foundation Press, 2003, pp. 22–5.
8 Greenberg, Kenneth S., *Honor and Slavery: Lies, Duels, Noses, Masks, Dressing as a Woman, Gifts, Strangers, Humanitarianism, Death, Slave Rebellions, the Proslavery Argument, Baseball, Hunting, Gambling in the Old South*, Princeton: Princeton University Press, 1996, p. 62.
9 Franklin, John Hope, *The Militant South, 1800–1861*, Cambridge: Harvard University Press, 1956, pp. 35–6.
10 Wyatt-Brown, *The Shaping of Southern Culture*, p. 73.
11 Franklin, *The Militant South*, pp. 54–5.
12 Berry, Stephen W. III, *All that Makes a Man: Love and Ambition in the Civil War South*, New York: Oxford University Press, 2003, p. 49.
13 Greenberg, *Honor and Slavery*, pp. 8 and 15.
14 High-stakes gambling was 'a distinguishing characteristic of gentry culture' in Virginia from as early as the late seventeenth century: Breen, T.H., 'Horses and Gentlemen: The Cultural Significance of Gambling among the Gentry of Virginia', *William and Mary Quarterly*, 1977, vol. 34, 242.
15 Groom, Winston, *Shrouds of Glory: From Atlanta to Nashville: The Last Great Campaign of the Civil War*, New York: Pocket Books, 1995, pp. 21 and 265.
16 Wyatt-Brown, *Southern Honor*, p. 111.
17 Smith, Gene, *Lee and Grant*, New York: McGraw-Hill, 1984, p. 300.

18 Cited in McPherson, James M., *For Cause and Comrades: Why Men Fought in the Civil War*, New York and Oxford: Oxford University Press, 1997, p. 27
19 Cited in Sword, Wiley, *Southern Invincibility: A Story of the Confederate Heart*, New York: St Martin's Press, 1999, pp. 41 and 50–1.
20 See for instance, Vandiver, Frank E., *Their Tattered Flags: The Epic of the Confederacy*, New York: Harper's, 1970, p. 207; and Fraser, John, *America and the Patterns of Chivalry*, Cambridge: Cambridge University Press, 1982, p. 33.
21 Eleanor S. Brockenbrough Library, The Museum of the Confederacy, Richmond VA (Henceforth referred to as MoC). J.Q.A. Nadenbousch Papers. Letter to wife, 31 July 1861.
22 MoC. Sgt Archie Livingstone Letters. Letter to Knox and Mec, 24 April 1864.
23 University of North Carolina Chapel Hill, Southern Historical Collection (Henceforth referred to as SHC). George Phifer Erwin Collection. Letter to sister, 25 January 1864.
24 Freeman, Douglas Southall, *Lee*, abridged by Richard Harwell, New York: Collier Books, 1993, pp. 530–1.
25 SHC, John Hooper Letters. Letter, 28 May 1864.
26 Smith, *Lee and Grant*, p. 238.
27 Wyatt-Brown, *The Shaping of Southern Culture*, p. 214.
28 Berlin, Jean V., 'Did Confederate Women Lose the War?', in Mark Grimsley and Brooks D. Simpson (eds), *The Collapse of the Confederacy*, Lincoln and London: University of Nebraska Press, 2001, pp. 172–3.
29 Cited in Gallagher, Gary W., *The Confederate War*, Cambridge: Harvard University Press, 1999, p. 75.
30 Crowther, Edward R., 'Holy Honor: Sacred and Secular in the Old South', *The Journal of Southern History*, 1992, vol. 58, no. 4, 620.
31 McPherson, *For Cause and Comrades*, p. 75.
32 MoC, William Samuel Woods, Letters. Letter to mother, undated.
33 Wyatt-Brown, *The Shaping of Southern Culture*, p. 184.
34 General John Gordon, cited in Buell, Thomas B., *The Warrior Generals: Combat Leadership in the Civil War*, New York: Three Rivers Press, 1997, p. 40.
35 Olsen, Christopher J., *Political Culture and Secession in Mississippi: Masculinity, Honor, and the Antiparty Tradition, 1830–1860*, Oxford: Oxford University Press, 2000, p. 182.
36 Franklin, *The Militant South*, p. 80.
37 McPherson, *Battle Cry of Freedom*, p. 79.
38 Olsen, *Political Culture*, pp. 49–51.
39 Sword, *Southern Invincibility*, p. 26.
40 Vandiver, *Their Tattered Flags*, pp. 38 and 40.
41 SHC, William Nelson Pendleton Papers. Note, 1 May 1861.
42 Weitz, Mark A., 'Shoot Them All: Chivalry, Honour, and the Confederate Army Officer Corps', in D.J.B. Trim (ed.), *The Chivalric Ethos and the Development of Military Professionalism*, London and Boston: Brill, 2003, p. 335.
43 SHC, Given Campbell Letters. Letter, 18 October 1863.
44 MoC, J.Q.A. Nadenbousch Papers. Letters, 31 July and 8 August 1861.
45 MoC, Sgt Archie Livingstone Letters. Letter to Enoch, 6 November 1863.
46 SHC, George Phifer Erwin Collection. Letter to mother, 8 October 1863.
47 McPherson, *For Cause and Comrades*, p. 169.
48 Ibid, pp. 25–6.
49 MoC, William Samuel Woods Letters. Letter to sisters, 8 February 1863.
50 McPherson, *For Cause and Comrades*, p. 80.
51 Ibid, p. 23.
52 Ibid, p. 80.
53 Berry, *All that Makes a Man*, pp. 179–82.
54 McPherson, *For Cause and Comrades*, p. 86.

55 Bonner, Robert E., *Colours and Blood: Flag Passions of the Confederate South*, Princeton: Princeton University Press, 2002, pp. 74–81.
56 Ibid, p. 85.
57 SHC, Calvin Leach Diary. Entry for 17 September 1862.
58 Cited in Mikaelian, Allen, *Medal of Honor: Profiles of American Military Heroes from the Civil War to the Present*, New York: Hyperion, 2002, p. 21.
59 McMurry, Richard M., *John Bell Hood and the War for Southern Independence*, Lincoln and London: University of Nebraska Press, 1982, p. 99.
60 Ibid, p. 141.
61 General Orders, no. 52, 23 July 1862, in *War of the Rebellion: Official Records of the Union and Confederate Armies,* Series IV, vol. 2, Washington: Government Printing Office, 1900, p. 14.
62 SHC, William Nelson Pendleton Papers. Letter to Northrope, 6 November 1861.
63 MoC, William F. Slemons Papers. Letter to Mattie, 23 April 1862.
64 SHC, John Hooper Letters. Letter, 9 June 1863.
65 SHC, Given Campbell Letters. Letter, 1 July 1862.
66 General Orders, no. 93, 22 November 1862 (passed by Congress, 13 October 1862), in *War of the Rebellion: Official Records of the Union and Confederate Armies*, Series 1, Vol. 20, Part 1, Washington: Government Printing Office, 1887, p. 972.
67 General Orders, no. 131, 3 October 1863, in *War of the Rebellion*, Series 1, Vol. 20, Part 1, p. 972.
68 McMurry, *John Bell Hood*, p. 56.
69 McWhiney, *Confederate Crackers*, p. 233.
70 Martin, Bessie, *A Rich Man's War, A Poor Man's Fight: Desertion of Alabama Troops from the Confederate Army*, Tuscaloosa: University of Alabama Press, 2003, pp. 224–6.
71 Greenberg, *Honor and Slavery*, p. 125.
72 Smith, *Lee and Grant*, p. 237.
73 Earle, Peter, *Robert E. Lee*, London: Weidenfeld & Nicolson, 1973, p. 191.
74 Groom, *Shrouds of Glory*, p. 205.
75 Smith, *Lee and Grant*, pp. 218–9; Winik, Jay, *April 1865: The Month that Saved America*, New York: Perennial, 2002, p. 97.
76 Buell, *Warrior Generals*, p. 294.
77 Fraser, *America and the Patterns of Chivalry*, pp. 64–5.
78 Weitz, 'Shoot Them All', p. 330.
79 Ibid, p. 334.
80 SHC, Given Campbell Letters. Letter, 2 September 1861.
81 Weitz, 'Shoot Them All', p. 336.
82 Fraser, *America and the Patterns of Chivalry*, p. 212.
83 West, Jeffry D., *Mosby's Rangers*, New York: Touchstone, 1990, p. 292.
84 Fraser, *America and the Patterns of Chivalry*, p. 212.
85 West, *Mosby's Rangers*, pp. 124 and 288.
86 SHC, John Hooper Letters. Letter to 'Friend', 7 June 1863.
87 For the law on reprisals, see: 'General Order No. 100', 24 April 1863, in Hartigan, Richard Shelly (ed.), *Lieber's Code and the Law of War*, Chicago: Precedent, 1983, Articles 27 and 28, p. 50.
88 Francis Lieber, cited in 'Introduction', in Hartigan (ed.), *Lieber's Code*, p. 11.
89 SHC, Given Campbell Letters. Letter, 11 May 1862.
90 Leslie, Edward E., *The Devil Knows How to Ride: The True Story of William Clarke Quantrill and his Confederate Raiders*, New York: De Capo Press, 1996, p. 284.
91 Davis, William C., *An Honorable Defeat: The Last Days of the Confederate Government*, San Diego: Harcourt, 2002, p. 188.
92 Winik, *April 1865*, p. 166.
93 Vandiver, *Their Tattered Flags*, p. 304.

94 Gallagher, *The Confederate War*, p. 28.
95 SHC, John Hooper Letters. Letter to Irene, 30 March 1864.
96 Groom, *Shrouds of Glory*, p. 270.
97 Smith, *Lee and Grant*, p. 129.
98 Earle, *Robert E. Lee*, p. 75.
99 Groom, *Shrouds of Glory*, p. 43.
100 McWhiney, *Confederate Crackers*, p. 118.
101 McMurry, *John Bell Hood*, p. 190.
102 For similar comments about General A.P. Hill, see McWhiney, *Confederate Crackers*, p. 243.
103 McPherson, *Battle Cry of Freedom*, p. 476.
104 Groom, *Shrouds of Glory*, pp. 61–2.
105 Evans, David (ed.), *Random Acts of Kindness: True Stories of America's Civil War*, Wilmington: Broadfoot, 2001, p. 12.
106 Ibid, pp. 86–8; Clemmer, Gregg S., *Valor in Gray: The Recipients of the Confederate Medal of Honor*, Staunton: Hearthside, 1998, pp. 20–1.
107 McPherson, *Battle Cry of Freedom*, p. 791.
108 Ibid, pp. 800–2.
109 West, *Mosby's Rangers*, pp. 245–50.
110 Leslie, *The Devil Knows how to Ride*, p. 97.
111 Davis, *An Honorable Defeat*, pp. 260–1.
112 McPherson, *For Cause and Comrades*, p. 152.
113 Davis, Burke, *The Long Surrender*, New York: Random House, 1985, p. 67.
114 Davis, *An Honorable Defeat*, p. 46.
115 William B. Feis, 'Jefferson Davis and the Guerrilla Option', in Grimsley and Simpson (eds), *The Collapse of the Confederacy*, p. 111.
116 Winik, *April 1865*, p. 322.
117 Ibid, p. 191.
118 Berry, *All that Makes a Man*, pp. 112–17.
119 Ibid, p. 216.
120 SHC, John Hooper Letters. Letter to 'Friend', 7 June 1863.
121 Leslie, *The Devil Knows how to Ride*, p. 168.
122 McPherson, *Battle Cry of Freedom*, pp. 551–2.
123 SHC, Given Campbell Letters. Letter, undated, from camp near Baldwin, Tishomingo Co., Mississippi.
124 Wyatt-Brown, *Southern Honor*, p. 35.
125 Gallagher, *The Confederate War*, p. 76.
126 Sword, *Southern Invincibility*, p. 59.
127 Weitz, Mark A., *A Higher Duty: Desertion among Georgia Troops during the Civil War*, Lincoln and London: University of Nebraska Press, 2000, p. 143.
128 Martin, *A Rich Man's War*, pp. 211–2.
129 Cited in Wyatt-Brown, *Southern Honor*, p. 172.
130 Weitz, *A Higher Duty*, p. 146.
131 Martin, *A Rich Man's War*, p. 148.
132 Cited in Weitz, *A Higher Duty*, p. 97.
133 MoC, Pvt Daniel Gilley Letters. Letter to sister, 2 January 1865.
134 McPherson, *For Cause and Comrades*, p. 137.

7 British imperialism, 1815–1918

Background

While the Americans were fighting one another, their former colonial masters, the British, were building themselves the largest empire ever known. In 1815, Britain's victory over Napoleonic France secured British hegemony in the Western world. But Britain's supremacy did not bring it peace. It is true that during the nineteenth century the British avoided major European conflicts (with the one exception of the Crimean war of 1854–1855), but elsewhere they were almost continually at war, fighting a succession of small campaigns in Africa and Asia. According to one list,[1] there were only two years (1869 and 1883) during the entire 64-year reign of Queen Victoria when Britain was not at war somewhere on the globe.

While much of British power rested on naval supremacy, the Royal Navy fought no major battles at sea between 1815 and 1914. For the most part, therefore, this chapter concentrates on land warfare, and on Britain's chosen instrument – its army of professional soldiers (with some reference also to the Indian Army, which was officered by Britons and manned by Indians).

Honour and virtue in imperial Britain

The industrial revolution turned Britain from a society of farmers into one of urbanized labourers, with an ever expanding middle class of professionals. The vast bulk of Middle England had little or no knowledge of military affairs. Members of the commercial classes looked to acquire honour through hard work and self-sacrifice. They valued law and order, and followed an Evangelical Christianity which emphasized inner conscience and sobriety. This led to 'the replacement of the [traditional] code of honour by what might be called the code of Christian commerce'.[2]

In the eyes of Victorian theorists, honour was internal in nature, and was related to terms such as conscience and integrity. As Kenelm Digby wrote in his book *The Broad Stone of Honour*: 'you must discharge your duty, not by giving yourself up, body and soul, to obtain the favour of a party, but by following the dictates of your honest judgment.'[3] And according to the Victorian moralist Samuel Smiles, 'The gentleman … values his character, not so much of it only as can be seen of others, but as he sees it himself, having regard for the approval of his inward monitor.'[4] It followed from this that anybody could be a gentleman, since that title depended 'not upon fashion or manners, but upon moral worth'.[5]

Despite this rhetoric, Victorians were greatly concerned about what others thought of them.[6] 'Respectability', the new term for external honour, was all important.[7]

Either way, to make a claim to honour, whether internal or external, one had to possess the necessary virtues. 'Obedience, submission, discipline, courage – these are among the characteristics which make a man; they are also those which make the true soldier', wrote Samuel Smiles.[8] The founder of the Boy Scout movement, Robert Baden Powell, drew up a comprehensive list in his book *Scouting for Boys* in a chapter entitled 'The Chivalry of the Knights'. His choice of virtues was: unselfishness, self-sacrifice, kindness, generosity, friendliness, politeness, courtesy to women, fair play, honesty, loyalty, obedience, humility, fortitude, courage, good temper and cheeriness, duty to God, thrift, and sobriety.[9]

The learning ground for these virtues was at first the public schools, although by the end of the nineteenth century their ethics had spread into the general population. These private boarding schools were of enormous importance to the British army because the overwhelming majority of military officers spent their childhoods there. According to Jan Morris, they instilled the very Roman values of discipline, teamwork, and self-control.[10] The great headmaster of Rugby School, Thomas Arnold, described his own priorities in education, saying: 'what we must look for here is, 1st religious and moral principles; 2ndly gentlemanly conduct; thirdly intellectual ability.'[11] J.E.C. Welldon, headmaster of Harrow, said that the public schools focused on four areas: sport; readiness (courage, resourcefulness, and so forth); character ('the supreme ruling quality of Englishmen'); and religion ('fear of God').[12]

'Character' was key. The poet Henry Newbolt wrote that the 'great merit' of the public school system was that 'it made men, and not sneaks or bookworms, and that its direct objects were character and efficiency.'[13] The result, claimed Robert Graves, was that at his school, Charterhouse, 'everybody despised school work.... the scholars ... unless good at games ... always had a bad time.'[14] This was not considered to be a shortcoming in the system. As Thomas Hughes wrote in *Tom Brown's Schooldays*: 'The object of all schools is not to ram Latin and Greek into boys, but to make them good future citizens.'[15]

To build all this character, schools taught the necessity of loyalty, of resisting bullies (a constant theme in literature on the subject), of standing one's ground (implying both moral and physical courage), of team work, fair play, and physical and sporting prowess. One of the prime means of doing this was team games. As Welldon said, 'The pluck, the energy, the perseverance, the good temper, the self-control, the discipline, the co-operation, the *esprit de corps* which merit success in cricket or football, are the very qualities which win the day in war or peace.'[16]

Closely connected to the idea of character was the idea of 'duty', but a duty which was far more specific than in the Civil War American South. As Robert Baden Powell advised the Scouts:

> In all that you do, remember to think of your country first; don't spend the whole of your time and money on games and tuck shops merely to amuse *yourself*, but think first how you can be of use in helping your empire ... 'Country first, self second', should be your motto.[17]

Concern for the collective over the individual led to a revived belief in discipline. Many Victorians looked back to the Spartans and Romans as examples, and like them, valued fortitude in the face of disaster. Consequently, they were fond of images of heroic 'Last Stands', with outnumbered British soldiers bravely fighting to the bitter end in the face of enormous odds. A favourite story was of the troopship Birkenhead, which sank off Africa in 1852. There were insufficient lifeboats for all, so, according to legend, the troops stood at attention on deck while the women and children boarded the available boats and rowed away. Then, to avoid masses of soldiers swimming out to the boats and overwhelming them, they stayed on parade and went down with the ship. A modern observer would probably focus on the incompetence of having too few safety measures. To Victorians, the Birkenhead was an exemplar of all that was most honourable – discipline, self-control, and self-sacrifice, in service of the weak.

One key difference between the British and their Classical forebears was that whereas heroic honour cultures encourage boastful behaviour, in nineteenth-century Britain this was considered 'bad form'. The truly honourable man excelled in what he did, but did not draw attention to it. Because of this, honour had the rather unusual effect of encouraging mediocrity. 'Don't talk too good, nor talk too wise', Rudyard Kipling advised in his poem *If*.[18] In the army, this meant that even if one did have a professional interest in studying military science, it was best not to let others know. One could not be a 'mug', which as Francis Younghusband wrote, was 'a brother officer who neither rode nor shot nor played games, who drank water at Mess, went to bed early and swotted at algebra, fortifications or French.' Being a mug, said Younghusband, was 'a fatal reputation to acquire'.[19] Unsurprisingly, this attitude gave the army an atmosphere of amateurism.

Victorians feared that modern luxury was resulting in 'degeneracy' and 'effeminacy'. They exhorted men to toughen themselves (cold baths in the morning being a favoured method), and exalted masculine virtues such as physical strength and bravery. One manifestation of this worry about manliness was the idea of 'Muscular Christianity', associated with, among others, the writers Thomas Hughes and Charles Kingsley.[20] With time, it developed into a form of 'Christian Militarism' which became very influential in the late nineteenth century.[21]

These attitudes led to a belief in some circles that a willingness to fight was the mark of a true man, a belief that competed with the more pacific honour code of the commercial classes. 'Cowardice is of all vices the most contemptible', wrote the children's novelist G.A. Henty.[22] This was counterbalanced by the idea of 'fair play'. 'Britons, above all other people', wrote Baden Powell, 'insist on fair play. If you see a big bully going for a small or weak boy, you stop him because it is not "fair play". And if a man, in fighting another, knocks him down, he must not hit or kick him while he is down.'[23]

In battle, the prime virtue was courage. The Duke of Cambridge, Commander in Chief of the Army for many years until 1896, once told a general: 'Brains! I don't believe in brains.'[24] Learning and professional knowledge were less important than leading by example, plunging headlong into the enemy at the head of one's troops during an attack, and standing firm to the last when on the defence. Ordinary soldiers had to show discipline, be obedient, and withstand hardship without complaining. During the 'small wars' which Britain fought in the nineteenth century, these values proved to be extremely effective in helping the army overcome numerous enemies. When tested by the stress of major continental conflict (the Crimean War and the First World War), they were to prove inadequate.

Honour and the causes of war

The expansion of the British Empire in the nineteenth century has troubled historians for decades. Beginning with socialist critiques in the early twentieth century,[25] many have focused on the economic motives for British imperialism, theorizing that Britain invaded and conquered much of the world in order to break down trade barriers, secure markets for its exports, and gain territories in which to invest surplus capital. Certainly, there is some evidence that various individuals and businesses looked at the Empire in this way, but from a national, economic point of view most of Britain's wars of conquest made little or no sense. Trade did not follow the flag. Less than a third of the country's exports went to the Empire.[26] Britain fought numerous wars in Africa, but not in the Americas, which were far more important in terms of trade. In fact, the cost of fighting foreign wars, and then governing and securing the conquered lands, far outweighed any income derived from them, with the one exception of India.

Bearing this in mind, historians have turned to an alternative explanation – that Britain expanded for reasons of security and strategy. In this view, as other states developed empires in Africa and Asia they came to threaten Britain's existing colonies and its lines of communication with India. Hence, Britain advanced into Afghanistan and Tibet as a defensive measure against Russian encroachments into Central Asia, and secured control of Egypt, and South and East Africa in order to protect the sea route to India.[27]

There are problems with this thesis as well. Although many Britons undoubtedly did feel that foreign powers threatened the Empire, their fears were often far-fetched. The 'Russian threat' to India, for instance, was absurd given the logistical practicalities of launching military operations through Central Asia. In addition, British governments were indifferent in many instances to expansion by other powers, such as that of the French in West Africa.[28] Material security only really mattered when something else was threatened, namely British honour.

Once honour is included in the analysis, a pattern emerges to Britain's imperial wars. The arrival of Europeans tended to disrupt indigenous societies, very often fuelling local conflicts. One side in the conflict might attack the Britons whom they held responsible for their trouble, or might seek to form an alliance with them against their enemies. Once Britons had been sucked into conflict, they appealed to the British government for support and the British government felt honour-bound to provide it.

Alternatively, non-European states might refuse Britain full diplomatic recognition while perhaps offering it to another European country. Such a snub was intolerable, and eventually there would be war in order to force the upstart natives to treat Britain with the respect which it felt it deserved.

Concern for British national honour grew stronger in the second half of the nineteenth century as Britain came to feel less secure about its position in the world. Germany, France and the United States were developing advanced industrial economies and catching up with Britain's economic, and consequently also military, power. Britain's status as number one nation was increasingly shaky. It became ever more important to maintain an image of strength. Britain took on a belligerent tone towards suspected insult.

In addition, Social Darwinism, Muscular Christianity, and Christian Militarism suggested to some that war was actually a positive good.[29] 'War', wrote Field Marshal Garnet Wolseley, was 'a manly, elevating aspiration ... War ... is the greatest purifier to the race or nation that has reached the verge of over-refinement, or of excessive civilization.'[30] In this climate, even if the government did not feel that important material or political issues were at stake in a given instance, if the public felt that national honour was on the line, then war was likely.

One can see this logic at work in Britain's wars against China. People often refer to these as the 'Opium Wars', reflecting popular prejudice that the purpose of the wars was to force a hitherto closed China to open up its markets to British imports, and particularly imports of opium, which the Chinese were trying to ban. In reality, when the Chinese prohibited the opium trade, the British accepted that 'Her Majesty's Government cannot interfere for the purpose of enabling British subjects to violate the laws of the country to which they trade.' Both the government and British public opinion considered the opium trade an immoral one. Policy changed only when the Chinese Imperial Commissioner for Canton, Lin, seized the warehouses of British traders in the city. He then ordered them to leave, and when they failed to obey, blockaded them and cut off their supplies to force their submission.[31]

At this point, British national honour came into play. Nobody in Britain sympathized with the traders but the methods used by Lin were an insult to British dignity. Britain would not tolerate its subjects being 'treated with violence'.[32] The government of Lord Palmerston was in a weak position at the time. This insecurity made it all the more important not to lose face in front of Oriental upstarts. Britain therefore declared war on China in 1838.

Similarly, when Afghanistan refused to allow Britain to establish an embassy in Kabul, British prestige was at stake, especially since the Afghans had allowed the Russians to send envoys into the country. Smarting at this insult, in 1878 the then Viceroy of India, Lord Lyttleton, in direct contradiction of orders from London, decided to send envoys into Afghanistan accompanied by a regiment of lancers. When the Afghans again refused the British entry, the insult had to be avenged.[33] Although Prime Minister Benjamin Disraeli was furious with

Lyttleton, national honour was now at stake, and in November 1878, the British government declared war on Afghanistan.

Even more preposterous was the 1903 invasion of Tibet. Like their notional suzerains, the Chinese, the Tibetans held themselves aloof from foreigners and refused to let them enter the country. Wishing to trade with Tibet, and fearing that the Russians might seize control of it, Britain signed two treaties with China in 1888 and 1890 delineating Tibet's frontier with India and reducing tariffs on trade. The Tibetans, however, did not recognize China's right to negotiate treaties on their behalf. They tore down the new border markers and continued to charge whatever tariffs they wished on goods coming over the border from India.

Lord Curzon, by then Viceroy of India, responded by sending two letters to the Dalai Lama. Both returned unopened. At this point, personal as well as national honour had been offended.[34] If the Tibetans would not take the letters willingly, they would be forced to take them. Curzon obtained permission from London to send an armed expedition under Francis Younghusband into Tibet with the express purpose of obtaining 'satisfaction' from the Tibetans.[35] The Tibetans' army was no match for the British forces, which captured Lhasa and forced Tibet to acknowledge Britain's authority. Beyond the 'satisfaction' this gave, it is hard to see what purpose the expedition achieved.

Honour played an equally important role in Britain's wars in Africa. In 1862, Captain Charles Cameron arrived in Abyssinia bearing gifts from Queen Victoria for the Abyssinian monarch, King Theodore. Pleased by the British envoy, Theodore sent a letter to Victoria asking her for safe conduct for his own representatives to visit London. For some unexplained reason, the Foreign Office failed to reply to this message. Aggrieved by this insult, Theodore became extremely suspicious of Cameron, and when a second British envoy arrived in Abyssinia in November 1863, still without a reply from Queen Victoria, he ordered the arrest of both British diplomats.

At first this did not matter too much, but by 1867 the British public had become aware of the problem and were demanding action.[36] The government feared losing face.[37] It therefore determined on war. A military expedition advanced into Abyssinia, where it defeated Theodore at Arogee and Magdala in April 1868. After handing the prisoners over to the British, Theodore committed suicide. The British, who had no desire to annex Abyssinia, withdrew from the country. Honour had been restored.

The Abyssinian expedition was a fairly minor military operation. Far more significant was the invasion of Egypt in 1882. In an effort to modernize his country, Egypt's ruler, the Khedive, had borrowed large sums of money from Britain and France, which he was subsequently unable to repay. In order to avoid bankruptcy, he had to accept British and French commissioners who took control of Egyptian finances, and ensured that the bulk of revenue went on debt repayments. This led to severe cuts in other government expenditure, and to a nationalist backlash against the British and French 'oppressors', which resulted in a coup d'etat by the army and riots which caused the deaths of 50 Europeans. Now both economic interests and honour were on the line. Britons feared that the new Egyptian leader, Colonel Arabi, might repudiate the Khedive's debts and seize the Suez Canal, and felt that the deaths of those killed in the riots had to be avenged.

Prime Minister William Gladstone wished to avoid war, but, under pressure to do something, agreed to a naval demonstration. The Royal Navy sent a fleet to Alexandria, hoping to intimidate Arabi into restoring the Khedive to power. Arabi, however, remained defiant. At this point, a perpetual problem with threats of force came into play: if you make them, you have to carry them out, or lose face. The government therefore issued orders for an invasion. Egypt remained under British sway for the next 70 years.

A few years later it was the turn of South Africa. After the British annexed the Boer republic of Transvaal in 1877, the Boers rose up in revolt and destroyed a British force at Majuba Hill in 1881. Gladstone's government conceded defeat and restored the Transvaal's independence, Gladstone himself having already stated his belief that the annexation was an unjust act. Others, though, regarded this outcome as a national humiliation. In 1899, it was their turn to be heard when Transvaal and the Orange Free State declared war on Britain and invaded the British-held Natal and Cape Colony.

The Boers' decision to declare war was a pre-emptive strike against what they accurately saw as an impending British invasion of their territory. Discoveries of gold and diamonds in the Transvaal had made the Boer republics extremely rich, threatening British domination in South Africa. Some British leaders, including the new High Commissioner in South Africa, Sir Alfred Milner, came to believe that unless Britain struck the Boers down soon their power would grow too great and South Africa would be lost to Britain. Milner therefore began preparing the ground for a pre-emptive strike of his own.

In essence what was happening was an old-fashioned Greek-style struggle for precedence. Milner's problem was to find a way of provoking the Boers into war. He settled on the plight of the 'Uitlanders', a group of non-Boers who lived and worked in the mines of Transvaal. Milner began lobbying British public opinion with statements that the Uitlanders were suffering under Boer tyranny, and that Britain must intervene to guarantee their political rights. He therefore sent a telegram, designed for publication, to Colonial Secretary Joseph Chamberlain, stating that: 'The spectacle of thousands of British subjects kept permanently chafing under undoubted grievances, and calling vainly to Her Majesty's Government for redress does steadily undermine the influence and reputation of Great Britain.'[38]

Milner's choice of language is telling. He understood that to justify war in South Africa he had to appeal to the public's sense of honour. In truth neither he nor Chamberlain cared for the Uitlanders, whom Chamberlain called 'a lot of cowardly, blatant selfish speculators who would sell their souls to have the power of rigging the market.'[39] But by persuading the British public that defending the Uitlanders was a matter of honour, he could force the Boers into a corner, and produce the war he wanted. Coaxed on by Milner, the government of Lord Salisbury agreed to send 10,000 troops to South Africa to put pressure on the Boers to give the Uitlanders the vote. The arrival of the troops convinced the

Boers that war was now inevitable, and in order to gain what little advantage they could, they decided that they might as well start it straight away. Milner's strategy succeeded.

By 1900 the spread of democracy had made public opinion a crucial element in decisions on war. This was best demonstrated in 1914 when Britain declared war on Germany and became a participant in the First World War.

Initially it seemed as if Britain might be able to avoid involvement in that conflict. The country had no obvious interests in the dispute between Austria-Hungary, Serbia and Russia in the Balkans, and, although Anglo-French military ties had expanded in the decade prior to 1914, Britain had not signed any treaty committing itself to defend France if attacked. When Germany declared war on France, Britain was not honour-bound to come to the latter's rescue.

Some members of the British government, fearful that a German victory over France would pose a serious long-term threat to Britain's security, were in favour of war from the beginning. But the Cabinet and public opinion were split. There was not as yet a majority for war. What tipped the balance was the German invasion of Belgium.

It is easy to see the invasion of Belgium as merely a 'pretext for intervention',[40] but as the Foreign Secretary, Sir Edward Grey, said of the war: 'But for Belgium we should have kept out of it.'[41] In his notes of a crucial Cabinet meeting on 1 August 1914, Prime Minister Herbert Asquith made it clear that, 'The main controversy pivots upon Belgium and neutrality.'[42]

When Belgium had become an independent country in 1830, the great powers, including Britain and Germany, had signed a treaty guaranteeing its independence. In 1914, however, Germany's war plans required its armies to advance through Belgium in order to sweep around the French flank. The invasion of Belgium put Germany in breach of its obligations while placing a burden on Britain to live up to its own. When the German chancellor Theobold von Bethmann Hollwegg described the treaty in question as 'a scrap of paper', British indignation reached new levels.

Interviewing Bethmann Hollweg in Berlin, Sir Edward Goschen told him that it was:

> A matter of life and death for the honour of Great Britain that she should keep her solemn engagement to do her utmost to defend Belgium's neutrality if attacked. That solemn compact simply had to be kept, or what confidence could anyone have in engagements given by Great Britain in the future?[43]

Sir Edward Grey affirmed later that:

> The real reason for going to war was that, if we did not stand by France and stand up for Belgium against this aggression, we should be isolated, discredited, and hated; there would be nothing for us but a miserable and ignoble future.[44]

Ordinary Britons agreed. 'War declared by England', wrote Patrick Gray in his diary on 5 August 1914, 'Intense relief, as there was an awful feeling that we might dishonour ourselves.'[45] Most did not want war, but felt that their sense of honour gave them no choice. Dr L.W. Batten who served on the Western Front, wrote years later of his motivations that:

> We in the British Expeditionary Force *didn't* serve 'to make the world safe for democracy' or any tripe like that. We came in because we *couldn't* let the Germans go on as they were going. The 'scrap of paper' remark … wasn't a nonsense; it moved us all. We *had* to come in – and I for one hated it (Sir Edward Grey hated it too … but had to declare war). We came in … for treaty-keeping and national honour … It was because German national behaviour had been intolerable.[46]

Honour as a motivation for fighting

Prior to 1914, the primary motivation for men to join the ranks was poverty. Soldiering was a low-status profession, the conditions of service were harsh, and the pay was poor. The army drew most of its recruits from the ranks of the unemployed, for whom it provided an escape from destitution. For others, it was a means of escaping family trouble or a prison sentence.

For officers, matters were very different. An officer was expected to participate fully in the social life of his regiment, and for this he generally needed a private income, since his army pay was unlikely to be sufficient. 'Good God', one subaltern is supposed to have said, when told that the War Office had deposited £100 in his bank account: 'I didn't know we were *paid*.'[47]

Once in the army, officers were not immune to the appeal of glory-seeking. Garnet Wolseley wrote:

> I can heartily say that the one dread I had – and it ate into my soul – was that if killed I should die without having made that name for myself which I had always hoped a kind and merciful God might permit me to win.[48]

Ambition meant that there was never any shortage of volunteers to go abroad on active service, where promotion prospects were better.

Once at war, a variety of motives motivated pre-1914 men and officers to stay in the ranks. For the men, harsh discipline was undoubtedly a factor.[49] Leadership was also important. As an engineer officer, Gerald Graham, wrote: 'Our men … will follow their officers through the heaviest fire, to certain destruction if necessary; but supposing the officers do not lead or direct, then the men are helpless.'[50] Aware of this, officers were terrified of looking bad in the eyes of their men.[51]

Another important factor for both officers and men was the honour of the regiment. Garnet Wolseley wrote of the British soldier:

> What can be finer than his love of regiment, his devotion to its reputation, and his determination to protect its honour? To him 'The Regiment' is mother, sister, and mistress. That its fame may live and flourish he is prepared to risk all and die without a murmur.[52]

In times of peace, regiments built up unit pride through ceremony and the use of symbols, as well as through inter-regimental sporting competitions. Troops took great pride in the distinctions of dress accorded to each battalion. The regiment very much did replace a soldier's family, especially as most soldiers were not allowed to marry until they had served for many years.

During the First World War, no single factor made men volunteer to fight, but honour continued to play an important role. Desertion rates were surprisingly low. Short-sighted Lieutenant Paul Jones explained to his father why he had obtained a transfer from his safe post in the Army Service Corps to the far more dangerous Royal Tank Corps:

> It is not only my own desire and own temperament that influence me, but the example of others. … Why that fellow that sat in the same form-room as I did two years back has won a V.C., paying, it is true, with his life for the honour. But what a glorious end! … The effect on me is as a trumpet call. All my old Welsh fighting blood comes surging up in me and makes me say, 'Short sight or no short sight, I *will* prove my manhood.'[53]

The language of duty had by this stage quite noticeably replaced the language of honour. Private A. Sagar wrote to his father in May 1917, 'We had a conscientious objector up this week. Well I would not be like that for something. I never grumbled yet at being called up, it's every single young man's duty to go.'[54] In a similar fashion, George Worthington wrote to his mother on 8 August 1915:

> It is impossible to be with you [on your birthday]. May you receive consolation from the fact that your sons are held by duty to the only place tenable by young men of military age and physique. We are here merely impelled by the sense of duty which is instinct (or at least ought to be) in every man. We simply cannot help ourselves, and there are millions like us. … I don't know whether you agree with me in what I say, but I really believe it myself.[55]

'Oh that this awful war were over!', wrote Private R. Ross-Douglas from his sickbed, 'I am rapidly getting well again and dread the idea of going back to the hell I have left. But I owe it to God … to do my clear duty.'[56] 'It is hard for you but remember Mother it is hard for me as well', wrote Corporal R.J.T. Evans, 'After all you know I am only doing the same as thousands of other fellows you would not be proud of me if I acted the coward now and tried to evade my Duty would you?'[57] Private W.H. Gardner similarly told his mother: 'I am not afraid of death and do not want any one to be badly upset if I go under. If I do, "God's will be done", only grant that I may be able to die saying "Thank God I have done my duty".'[58] 'I am glad I came', said Private Pennell who served with the ANZACs at Gallipoli, 'I do not think I should have forgiven myself had I stayed behind.'[59]

Those who did stay behind often did feel guilty about it. Captain J.R. Tibbles of the 1st Battalion, East Kent Regiment (the Buffs), reported to hospital where he underwent an operation, but regretted it: 'I was ill, yes, but I could have carried on. No one has ever reproached me for going; but the thing is there, my one great regret in the war; that I did let the battalion down.'[60]

During the nineteenth century, regiments like Tibbles' Buffs carried colours into battle. The honour of a regiment was embodied in its battle flags, and in the battle honours inscribed upon them. Infantry had 'colours', the Household Cavalry and Dragoon Guards 'standards', and the Hussars and Lancers 'guidons'. The colours of the Royal Artillery were its guns.[61]

In accordance with a royal warrant of 1743, each infantry regiment had two colours – the King's or Queen's Colour and the Regimental Colour. Defending the colours was a matter of honour. Regiments of the Indian Army regarded their colours with particular veneration. The example of the 31st Bengal Native Infantry is especially remarkable. In 1805 during an assault on the fortress of Bhurtpore, the regiment managed to get its colours near the summit of the fortress before being forced to withdraw. The tattered colours were replaced after this unsuccessful battle, but the night before the new colours were to be consecrated the old ones disappeared. Twenty-one years later, the regiment again found itself before Bhurtpore. Suddenly, as the 31st prepared to launch an assault, the old, lost colours reappeared. They had been preserved by members of the regiment, ready for a time when they could be brought out again to redeem the unit's honour.[62] This time the attack succeeded.

The last time colours were carried into battle was during a failed assault on Boer positions near Laing's Neck on 28 January 1881, shortly before the defeat at Majuba Hill. After that, changes in tactics and technology meant that colours no longer served a useful battlefield purpose.

Honours and rewards

Although they claimed that the satisfaction of duty done was sufficient reward, the British did not dispense with a more formal system of external rewards, both individual and collective.

The simplest reward remained money. Soldiers were entitled to a share of any captured goods which were designated as 'prizes'. In India, the overall value of the prize money was often substantial, but it could take years for the goods to be sold and the money distributed. Furthermore, prize money varied according to rank in a disproportionate manner. After the capture of Bhurtpore, the Commander-in-Chief received nearly £60,000, generals £6,000, subalterns £238, and privates only £4.[63] Senior officers could also receive very large sums of money, as well as titles, as rewards for noteworthy victories. Field Marshal Roberts, for instance, received an Earldom and £100,000 for his successes against the Boers, and

Wolseley a baronetcy and £30,000 for his victory in Egypt.[64] They might also get statues in their honour, such as those of Generals Napier and Havelock which stand in Trafalgar Square near to Nelson's Column.

Promotion was another method of honouring excellence. Since there was no mandatory retirement age for most of this period, it could take a very long time to rise in rank. On average, it took almost 19 years to become a major, 23 and a half to become a lieutenant colonel.[65] Standard promotions were based on seniority, so that when, for instance, a major retired, the most senior captain in his regiment would take his slot (in the era of purchased commissions, this depended also on being able to afford to buy the commission in question). However, when an officer died in combat, the slot could be taken by anybody, opening the way for officers to be promoted as a reward for gallantry or excellent leadership. Not surprisingly, officers were keen to attach themselves to units going to fight overseas, as the opportunities for advancement (due to deaths in action) increased significantly. In this respect, the promotion system did actually succeed in encouraging officers to fight.

Especially distinguished non-commissioned officers might be honoured with a commission. In peacetime this was rare. The prevailing view was that ordinary soldiers did not make good officers because of their lowly social backgrounds. Still, such promotions did take place. Sergeant Bernard McCabe of the 31st Foot, for instance, won a commission as a reward for planting the regimental colour on the Sikh parapet at Sobraon.[66] Most spectacularly, William Robertson rose from the very lowest rank, trooper, to the very highest, Field Marshal, and to the position of Chief of the General Staff in the First World War. This was beyond exceptional. In the 1870s only 5 per cent of the army's officers had been commissioned from the ranks.[67]

Until the Crimean War, there were only three methods of honouring bravery – the Order of the Bath, promotions, and 'mentioning of an individual in the field dispatch of the Commander-in-Chief'. The latter, however, had become rather debased because the Commander-in-Chief tended to mention mostly those who came to his personal attention, which normally meant members of the staff who had performed well but quite likely had not risked their lives in battle.[68]

Complaints about this led to demands for a medal for gallantry. In 1854 the armed forces established the Distinguished Conduct Medal (DCM) for the army, and the Conspicuous Gallantry Medal (CGM) for the Navy. Not everybody approved. Critics feared that soldiers might engage in rash actions in pursuit of medals, undermining the discipline which was the basis of the British army's success in battle.[69] However, the idea of medals won the support of the Prince Consort, and in January 1856 Queen Victoria signed a Royal Warrant instituting the Victoria Cross (VC) as a reward for bravery.

The salient feature of the Victoria Cross was that it was open to all ranks. At first, the army issued it fairly liberally, but within a few years the criteria for winning it became stricter, with only the most conspicuous deeds being rewarded with VCs, and lesser acts of gallantry with DCMs and CGMs (or the DSO, instituted in 1886, for officers). During the First World War, the number of acts needing recognition rose substantially, so the army created yet another pair of awards – the Military Medal (MM) for other ranks and the Military Cross (MC) for officers.

Some were sceptical. J.C. Wakeford, for instance, wrote: 'I desire a whole skin more than many MCs. It is more valuable in after life.'[70] But there can be no doubt that most soldiers valued the honour bestowed by medals enormously. Lieutenant, later Field Marshal, Roberts wrote to his mother that he wanted the VC 'more than any other … Oh! If only I can manage it, how jolly I should be!'[71] (Roberts got his wish.) 'No news of the MC coming through', wrote 2nd Lieutenant P.G. Kennedy in September 1918, 'I'm keen on getting it, as it will be all to my credit for getting it at 18.'[72] John Charter did get the MC and told his mother in June 1916: 'Of course, I'm awfully pleased about it, and I know you will be too. I've always had a great ambition to get the cross … I wish I could come back home again with the ribbon on, just to show it to you.'[73] Tom Worthington was equally pleased with his MC, and told his nephew Rollo:

> Many thanks for your letter of the 11th, and for your congratulations on my MC. It is very gratifying to feel that one has done something in the War that the authorities consider worthy of honour, and when you get yours I expect you will be as pleased as I do.[74]

Most men preferred medals to promotion. P.L. Ibbetson, for instance, noted in his diary that he and a friend, Fred, had been recommended for the MM:

> I was told I had missed it. Fred had got the MM of course I was disappointed as I expected to get it, however the next morning it came out in order's and I was made a temp. Bombardier signaller, but of course that was not as good as the medal.[75]

The desire for medals was such that another soldier wrote:

> I have known good men eat their hearts out through want of recognition. How petty this sounds. Yet a ribbon is the only prize in war for the ordinary soldier. It is the outward visible proof to bring home to his people that he has done his job well. And, say what you may, a man's prowess will be assessed by the number of his ribbons.[76]

Soldiers in the First World War wrote about the frustration of seeing others get medals when they felt they did not deserve them. As H.R. Osborne wrote on 26 February 1915:

> There is only one thing that grieves me in this war so far, and that is this no doubt you have seen it in the papers about Lc Cpl Dyson of our Regt getting the DCM medal for reconnoitering … German guns, this is a thing that me and a private of our Regt done, we done the work another fellow gets the honour.[77]

S.H. Burt complained similarly after some of his friends captured five Germans in 1915:

> I suppose if a Colonel or some big bug had seen it they would have got DCMs but I guess that they get nix now. It is a confounded shame that all the officers take the credit for it and they get the distinctions instead of the men who deserve them.[78]

Given the importance of regimental honour, the army also gave collective rewards in the form of battle honours and honorific titles. Battle honours dated back to 1784, when the King authorized several regiments to emblazon the word 'Gibraltar' on their Regimental colour.[79] Thereafter the army issued such honours in abundance, many of them being awarded retroactively for deeds long in the past. The earliest-dated battle honour, 'Tangier, 1662–1680', was awarded only in 1909.

It is not clear exactly what effect medals and battle honours had on behaviour. It does not seem that most recipients of medals actively sought them, deliberately showing ostentatious courage in the style of ancient warriors in order to gain recognition. Some did. In the First World War, for instance, Lieutenant F.L.C. Jones announced that he intended to win a VC, and when his men ran up against a German machine-gun post shouted, 'Here's my chance, I'm after that VC.' He charged the machine-gun, but fell dead, a bullet in the head.[80] Generally, though, the impact of medals was probably more indirect, raising morale by creating the impression that courage and excellence gained suitable recognition.

Honour and death

Glory attached itself not just to medals, but also to death in combat. If the First World War poet Wilfred Owen felt it necessary to nail the 'old lie' – 'dulce et decorum est pro patria mori' – it was precisely because the sentiment expressed in Horace's dictum was so widespread in the period under study. For all the spread of middle class commercial values, many Britons still believed that dying in battle was the finest end a man could hope for. Whereas until the eighteenth century depictions of heroes avoided showing their deaths, now images of heroic death suddenly became popular, whether it was the dying Nelson, Gordon fighting to the last at Khartoum, or the last stand of the British forces at Gandamak in the Afghan War of 1842.[81]

Nineteenth- and early twentieth-century moralists urged men to consider their lives of little worth compared to the glory of the greater whole. As Baden Powell advised his Boy Scouts:

> We have all got to die someday; a few years more or less of our own lives don't make much matter in the history of the world, but it is a very great matter if by dying a year or two sooner than we should otherwise do from disease we can help to save the flag of our country from going under.[82]

Many bought this line wholesale. Charles Gordon, who gained fame dying in defence of Khartoum, told friends that as a young man he had volunteered for service in the Crimea in order 'to be killed', and during the Ashanti War of 1874, Garnet Wolseley was heard commenting on his soldiers' 'good fortune to be killed in battle'.[83] P.H.B. Lyon wrote in 1917:

> And if beyond the day's long labour Death
> Stand in our path and shroud us in his pall,
> Bartering honour for this wasted breath,
> Ah then! It were the greatest good of all.[84]

If glory was to attach to death, it followed that the living must honour the dead, and it became increasingly necessary to do so in the case of each and every dead soldier. At the start of the nineteenth century, the remains of war dead were treated with little or no respect. The bodies of the dead at Waterloo were later dug up, and their bones were crushed and turned into fertiliser, while their teeth were used to make dentures, popularly known as 'Waterloo teeth'. By the mid-nineteenth century, officers' families had started to erect individual monuments for their fallen relatives in the form of plaques in churches and on the walls of public schools. Simultaneously, ordinary soldiers began to appear on public war memorials for the first time. The Guards Crimean Memorial in London shows three guardsmen in front of a statue of Victory. Honour now belonged to every soldier, however humble.

The First World War completed the process of the democratization of honour. Towns, villages, businesses, schools, universities, and clubs all issued 'honour rolls' listing the name of every member of their collective who had lost his life. 'Casualty lists' like those of ancient Athens reappeared. The Menin Gate at Ypres lists the names of almost 60,000 men who have no known grave, and another 30,000 are listed on long walls at the nearby Tyne Cot cemetery.

The First World War soldiers of the British Empire remain where they were buried, in scores of formal war cemeteries across northern France and Belgium. Imperial authorities actually refused families the right to repatriate their loved ones' bodies.[85] This had nothing to do with the logistical difficulties of transporting thousands of corpses back to Britain, Canada, Australia, or elsewhere. Rather it was a political and symbolic decision that every soldier would receive exactly the same treatment regardless of wealth or rank. The organization in charge of the war cemeteries, the Graves Registration Commission (later renamed the Imperial (now Commonwealth) War Graves Commission) believed that if repatriation was allowed, the wealthy would take advantage of it, while the poor would be left behind. Similarly, the commission decided that all graves should have identical markers, that: 'in death, all, from General to Private, of whatever race or creed, should receive equal honour.'[86]

One of the few variations permitted on headstones was the addition of military insignia. In the case of British soldiers these are regimental crests, for as Rudyard Kipling, a member of the graves commission, said: 'when a man is once in the service, it is for his regiment that he works, with his regiment that he dies, and in his death he wishes to be remembered as one of the regiment.'[87] Interestingly, though, the stones of all Canadian soldiers bear not a regimental crest but a maple leaf, identifying them as Canadians first and foremost. In this we can see a deliberate effort to exploit the dead to promote a sense of national identity. This formed part of what historian George Mosse calls the 'cult of the fallen soldier', which 'became the centrepiece of the religion of nationalism after the [First World] war'.[88]

Honour and the conduct of war

The heavy casualties of the First World War were a product of an offensive strategy which was possibly necessary for final victory, but proved to be extremely costly in terms of lives. In its numerous small wars around the world, the British army had often faced greatly superior forces and had relied on inflicting a very rapid defeat on the enemy in order to demoralize him from the outset. This fitted in very well with the preference for character over technical proficiency. Quick action and offensive spirit were seen as the key to victory.

Inevitably this led to rash actions on the battlefield. Sometimes, boldness garnered stunning success. At the start of the Boer War, the 60th Rifles, one of whose battalions had been destroyed at Majuba, sought to restore the regimental honour by launching a direct assault on Boer positions near Dundee in northern Natal. When the attack stalled, Major General Sir W. Penn Symons personally took command, riding to the front of the troops carrying a red pennant. Mortally wounded, he observed a fine stiff upper lip and only allowed himself to be stretchered away to the dressing station when he was out of sight of his men. The attack recovered its momentum, and drove the Boers from the field.[89]

Equally often this approach led to disaster. At Omdurman in 1898, the commanding officer of the 21st Lancers launched a charge against the Sudanese which resulted in the deaths of five officers and 65 men out of a force of 400. The reason for his action may well have been that the regiment had never seen combat, and thus had no battle honours; it was mocked by other regiments with the motto, 'Thou shalt not kill.'[90]

Many officers deliberately exposed themselves to danger. In the First World War, Robert Graves noted that 'the only thing respected in young officers was personal courage'. He therefore recorded that in order to gain respect, 'I went on patrol fairly often.'[91]

Circumstances sometimes dictated that the British adopt a defensive posture, and on occasion British units were overwhelmed by vastly superior enemy forces. In these circumstances, the honourable thing was not to panic, to show self-control and a stiff upper lip, and if necessary die heroically. One of the most renowned examples was that of 'Wilson's Last Stand'. Fighting the Matabele in Rhodesia in 1895, Major Alan Wilson and a patrol of 32 men were assaulted by several thousand enemy troops. When they had run out of ammunition, the survivors shook hands and sang *God Save the Queen*, and then calmly waited for their deaths.[92] On 31 May 1900, the Irish Hunt Company (whose complement consisted primarily of volunteer gentleman-rankers) found itself surrounded by Boers. Despite the hopeless position, the unit's commander, Lord Longford, ordered his troops to fight on. 'I knew it to be madness', said one of the survivors afterwards, 'and so did everyone else, I think, but not a man refused.'[93]

The very name of the Irish Hunt Company illustrates beautifully the manner in which many British gentlemen identified war with sport. In the First World War, Second Lieutenant W.E. Giffard, who had already lost one leg in action, volunteered to continue working in observation balloons and refused a safe job on the ground. 'I do not think it is playing the game', he wrote.[94] 'Playing the game' might also imply not using certain methods of warfare which were in some way 'unsporting'. General Herbert Plumer refused to distribute propaganda leaflets on the German front lines in his sector: 'No that wouldn't be fair', he announced, 'We have to defeat these boys on our own merits.'[95] The British similarly disclaimed the use of snipers. 'Our souls abhorred anything unsportsmanlike', said General Lord Horne. The army refused to give funds to Major 'Hex' Hesketh-Pritchard when he tried to start a sniping course, and he had to raise the money for the rifles he needed from the public.[96] As a result, for most of the war, the Germans held a distinct advantage over the British in this area of warfare.

The pressures of war meant, however, that few means remained unacceptable for very long. The British eventually overcame their reluctance to use gas, propaganda, and sniping, as well as many other methods of war. They also targeted enemy civilians directly, despite chivalric pretensions to be fighting to defend the innocent. Many military operations on the imperial frontier were deliberately punitive, designed to deter future aggression by means of harsh reprisals against the enemy's population. Racist assumptions meant that the British often massacred African and Asian people without remorse. Rifleman John Rose described operations against a Matabele village in 1896, saying: 'all over the place it was nothing but dead or dying niggers. We burnt all the huts and a lot of niggers that could not come out were burnt to death, you could hear them screaming, but it served them right.'[97] 'There is no doubt that we are very cruel people', wrote Winston Churchill.[98]

The Boer War showed that even white peoples were not immune from British cruelty. In order to curb the guerrilla warfare being waged by the Boers, the British burned down farmhouses, destroyed crops, and drove away livestock, leaving Boer women and children utterly destitute. The intent was that the men would be deprived of the means to continue resisting, while their womenfolk would beg them to return home and lay down their arms. The tactic did not prove very successful, and to avoid starving, the women and children fled to 'concentration camps' set up by the British to provide them with shelter. Conditions in the camps were appalling, although because of incompetence rather than deliberate policy. Some 28,000 Boers died in the camps, which the leader of the opposition Liberal Party in Britain, Henry Campbell-Bannerman, denounced as the 'methods of barbarism'.[99]

In the case of the concentration camps, an enormous public outcry forced the British government to act to improve conditions, and by the end of the war, Boer families were possibly better off in them than out of them. In another example, when the army helped white colonists massacre hundreds of Hlubi tribesman and kidnap thousands of women and children, the government, after protests by Bishop John Colenso of Natal, ordered that the captives be set free.[100] The new factor of public opinion meant that the army was not entirely free to use whatever tactics it chose.

Honour and the enemy

One area in which people did feel that the old ideals did survive was air warfare. 'In many ways', wrote the American pilot Bennett A. Molter, 'the fighting aviators are living much like the lives of the heroes of chivalry. Their warfare is that of man to man.'[101] British pilot Cecil Lewis echoed this sentiment, writing that the war in the air 'was like the lists of the Middle Ages, the only sphere in modern warfare where a man saw his adversary and faced him in mortal combat, the only sphere where there was still chivalry and honour'.[102] Like knights of old, pilots on occasion issued challenges to single combat, and captured pilots might be entertained by their enemies at officers' messes before being sent off to prison camp.[103] 'Air fighting', Molter claimed, 'retains whatever is possible, in a life where the object is to kill, of consideration for the enemy and exchange of civilities, much as there was between opposing knights.'[104] Molter describe how French pilots dropped wreaths on a German airbase in respect of the death of the great German ace Captain Boelke. He also noted that aviators would give a separate burial to enemy pilots who crashed on their side of the front, marking the spot with a cross made of propellers.

Land forces sometimes behaved similarly. In the Boer War, for instance, Sir John French and a Boer general, Christiaan Beyers, exchanged Christmas presents.[105] Nonetheless, when the Boers resorted to guerrilla tactics, some British officers felt that they were in breach of the laws of war and so had lost the right to decent treatment. Part of the problem was that the Boers relied on captured British equipment, including uniforms (the standard Boer practice with captured British troops was to strip them of their clothes and release them naked to find their way home). On occasion, this led to confusion when British troops mistook Boers for friendly forces. After one such incident, Douglas Haig ordered that all Boers found in British uniforms should be executed on the spot.[106] British troops undoubtedly did sometimes murder Boer prisoners, the notorious case of the Australian officer Lieutenant 'Breaker' Morant being the most famous. However, the fact that the British authorities convicted and executed Morant for murder showed that this was not generally considered acceptable behaviour.

Similarly, the attitude of British soldiers towards German prisoners in the First World War was normally in conformity with the rules of war. Again, there were instances of soldiers murdering prisoners,[107] but this was not general practice.

One area in which the First World War fundamentally altered the relationship between enemies was in the conduct of troops after capture. The Hague

Conventions of 1899 and 1907 made specific reference to parole, giving it a formal legal status, and stating that:

> Prisoners may be set at liberty on parole if the laws of their country allow, and, in such cases, they are bound, on their personal honour, scrupulously to fulfil, both towards their own government and the government by whom they are made prisoners, the engagements they contracted.[108]

In the First World War, however, the practice ceased almost entirely. Both sides forbade their men from giving their paroles. After capture, a man was now expected to regain his honour by trying to escape.

Prisoners in the Boer and First World Wars could probably rely on receiving decent treatment. On the whole, white men treated other white men properly. The British were not so generous to the coloured soldiers they encountered in their numerous imperial wars. After fighting on the Jhelum river in the Sikh War of 1849, the British killed all the enemy wounded.[109] Similarly, after the Battle of Omdurman, the British left thousands of wounded Sudanese on the battlefield to die. The British commander, General Kitchener, merely complained about the 'dreadful waste of ammunition'.[110]

The British response to the Indian mutiny was especially brutal. After taking the city of Allahabad, for instance, British troops massacred the population 'regardless of age or sex'. Advancing towards Cawnpore, Colonel Neill issued instructions that 'friendly' villages were to be left alone, but 'hostile' ones were, in Neill's words, 'to be destroyed; all men in them to be slaughtered.'[111] A soldier in a force advancing to recapture Delhi, noted that, 'We burnt every village and hanged all the villagers who had treated our fugitives badly until every tree was covered with scoundrels hanging from every branch.'[112] Mutinous troops who fell into British hands suffered painful and humiliating deaths. The British deliberately offended religious taboos by sewing up Muslim prisoners in pigskins prior to executing them.[113] In other cases, they strapped their prisoners to the mouths of cannon, which they then fired, spreading the shattered body over a large area.

Honour had developed since the days of chivalry in that the rules which once applied only to knights now applied to all Western soldiers. But they still applied only to Westerners.

Honour and the ending of wars

The contempt shown for 'savage' peoples meant that it was difficult to keep the peace with them, except by continuous shows of force and the never-ending application of fear. Sometimes, the subject peoples of the Empire would react against the dishonours thrust upon them and rise up in revolt. The Indian Mutiny was a classic example. Another was the revolt of the Ndebele people in 1896. After their defeat by Cecil Rhodes' British South Africa Company, the company had deprived them of most of their land and cattle. This was a practice the Ndebele understood, even if they did not like it, as it was the traditional manner in which victorious Africans punished their defeated enemies. However, the British South Africa Company went one step further and forced the Ndebele to work for it.[114] Humiliated, they rose up in a doomed effort to drive the British from their land.

In contrast, the British could be generous in victory with white opponents. Their treatment of the Boers showed an understanding of the need to give their enemies honour in defeat. The treaty which brought the Boer War to an end forced the Boers to recognize British sovereignty and the loss of their own independence. In this sense, the British were clear winners. In all other respects, the British conceded the Boers' demands. They granted an amnesty, and compensated the Boers for their losses in the war. They also promised not to grant the vote to the blacks prior to South Africa gaining self-rule, a promise which assured white domination for another century as there was no prospect of a self-governing white South Africa enfranchising the blacks. So well integrated did many Boers become in the British Empire that one leading Boer general, Jan Smuts, went on to become a British Field Marshal. From the British point of view this was a very successful peace.

Less successful was the peace signed at Versailles in 1919 after the First World War, which many have held responsible for the outbreak of the Second World War 20 years later. When French negotiators proposed detaching all Germany's possessions west of the Rhine, British Prime Minister David Lloyd George denounced their ideas as 'a definite and dishonourable betrayal of one of the fundamental principles for which the Allies had fought', and suggested that they 'would cause endless friction and might provoke another war.'[115]

Germans saw three facets of the Versailles Treaty as particularly ignominious. The first was the fact that the Allies had not negotiated the treaty with them but imposed it on them. In the process, Germans claimed, the Allies had broken the terms of the original armistice of November 1918, rendering the treaty 'illegitimate'.[116] Second, the treaty imposed onerous reparations on Germany. Third, it included a clause requiring the Germans to admit their guilt in starting the war. The Allies included the 'war guilt' clause for legal reasons, to justify the reparations, but it was unnecessarily humiliating, and did much to stoke up nationalistic opposition to the terms of the Versailles treaty.[117]

The terms of the treaty were not really that harsh, and the Allies probably treated Germany rather better than Germany would have treated them if it had emerged victorious. The problem was that many Germans felt that their country had surrendered at a time when its army had not been decisively defeated. This meant that they had shown themselves unworthy by giving in when they still had the ability to resist. They would have to prove their honour by taking up arms once again.

Women and honour

In the First World War, for the first time, women put on uniform and officially joined the armed forces of their countries, albeit still in non-combatant roles. Britain formed the Women's Army Auxiliary Corps in July 1917, and later the

Women's Royal Naval Service and the Women's Royal Air Force. Their purpose was to relieve men from rear echelon duties to fill the ranks at the front. Women also joined in industrial production and as nurses, most notably in the Volunteer Aid Detachments, which had some 80,000 members by 1916.[118]

Unlike the Confederate soldiers examined in Chapter 6, nineteenth-century British soldiers do not generally seem to have measured their honour in terms of their image in front of women. This was in part because until 1914 they were professionals, not family men sucked into war. The honour group of their fellow soldiers mattered much more than the honour group of female opinion.

The army had long done what it could to keep female influence out of army life. Soldiers could not marry without permission, and this was generally withheld until they had already served for a considerable amount of time. Officers could not marry until they became captains, which was usually not until their mid or late 30s. By 1900, other ranks had to have served for five years and be at least 26 years old in order to marry. Even then, not all wives were allowed to live in barracks, and few were permitted to accompany a regiment on a tour of duty overseas.[119] The deliberate effect of this policy was that the regiment replaced the family as the soldier's primary focus of loyalty. Ian Hamilton, who became a general in the First World War, wrote unromantically to his wife: 'The fact is a soldier has no business to be married. He is no longer whole-hearted in his pursuit of glory.'[120]

The male atmosphere of the army combined with the obsession with manliness to produce a climate unresponsive to female opinion. Eliza Amelia, Lady Errol, accompanied her husband on campaign to the Crimea, where she shared his tent. Asked if the bed was comfortable, she replied: 'I don't know, my dear. His lordship had the bed and I slept on the floor.'[121] Rudyard Kipling summarized the attitude well in his poem *The Betrothed*: 'And a woman is only a woman, but a good Cigar is a Smoke.'[122]

During the First World War, the army ceased to be so divorced from the society it served. As in ancient Sparta, the women of Britain acted to shame their men into taking up arms, and government authorities exploited images of women in wartime propaganda to persuade men that women wanted them to fight and would shun them if they did not. Recruiting posters played heavily on this theme. One poster shows a woman talking to a man, while pointing to Belgium burning in the background with her hand. 'Will you go, or must I?', she asks. 'Go, it's your duty', says a grandmother to a young man in another. 'Women of Britain say Go!', says a third.[123]

Other propaganda targeted women, to persuade them to pressure their men to enlist. An example was a poster which asked 'the women of London' to consider that if their 'best boy does not think that you and your country are worth fighting for – do you think he is WORTHY of you?'[124] A recruiting leaflet addressed to 'Mothers and Sweethearts' told them: 'If you cannot persuade him to answer his Country's Call and protect you now *Discharge him* as unfit.' 'Don't pity the girl who is alone', said a poster:

> Her young man is probably a soldier – fighting for her and her country – and for *You*. If your young man neglects his duty to his King and Country, the time may come when he will *Neglect You*. Think it over – then ask him to JOIN THE ARMY TODAY![125]

Some women heeded the call. Most famously, women handed out white feathers, a mark of cowardice, to men they found not in uniform. This practice began when Admiral Charles Penrose Fitzgerald persuaded 30 women in Folkestone to hand out white feathers on 30 August 1914, and was soon copied by women across the country.[126] The Suffragette movement took up the practice with particular zeal, hoping thereby to prove that women were playing their part in the war and so were worthy of full citizenship and the vote.[127]

Shaming men in this fashion appears to have had some effect. H. Symonds described how when a ginger-headed girl 'gently tucked a white duck feather into my button-hole I went off to the recruiting office and, putting two years on my age, joined up'. Similarly, Granville Bradshaw described how he and Basil Hallam 'were both surrounded by young, stupid, and screaming girls who stuck white feathers into the lapels of our coats … When we extricated ourselves Basil said "I shall go and join up immediately" – and he did', only to die in a parachute accident shortly afterwards.[128]

Many contemporaries found the white feather campaign uncouth.[129] Accosting strange young men was hardly becoming to a lady, especially when some of the men were actually soldiers out of uniform. Major Leonard Darwin, exhorting a meeting of the Women's League of Honour to persuade their men to enlist, nonetheless stated that he 'was very far from admiring those women who go up to young men in the street … and abuse them for not enlisting, a proceeding which requires no courage on the woman's part, but merely complete absence of modesty.' Echoing the major, recruiting sergeant Coulson Kernahan said that a woman who behaved in such a way 'thereby classes herself … as what in the other sex would be called a "cad".'[130]

In the twentieth century, a progressive increase in the value of individual dignity means that it is still acceptable to punish the guilty, but much less acceptable to humiliate them. The fate of the white feather campaign indicates that at the time of the First World War many already no longer regarded shaming as a fitting practice. In this sense, it turned out to be the last major fling of an ancient method of enforcing the male code of honour.

Conclusion

Britain dominated the world for a century. During that time, ideas of honour underwent a significant evolution, with the clear harnessing of duty to the nation, and a gradual lowering in importance of the concept of personal glory. 'Character' replaced prowess as the primary virtue, while the First World War dealt serious blows to the heroic and chivalric models of honour. The greatest change was the expansion yet again of the honour group. The military code of honour now no longer applied only to knights or gentlemen, but included European men of all ranks and social classes, and in some respects even women. Meanwhile, the First World War dealt a blow to Britain's power from which it never fully recovered. The United States of America was emerging in Britain's place as the foremost power in the world, a trend accentuated by the Second World War of 1939–1945. In the second half of the twentieth century, it was American honour which was to come to the fore.

Notes

1 Appendix 2 to Bond, Brian (ed.), *Victorian Military Campaigns*, London: Hutchinson, 1967, pp. 309–11.
2 Andrew, Donna T., 'The Code of Honour and its Critics: the Opposition to Duelling in England, 1700–1850', *Social History*, 1980, vol. 5, no. 3, 434.
3 Digby, Kenelm, *The Broad Stone of Honour: Or Rules for the Gentlemen of England*, London: C. & J. Rivington, 1823, p. 579.
4 Smiles, Samuel, *Self-Help*, London: John Murray, 1897, pp. 388 and 398.
5 Ibid, p. 397.
6 Girouard, Mark, *The Return to Camelot: Chivalry and the English Gentleman*, New Haven: Yale University Press, 1981, p. 263.
7 Flanders, Judith, *The Victorian House: Domestic Life from Childbirth to Deathbed*, London: HarperCollins, 2003, p. xxxiv.
8 Smiles, Samuel, *Duty*, London: John Murray, 1897, p. 190.
9 Baden-Powell, Robert, *Scouting for Boys*, London: Horace Wilcox, 1908, chapter VII. (Reprinted Oxford: Oxford University Press, 2004.)
10 Morris, James, *Pax Britannica: The Climax of an Empire*, London: Faber & Faber, 1968, p. 220.
11 Thomas Arnold cited in Rutherford, Jonathan, *Forever England: Reflections on Race, Masculinity and Empire*, London: Lawrence & Wishart, 1997, p. 13.
12 Rutherford, *Forever England*, p. 15.
13 Ibid, p. 16.
14 Graves, Robert, *Goodbye to All That*, revised edition, London: Penguin, 1957, pp. 37–42.
15 Hughes, Thomas, *Tom Brown's Schooldays*, London: W. Foulsham & co., no date given, p. 21.
16 Rutherford, *Forever England*, p. 17.
17 Baden-Powell, *Scouting for Boys*, p. 28.
18 Kipling, Rudyard, 'If', in *Complete Verse*, New York: Doubleday, 1940, p. 578.
19 Mason, Philip, *A Matter of Honour: An Account of the Indian Army, Its Officers and Men*, London: Macmillan, 1986, p. 364.
20 Hall, Donald E., *Muscular Christianity*, Cambridge: Cambridge University Press, 1994, p. 9.
21 Peck, John, *War, the Army and Victorian Literature*, Basingstoke: Palgrave, 1998, p. 74. See also, Anderson, Olive, 'The Growth of Christian Militarism in mid-Victorian Britain', *English Historical Review*, 1971, vol. 84, no. 338, 46–72.
22 Henty, G.A., *The Dash for Khartoum*, London: Blackie & Son, 1892, p. v.
23 Baden-Powell, *Scouting for Boys*, p. 223.
24 Morris, *Pax Britannica*, p. 409.
25 See, for instance, Hobson, J.A., *Imperialism: A Study*, 3rd ed., London: G.A. Allen & Unwin, 1938.
26 Eldridge, C.C., *Victorian Imperialism*, London: Hodder & Stoughton, 1978, p. 75.

27 This thesis was most famously propounded by Ronald Robinson and John Gallagher in *Africa and the Victorians: The Official Mind of Imperialism*, London: Macmillan, 1961.
28 Eldridge, *Victorian Imperialism*, p. 138.
29 Porter, Bernard, *The Lion's Share: A Short History of British Imperialism, 1850–1983*, London: Longman, 1984, pp. 128–9.
30 Spiers, Edward M., *The Late Victorian Army, 1868–1902*, Manchester and New York: Manchester University Press, 1992, pp. 185–6.
31 Selby, John, 'The Third China War, 1860', in Bond (ed.), *Victorian Military Campaigns*, pp. 71–2.
32 Ibid, p. 72.
33 Porter, *The Lion's Share*, p. 86.
34 Hopkirk, Peter, *Trespassers on the Roof of the World: The Race for Lhasa*, Oxford: Oxford University Press, 1982, p. 162.
35 Ibid, p. 163.
36 Chandler, D.G., 'The Expedition to Abyssinia, 1867–8', in Bond, *Victorian Military Campaigns*, p. 116.
37 Ibid, p. 110.
38 Cited in Smith, Simon C., *British Imperialism, 1750–1970*, Cambridge: Cambridge University Press, 1998, p. 96; also, Spiers, Edward M., *Army and Society, 1815–1914*, London and New York: Longman, 1980, p. 236; and Pakenham, Thomas, *The Boer War*, London: Futura, 1982, p. 59.
39 Pakenham, *The Boer War*, p. 30.
40 James, Lawrence, *Warrior Race: A History of the British at War*, London: Little, Brown & Company, 2001, pp. 404–5.
41 Robbins, Keith, *Sir Edward Grey*, London: Cassell, 1971, p. 297.
42 Trevelyan, G.M., *Grey of Fallodon*, London: Longman, Greens & Co., 1937, p. 269.
43 Cited in Gullace, Nicoletta F., 'Sexual Violence and Family Honor: British Propaganda and International Law during the First World War', *The American Historical Review*, 1997, vol. 102, no. 3, 720, f. 31.
44 Cited in Kagan, Donald, 'Honor, Interest, and the Nation-State', in Elliott Abrams (ed.), *Honor among Nations: Intangible Interests and Foreign Policy*, Washington, DC: Ethics and Public Policy Center, 1998, p. 5.
45 Cited in Girouard, *The Return to Camelot*, p. 283.
46 Liddle Collection, Brotherton Library, University of Leeds, Dr L.W. Batten (GS), Letter to Tristram, 18 March 1970.
47 Morris, *Pax Britannica*, p. 408.
48 Farwell, Byron, *For Queen and Country*, London: Allen Lane, 1981, p. 116.
49 Holmes, Richard, *Redcoat: The British Soldier in the Age of Horse and Musket*, London: HarperCollins, 2001, p. 313.
50 Farwell, *For Queen and Country*, p. 136.
51 Holmes, Richard, *Tommy: The British Soldier on the Western Front, 1914–1918*, London: HarperCollins, 2004, p. 578.
52 Garnet Wolseley, cited in Lendon, J.E., *Empire of Honor: The Art of Government in the Roman World*, Oxford: Oxford University Press, 2001, p. 250.
53 Brodsky, G.W. Stephen, *Gentlemen of the Blade: A Social and Literary History of the British Army since 1660*, Westport: Greenwood Press, 1988, p. 111.
54 Liddle Collection, Pte A. Sagar (GS). Letter to Father, 18 May 1917.
55 Liddle Collection, General Aspects, Love, Item 4. Letter, George Worthington to Mother, 8 August 1915.
56 Liddle Collection, Pte R. Ross-Douglas, Diary, Friday 14 May 1915.
57 Liddle Collection, Cpl R.J.T. Evans (GS). Letter to Mother, 4 November 1914.
58 Liddle Collection, Pte W.H. Gardner (GS). Letter to Mother, 21 June 1916.
59 Liddle Collection, E.W. Pennell (ANZAC, Aust). Letter to Mr and Mrs Murray, 24 July 1915.

60 Liddle Collection, Capt. J.R. Tibbles, Memoir, vol. D, November 1917, p. 103.
61 Ascoli, David, *A Companion to the British Army*, London: Harrap, 1983, p. 183.
62 Mason, *A Matter of Honour*, pp. 129–30.
63 Ibid, p. 206.
64 Pakenham, Thomas, *The Scramble for Africa*, London: Abacus, 1992, p. 575; Farwell, *For Queen and Country*, p. 174.
65 Spiers, *The Late Victorian Army*, p. 90.
66 Holmes, *Redcoat*, p. 168.
67 Spiers, *The Army and Society*, p. 3.
68 Crook, M.J., *The Evolution of the Victoria Cross: A Study in Administrative History*, Tunbridge Wells: Midas, 1975, p. 7.
69 Ibid, pp. 252–3.
70 Liddle Collection, J.C. Wakeford (GS). Letter to mother, 31 May 1918.
71 Spiers, *The Army and Society*, p. 128.
72 Liddle Collection, 2Lt P.G. Kennedy (Dunster Force). Letter to mother, 29 September 1918.
73 Liddle Collection, Jasper Charter (GS). Letter to mother, 2 June 1916.
74 Liddle Collection, Tom Worthington (GS). Letter to Rollo, 15 January 1917.
75 Liddle Collection, Sgt Maj. P.L. Ibbetson (GS). Diary, p. 69.
76 Winter, Denis, *Death's Men: Soldiers of the Great War*, London: Penguin, 1979, pp. 189–90.
77 Liddle Collection, H.R. Osbourne (GS). Letter to Ellen and Tom, 26 February 1915.
78 Liddle Collection, S.H. Burt (GS). Diary, 26 June 1915.
79 Ascoli, *Companion to the British Army*, p. 177.
80 Holmes, *Tommy*, p. 586.
81 Borg, Alan, *War Memorials from Antiquity to the Present*, London: Leo Cooper, 1991, pp. 47–8.
82 Baden-Powell, *Scouting for Boys*, p. 292.
83 Strawson, John, *Beggars in Red: The British Army, 1789–1889*, London: Hutchinson, 1991, pp. 165 and 194.
84 P.H.B. Lyon, 'Comrades in Arms', in Hibberd, Dominic and Onions, John (eds), *Poetry of the Great War: An Anthology*, Basingstoke: Macmillan, 1986, p. 172.
85 Winter, Jay, *Sites of Memory, Sites of Mourning: The Great War in European Cultural History*, Cambridge: Cambridge University Press, 1995, pp. 24–7.
86 Longworth, Philip, *The Unending Vigil: A History of the Commonwealth War Graves Commission, 1917–1967*, London: Constable, 1967, p. 33.
87 Ibid, p. 35.
88 Mosse, George, *Fallen Soldiers: Reshaping the Memory of the World Wars*, New York and Oxford: Oxford University Press, 1990, p. 7.
89 Pakenham, *Boer War*, pp. 129–30.
90 Pakenham, *Scramble for Africa*, p. 545; Farwell, *For Queen and Country*, p. 31.
91 Graves, *Goodbye to All That*, p. 111.
92 Morris, *Pax Britannica*, p. 95.
93 Pakenham, *Boer War*, p. 436.
94 Holmes, *Tommy*, p. 531.
95 Schivelbusch, Wolfgang, *The Culture of Defeat: On National Trauma, Mourning, and Recovery*, London: Granta, 2002, p. 219.
96 Dougan, Andy, *The Hunting of Man: A History of the Sniper*, London: Fourth Estate, 2004, Chapter 10, pp. 158–83.
97 James, Lawrence, *The Rise and Fall of the British Empire*, London: Abacus, 1998, p. 262.
98 Morris, *Pax Britannica*, p. 418.
99 Spiers, *The Late Victorian Army*, p. 311.

100 Pakenham, *Scramble for Africa*, pp. 47–9. For more details, see Pakenham, *Boer War*, pp. 508–18.
101 Molter, Bennett A., *Knights of the Air*, New York and London: D. Appleton and Company, 1918, p. 21.
102 Cecil Lewis, cited in Hastings, Max, *Warriors: Extraordinary Tales from the Battlefield*, London: HarperCollins, 2005, p. 169.
103 Mosse, *Fallen Soldiers*, p. 121.
104 Molter, *Knights of the Air*, p. 22.
105 Farwell, *For Queen and Country*, p. 111.
106 Pakenham, *Boer War*, p. 525.
107 Holmes, *Tommy*, pp. 547–53. Also, Graves, *Goodbye to All That*, pp. 153–4.
108 Article 10 of the POW section of the Hague Convention, cited in Rachaminov, Alon, *POWs and the Great War: Captivity on the Eastern Front*, Oxford and New York: Berg, 2002, p. 74.
109 Crawford, E.R., 'The Sikh Wars, 1845–9', in Bond (ed.), *Victorian Military Campaigns*, p. 63.
110 Porter, *The Lion's Share*, p. 165.
111 Mason, *A Matter of Honour*, pp. 299–301.
112 Dawson, Graham, *Soldier Heroes: British Adventure, Empire and the Imagining of Masculinities*, London and New York: Routledge, 1994, p. 93.
113 Eldridge, *Victorian Imperialism*, p. 70.
114 Pakenham, *Scramble for Africa*, p. 497.
115 Macmillan, Margaret, *Peacemakers: The Paris Conference of 1919 and its Attempt to End War*, London: John Murray, 2001, p. 184.
116 Ibid, p. 28.
117 Ibid, p. 204.
118 Ouditt, Sharon, *Fighting Forces, Writing Women: Identity and Ideology in the First World War*, London and New York: Routledge, 1994, pp. 15–16.
119 Holmes, *Tommy*, p. 117. See also Holmes, *Redcoat*, pp. 293–4.
120 Brodsky, *Gentlemen of the Blade*, p. 231.
121 Ibid, p. 237.
122 Kipling, Rudyard, 'The Betrothed', in *Complete Verse*, p. 49.
123 Grayzel, Susan R., *Women and the First World War*, London: Longman, 2002, pp. 11–18.
124 Ibid, p. 20.
125 Gullace, Nicoletta F., 'White Feathers and Wounded Men: Female Patriotism and the Memory of the Great War', *Journal of British Studies*, 1997, no. 36, 184–5.
126 Ibid, pp. 178–9.
127 Ouditt, *Fighting Forces, Writing Women*, p. 246.
128 Gullace, 'White Feathers', pp. 197 and 203.
129 Grayzel, *Women and the First World War*, p. 20.
130 Gullace, 'White Feathers', p. 186.

8 The Cold War and after

Background

The First World War was thought to be the 'war to end all wars', but proved rather to be just the prelude to the even greater blood-letting of 1939–1945. From 1945 to 1990, Western Europe and North America were engaged in a prolonged struggle for dominance with the communist world led by the Soviet Union, a struggle which often erupted into violence. Following the collapse of communism, new wars, such as that in Iraq, continue to break out. War remains a constant in international relations.

Some commentators now consider the idea of honour to be 'obsolete'.[1] We tend to contrast our modern rationality with the 'irrational' behaviour of the honour-conscious past. On this, our perceptions are wrong. Honour continues to exercise its influence on the world, and on war no less than any other activity.

Honour and virtue in the modern era

The carnage of the First World War made it harder thereafter for men to believe in the glory of war. Military honour would never be quite the same again. Nevertheless, it is a mistake to think that the war entirely destroyed the intimate connection between war and honour. Indeed, in the 1920s, 1930s and 1940s there was a revival of interest in martial honour in parts of Europe. Faced with what many felt was a collapse in the morals of contemporary society, some believed that the best way of revitalizing their nations was through an elite 'chivalric' organization which would set the example. This was especially true among the people of defeated nations – Russia, Germany, and France post-1940 – who saw in knightly honour a means of resurrecting the battered spirits of their nation. The White officers who led the resistance to the Bolsheviks after the Russian revolution repeatedly used the language of honour, and in some instances liked to see themselves as 'monk knights'.[2] In the Second World War Vichy France established the *Ecole Nationale des Cadres d'Uriage*, whose students directly paralleled the White veterans by referring to themselves as 'knight-monks'.[3] Similarly, in Nazi Germany, Heinrich Himmler envisioned the SS as a sort of knightly order, and even attempted to reintroduce duelling and a system of courts of honour.[4]

This continued fascination with traditional military honour helped provoke the slaughter of the Second World War. Since those who most loudly used the language of honour, such as the members of the SS, often behaved with utter barbarity, post-Second World War that language has become largely discredited. In particular, it has become harder to speak of honour in its external sense. Nowadays, when people use the word 'honour', it is usually in the sense of an internal moral code. Typically, one officer interviewed for this book described honour as 'like a code of ethics … an internal characteristic a person lives by … a moral code'. Many others defined it in terms of 'doing the right thing'.[5]

We should not, however, jump from this to the conclusion that we no longer care for external honour or for the judgements of others. In fact, philosopher Alain de Botton claims that we may even be more prone to status anxiety than past generations, because of the way in which status has become detached from birth. This means that we are no longer so sure of our relative status, and that status, once acquired, is very unstable and easily lost.[6] Historian William Miller echoes this sentiment, claiming that external confirmation of worth remains essential for self-esteem: 'So we … care about honor, about how we stack up against all those with whom we are competing. … honor still looms large in many areas of our social life, especially in those, I would bet, that occupy most of our psychic energy.'[7]

In fact, recent research suggests that modern people care so much about their status that their anxiety can actually make them physically sick. In his book *Status Syndrome*, doctor Michael Marmot demonstrates that those who feel valued and honoured by their society are healthier than those who do not.[8] Modern man remains as attached to external recognition as any ancient hero.

Theoretically, honour still derives from virtue, but today's list of relevant virtues has evolved enormously from the time of Achilles. Physical strength, for instance, has lost much of its importance. One can be a weakling, but still a person of great honour. A man could even be a coward, as most Westerners no longer ever face a situation in which their physical courage is tested. Today, excellence in almost any socially valued activity is likely to bring one honour, and since such excellence often leads to wealth, people still strongly associate wealth with honour.[9] Fortunately, there are better sources of wealth than loot nowadays. In fact, since war is expensive, and so may have a negative effect on wealth, and thus on honour, there is a disincentive to fight.

At the same time, shame has lost much of its power, for the simple reason that it has become increasingly difficult to enforce it. In a small society, where everybody knows everybody else, a person cannot avoid the eyes of others. Today, it is quite easy to do so.[10] Many people do not even speak to their neighbours, let alone know or care about their moral characters.

Lingering fears of shame and concerns with honour are likely to be greatest in communities in which such a separation of professional and private life is not possible. The international community is one such. A state which dishonours itself cannot hide its face. This is especially true for the rich and powerful. If the United States misbehaves, everybody knows it. We might, therefore, expect powerful states like the USA to be particularly sensitive to matters of national honour.

Military forces are another type of close community. Soldiers live and work together in conditions of great intimacy. The influence of honour is, therefore, strong among them, and indeed Western armies make much use of the language of honour, even if other words (such as 'integrity') often substitute for the actual word 'honour'. The most notable example is the United States, whose military academies continue to explicitly indoctrinate officer cadets in a fashion which is in some respects quite archaic.

The epitome of this is the 'Honor Code' of the United States Military Academy West Point.[11] The code states that 'A Cadet will not lie, cheat, steal, or tolerate those who do.' Its purpose is 'to foster a commitment to honorable living in cadets in preparation for their service as leaders of character for the Army'.[12] The honour code of the US Naval Academy Annapolis is almost identical, but without the infamous 'non-toleration clause'.[13] Until the late 1970s, these honour codes were extremely rigid, and based almost entirely on negatives. In recent years, the moral education of cadets has become more sophisticated. The West Point honour code is now described merely as 'a baseline standard of behavior to which all cadets are expected to adhere. But … cadets are expected to go beyond this baseline and develop an understanding of the "spirit of the code".'[14] The key, I was informed at West Point in 2002, is not just to 'adhere' to the code, but to 'believe'.[15]

Whether the system does indeed instil a sense of honour as desired cannot easily be determined. Some people clearly abide by the code solely out of fear, and never internalize its values. Conversations at both West Point and Annapolis suggested some cynicism. Some cadets also distinguish between the honour code and other regulations, saying 'I break regulations, but not honour' – a phrasing which suggests the system may be somewhat counterproductive, if it teaches them, even inadvertently, that honour is solely a matter of not lying, cheating and stealing.[16] Nonetheless, in many other cases it was clear that the system had succeeded in indoctrinating young men and women into believing that honour mattered and that it demanded an absolute commitment to truth and honesty.

The honour codes of the US military academies are unique to the USA, but the virtues which Americans consider essential for the honourable soldier are very similar to those of other Western armed forces. The main attributes required are courage, loyalty, service, and honesty. The obvious breaks with the past are the disappearance of God and monarch, the increased stress on conscience and integrity, and the reduced emphasis on physical strength and skill with weapons.

The United States Army lists its 'Army Values' as:

- Loyalty
- Duty
- Respect
- Selfless Service
- Honour
- Integrity
- Personal Courage

By contrast, the 'Core Values' of the British Army are:[17]

- Selfless Commitment
- Courage
- Discipline
- Integrity
- Loyalty
- Respect for Others

While those of the Canadian Forces are:[18]

- Duty
- Loyalty
- Integrity
- Courage

The ethical training of Western soldiers teaches that soldiers must uphold these values not as ends in themselves, but because they are essential for military effectiveness. As the British pamphlet *Values and Standards of the British Army* states, commanders must consider cases of possible misconduct against the following Service Test: 'Have the actions or behaviour of an individual adversely impacted or are they likely to impact on the efficiency or operational effectiveness of the Army?'[19]

There is no honour in defeat in the modern world. Winning remains the priority. Consequently, as one officer told me: 'The "good" soldier is not necessarily the good soldier.'[20]

Honour as a cause of war

Barry O'Neill comments in a study of honour in modern international relations that, 'Leaders talk about showing "will", "resolve", "strength", or "credibility", but their patterns of behavior are typical of past disputes over honor.'[21] 'Credibility', in fact, appears to be the word most often used to justify war in the modern era. American governments claimed of their military involvement in Central America in the 1980s that: 'Our credibility worldwide is engaged'; and Ronald Reagan repeated that, 'If Central America were to fall … our credibility would collapse.'[22] In 1999, leaders of the North Atlantic Treaty Organization (NATO) warned that the 'credibility of the alliance' was on the line when it launched a military campaign against Yugoslavia; and in 2002, President George W. Bush warned others that 'their credibility is at stake' when deciding whether to support the United States in its invasion of Iraq.[23]

Democratic politics may even reinforce the role of credibility/honour in causing wars. First, democratic politicians' positions depend on reputation, and the process of democracy is likely to push to the fore those who most crave the acclamation of others. A journalist once asked the psychiatrist Anthony Storr, many of whose clients were British politicians, what he thought motivated them. 'They all have an irresistible urge to be recognized and applauded', he replied.[24]

Second, modern nationalism means that people define their own personal honour in part through the honour and status of their country. They are liable to take issues of national honour very seriously.

Third, honour systems flourish where legal apparatuses are weak, acting as de facto bills of rights, protecting peoples' right to respect. The international arena is such a place. As a result questions of honour can acquire a great importance in international relations.[25]

Fourth, in the political world antique virtues continue to be seen as desirable. Supporters of British Prime Minister Tony Blair's decision to join the 2003 invasion of Iraq regularly praised him for his political 'courage' and 'strength'. Politicians who oppose war regularly find themselves accused of 'appeasement' and 'weakness'. Not all share the obsession with strength, but the traditional outlook still retains considerable power.

War is most likely to occur when matters of honour coincide with questions of security, demonstrating once again that the two are not mutually exclusive causes of war, but rather mutually supporting ones. A prime example is America's war in Vietnam. When the former French colony split into North and South Vietnam after the French failed to defeat a communist and nationalist insurgency in the 1950s, South Vietnam became an ally of the USA, while the communist North attempted to conquer the South. In America, President John F. Kennedy voiced his fear, 'that US credibility would suffer a grievous blow if [South] Vietnam were "lost".'[26] His staff concurred. A report written for Kennedy in 1961 by his Secretary of State Dean Rusk and his Secretary of Defence Robert McNamara warned him that, 'The loss of South Vietnam would ... undermine the credibility of American commitments elsewhere.'[27] National honour in this way became linked with security. Defeat in Vietnam would damage American prestige, which would lead to other countries falling under the communist sway – the infamous 'domino theory'.

By 1964 it was obvious that without direct American military involvement in combat operations, the South Vietnamese regime would fall. Explaining his decision to escalate rather than withdraw, Kennedy's successor, Lyndon Johnson, said in 1965: 'If America's commitment is dishonoured in South Vietnam, it is dishonoured in forty other alliances or more.' He also said: 'We love peace. We hate war. But our course is charted always by the compass of honor.'[28]

President Johnson felt very insecure about his personal honour, and regarded Vietnam as a test of it. He told his biographer, Doris Kearns: 'if I left that war and let the Communists take over South Vietnam, then I would be seen as a coward and my nation would be seen as an appeaser.'[29] People would say, he told her, 'That I was a coward. An unmanly man. A man without spine.' Johnson was not the only one who saw the war as a matter of honour. This perception was vital in generating political support for the war. Senator Richard Russell of Georgia, who had long harboured reservations about American involvement in Vietnam, cast aside his doubts in the end: 'Our national honor is at stake', he said, 'We cannot and we will not shrink from defending it.'[30]

More recently, we have seen honour contributing towards another war, in Iraq. American and British politicians presented their attack on Iraq in 2003 as motivated by fears that sooner or later Iraqi 'weapons of mass destruction' would be used against them. The problem with this scenario was that (in the eyes of this author at least) it bore no relation to the known facts about Iraq. The idea that an impoverished Arab state, whose army had been shattered ten years earlier, which had suffered over a decade of economic sanctions, and for whose weapons capacity and links with terrorism there was no reliable evidence, could pose any sort of threat to the most powerful nations on earth was as absurd as Julius Caesar's claim that Ariovistus's Germans might march on Rome. This does not mean that President Bush, Prime Minister Blair, or their ministers deliberately lied. More probably, they believed their own propaganda. The question is why they and so many others were psychologically inclined to believe such absurdities.

In a recent book, Walter Russell Mead identified four strands of American foreign policy. Of these, Jacksonianism (named after the honour-obsessed American President Andrew Jackson) now appears to be dominant. 'The Jacksonian school', says Mead, is based on a powerful sense of honour, and 'represents a deeply embedded, widely spread populist and popular culture of honor, independence, courage and military pride among the American people.'[31] After declining in importance in the early twentieth century, it has recently undergone a revival. As Mead explains:

> [H]onor remains a core value for tens of thousands of middle-class Americans. The unacknowledged code of honor that shapes so much of American behavior and aspiration today is a recognizable descendent of the honor of early Jacksonian America.[32]

Academic research suggests that sensitivity to honour is particularly strong in the southern states of the USA. Southerners, according to one survey, still 'belong to a society in which insults are a very serious matter, [and] are more violent than non-southerners', as well as being more likely to support military undertakings.[33] This matters both because Southerners are over-represented in the US military, and because, according to American commentator Michael Lind, during the Presidency of George W. Bush there has been a 'Southern takeover of American politics',[34] with which the US government has fallen into the hands of 'the political and philosophical heirs of the Jacksonians, Confederates, and segregationist Democrats'.[35]

For these people, the problem with Iraq and its leader Saddam Hussein was not that they posed a serious direct threat to America, but rather that they defied the United States, and even worse, were seen to get away with it. This was a blow to America's honour which could not be tolerated. Iraqi defiance was a 'challenge' which sooner or later demanded a violent 'response'.

The 2003 confrontation had been brewing for ten years. Under the terms of United Nations resolutions passed at the end of the 1991 Gulf War, when America led the world in reversing an Iraqi invasion of Kuwait, Iraq had to destroy all its chemical and biological weapons and terminate all its chemical, biological and nuclear weapons programmes. To enforce compliance, the UN imposed economic sanctions on Iraq, and the US and UK air forces regularly bombed targets in Iraq, claiming that the Iraqis had not destroyed all their weapons as required. The disputed weapons had become points of honour.[36]

Defence of honour had become doubly important, many felt, because the flight of American forces from Somalia in 1993 had created an impression among some of America's enemies that Americans were cowardly.[37] Many Americans attributed the terrorist attacks on New York and Washington on 11 September 2001 to this loss of prestige.[38] The purpose of the offensive against Iraq was, more than anything, to restore America's reputation for strength and courage in order to deter future attacks. This is one explanation of why so little effort was put into post-war planning. To those spearheading the war, war was an end in itself.

British leaders seem to have shared the sentiment that Iraqi defiance represented a test of their credibility. British Foreign Secretary Jack Straw told the United Nations Security Council on 14 February 2003, one month before the invasion of Iraq, that, 'This period of twelve years has frankly been a period of humiliation for this body.'[39] British Prime Minister Tony Blair used similar language to justify his support for the invasion in an interview two years later, saying, 'I had a decision to make as to whether to leave Saddam there, in breach of UN resolutions, and end up in a situation with the international community humiliated and him emboldened, or to remove him. I decided to remove him.'[40] Furthermore, having once threatened force against Iraq, the British and Americans then had very little choice but to use it if they were to maintain their reputations. As one British official said shortly before the invasion: 'The quicker it is done the better. To back down now would be the worst result possible. We would have no credibility if Saddam Hussein was still in place.'[41]

Honour as a reason for fighting

A survey of American soldiers after the 2003 Iraq war identified the following reasons for their decision to join up: 'to get money for college, to gain experience before looking for a job, to follow in the footsteps of a family member who had been in the military, or just to find some adventure before settling down.'[42] American journalist Evan Wright, who accompanied US Marines during the invasion of Iraq, noted that many of them had joined to escape poverty, but others were motivated by patriotism. Some even turned down commissions to serve in the ranks.[43] British journalist Oliver Poole made similar observations.[44]

A generation earlier, a similar mixture of motives seems to have led Americans to volunteer for service in Vietnam. One veteran, Dale Reich, 'imagined himself to be "a soldier like John Wayne, a dashing GI who feared nothing and either emerged with the medals and the girl, or died heroically".'[45] Robert Bower said that he joined the army because 'I got into a real patriotic attitude. I went into this real heavy God-and-Country thing. And I thought I should go to Vietnam and, you know, help the free world out.'[46] Having interviewed many veterans, psychiatrist

Jonathan Shay concluded that some of them were motivated by patriotism and a desire to defend the world against communism, others by a belief that war would allow them to prove their worth as men.[47]

Once in the army, the willingness of men to fight was far greater in Iraq than in Vietnam. While most US troops in Vietnam did their duty properly, there was a significant amount of desertion and insubordination, and other indications of poor morale, such as the assassination of officers.[48] There was a considerable degree of dissent as to whether the Vietnam war was just, as well as an awareness that it was not popular back home. In addition, according to Richard Gabriel and Paul Savage, officers in many cases set a poor example, and provided bad leadership. They claim that the reason was that officers had abandoned traditional military values in favour of 'a new ethical code rooted in the entrepreneurial model of the modern business corporation'. With this change, 'managerial efficiency instead of "honor" became the standard of performance.'[49] It did not help that units did not deploy to Vietnam *en masse* after a period of training together. Rather, the units stayed in theatre while individuals rotated in and out of them on an individual basis. This disrupted small unit cohesion. As Dale Reich noted:

> The old clichés about camaraderie under fire did not seem to apply … I was crushed by the combination of slipping one step closer to combat, and finding no one to pat me on the back and assure me that I would survive. Instead, I found that even my fellow soldiers had no real interest in my welfare.[50]

The American army of 2003 was a greatly improved institution, and its members had a much stronger belief in the morality of their cause. Oliver Poole noted that the soldiers of the battalion which he accompanied into Iraq universally believed that in removing Saddam Hussein from power they were both liberating Iraqis and making America safer.[51]

Primary group cohesion was strong in Iraq, as US soldiers had trained together for a long time prior to the war and had bonded into strong teams. In a survey of soldiers undertaken after the war, 'the most frequent response given for combat motivation was "fighting for my buddies".'[52] As one soldier said, 'I am the lowest ranking private on the Bradley [fighting vehicle] so I am trying to kind of prove something in a way that I could do things. I did not want to let anyone down.'[53] 'Here we're brothers', Corporal Walter Hauser told Evan Wright, 'and we all look out for each other. That's the best part of being in a war. We all get to be together.'[54]

The presence of comrades is reassuring, but it also adds pressure to perform well. As Tim O'Brien said, looking back on his service in Vietnam: 'fear is paralyzing … but when you are afraid you must hide it to save respect and reputation.'[55] Similarly, a British parachute regiment commander told historian Richard Holmes that during the Falklands War, 'his soldiers were sustained by the desire not to let their comrades down, or to be seen to fail. "Their own self-respect", he said, "would not permit them to funk".'[56]

At the individual level, the one virtue which invariably wins soldiers honour from their group is still physical courage. Tim O'Brien's company commander in

Vietnam, Captain Johansen, reflected a commonly held sentiment in telling him, 'I'd rather be brave … I'd rather be brave than almost anything.'[57]

In theory, people are now more sympathetic to the psychological casualties of war, whom they do not necessarily any longer denounce as cowards. There is a recognition that every man has his limits, and that there is 'no clear-cut distinction between the weak and the strong, the "honourable" and the "dishonourable".'[58] Asked how they would react to a colleague or subordinate who was unable to control his or her fear, only one officer interviewed for this book expressed a negative sentiment: 'I wouldn't think much of the guy. … They've let the team down.' Others said that they 'would be sympathetic. It's normal to expect it. Everyone would cave at some point.' 'Is he acting dishonourably? That's probably too strong a word. That's just the way some people are'. 'I would not consider it disgraceful. I would not hold it against an individual. We all have our tolerance levels. We had people in Desert Storm who couldn't cope, and were sent home, but that's o.k.' 'We've come on, with ideas of PTSD [Post Traumatic Stress Disorder] etc. I would not hold them accountable … It's not in everybody's nature [to be courageous].'[59]

The ordinary soldier in a fighting unit on the front line seems to have a rather different attitude. In Iraq, Evan Wright observed Marines abusing a colleague they suspected of being a coward, calling him, 'fucking pussy', 'fucking pussy wimp', 'scared little bitch'. Sergeant Brad Colbert of the Marine reconnaissance battalion in Iraq told Wright that, 'his life is driven by a simple philosophy: "You don't want to ever show fear or back down, because you don't want to be embarrassed in front of the pack".'[60] 'The judgement of the pack', noted Wright, 'is relentless and unmerciful.'[61]

Wright also commented that, as well as courage, the US Marines valued strength, 'hardness', and an ability to kill – in short, their primary value appeared to be old-fashioned prowess:

> Among them [Marines], few virtues are celebrated more than being hard – having stronger muscles, being a better fighter, being more able to withstand pain and privation. They refer to extra comforts – foam sleeping pads, sweaters, even cold medicine – as 'snivel gear', and relentlessly mock those who bring it as pussies.[62]

This has the preposterous effect of inducing soldiers to forego equipment which would make their life in battle more comfortable (and thus probably make them more efficient) in order to gain honour through showing their toughness.

The emphasis on prowess creates a desire for a reputation as an efficient killer. A Marine corps chaplain told Wright in the middle of the Iraq war that:

> Many of them [the Marines] have sought my counsel because they feel guilty … But when I ask them why, they say they feel bad because they haven't had a chance to fire their weapons. They worry that they haven't done their job as Marines. … The zeal these young men have for killing surprises me.[63]

While their own sense of honour remains strong, US forces have sometimes failed to remember that the enemy also has honour to defend. Tactics used by the occupation forces to tackle the insurgency in Iraq have too often served to humiliate Iraqis. As an Iraqi told Mark Danner in the city of Fallujah, one of the centres of resistance to American occupation:

> For Fallujans it is a *shame* to have foreigners break down their doors. It is a *shame* for them to have foreigners stop and search their women. It is a *shame* for the foreigners to put a bag over their heads, to make a man lie on the ground with your shoe on his neck. This is a great *shame*, you understand. This is a great *shame* for the whole tribe. It is the *duty* of that man, of that tribe, to get revenge on this soldier – to kill that man. Their duty is to attack them, to *wash the shame*. The shame is a *stain*, a dirty thing: they have to *wash* it. No sleep – we cannot sleep until we have revenge. They have to kill soldiers. ... The Americans *provoke* the people. They don't *respect* the people.[64]

As James Bowman says: 'The real reason for the acts of war committed by both sides is not a species of sickness but the old imperatives of honor that we have almost forgotten.'[65]

Honour and rewards

Nowadays soldiers no longer receive monetary rewards or prize money in the manner of old. The prevailing sentiment is one expressed by an officer in an interview for this book: 'I'm not in it for the money.'[66] The notion of financial reward is actually somewhat despised.

This has left modern Western armies with only two means of honouring their soldiers: promotions and medals. Soldiers appear to value the latter more highly. Asked which they would prefer as recognition of their excellence, personnel interviewed by the author said: 'Medals. It's a pride thing, showing that someone valued you ... the people that know, know they don't just give out this medal'; 'Medals are more unique'; 'Promotion is not a reward but recognition of someone's ability to work at a given rank', said one officer, whereas a medal 'is recognition of conduct above and beyond, and shows the troops that this person has done something.' Soldiers expressed the feeling that such recognition was important: 'If you do well, you need to be recognized in front of your troops.'[67]

The deeds which garner the most important medals have changed since the nineteenth century. In the American Civil War, US soldiers most often won the Medal of Honor for capturing or rescuing a battle flag. Now, rescuing comrades is the most common cause mentioned in citations for the highest awards.[68] The most significant medals awarded by the British after the invasion of Iraq were a Victoria Cross and a George Cross, both given to soldiers for rescuing comrades while under fire.

A second change is that awards have become, at least officially, more egalitarian, in that they are supposedly no longer dependent on rank. Having said that, it remains the case that the more senior one's position, the more likely one is to win a medal, even a medal for gallantry. A list of medals granted to the American brigade which captured Baghdad in 2003 shows that of 26 Silver Stars, four went to colonels, 11 to captains, and only 11 to non-commissioned officers. Private soldiers did not receive any. Of 104 Bronze Stars with a 'V' for valour, 32 went to officers, and 72 to other ranks, including four privates. Of 275 plain Bronze Stars, 149 went to officers, 133 to non-commissioned officers, and only three to privates. Purple Hearts, which go to those who are wounded, and thus perhaps represent better the actual level of danger troops were in, were rather differently distributed. Of 88 Purple Hearts, ten went to officers, 36 to non-commissioned officers, and 42 to privates.[69]

What these figures suggest is that higher ranked personnel are more visible to those who grant medals, and that medals are used for reasons other than honouring bravery. In Vietnam the US military leadership seems to have tried to use them as a tool for raising morale by dealing them out with apparent abandon. The 'ultimate absurdity', according to Gabriel and Savage, was the 'presentation of award "packages" … Under this practice a stipulated number and type of medal was automatically given to individuals depending upon their rank and position.'[70] The result was that medals lost much of their value. Tim O'Brien described his work processing the paperwork for medals in his battalion headquarters: 'We dispensed awards – Purple Hearts, one and the same for a dead man or a man with a scraped fingernail; Bronze Stars for valor, mostly for officers who know how to lobby.'[71] Another veteran went even further: 'Medals are a farce', he said, 'Officers get them for just being there, you know. They give them to each other.'[72]

The Iraq war has brought similar complaints of medal inflation. After the initial conquest of Iraq, the US Air Force handed out over 69,000 medals, commendations and other awards, and the US Army 40,000 (an odd contrast, since most Army soldiers were in considerably more danger in the war than most Air Force personnel). These figures include over 2,000 Bronze Stars for the Air Force and 17,000 for the Army, a ratio of 91 medals per fatality for the former, and 27–1 for the latter. Only the Marine Corps seems to have kept the inflation in check, awarding about 1,000 medals, a ratio of a mere three medals per fatality. Clearly, different services adopt very different practices when giving out honours. Noting a case in which the crew of a B2-B bomber received the Distinguished Flying Cross for dropping a bomb on a Baghdad restaurant in which Saddam Hussein was suspected (incorrectly) of being, retired US Colonel David Hackworth complained:

> In World War II, when I saw a Distinguished Flying Cross that meant the guy had made 25 or 30 missions over dangerous places like Hamburg or Berlin. Those places sometimes had 50 percent casualty rates. Now, they give medals out to guys who fly bombers invisible to radar whose bombs miss Saddam and kill civilians in a restaurant. It's an outrage.[73]

Medals seem to generate the most excitement not among those who get them but among those who resent others getting them. Medal winners in the modern world tend to adopt a rather nonchalant attitude. It is no longer considered honourable to boast. Besides, the modest medal winner gains honour twice – once for his bravery, and again for his modesty. VC winners have a reputation for humility.[74]

Occasional examples of unabashed medal hunting do still occur. In the Korean War, for instance, a Canadian officer arrived at his unit and announced that he planned to win the Victoria Cross. Lieutenant Doug Banton then led his men straight into an ambush and died.[75] This is perhaps exceptional. Still, even if most soldiers do not quite so actively seek rewards, they undoubtedly value them when they receive them, and dislike seeing them in the hands of others they regard as unworthy.

Honour and death

In the nineteenth century, Romantic notions attached a degree of glory to death in combat. Military personnel interviewed for this book mostly did not see it that way. 'Dying for your country is one thing, but dying for a good cause could have glory in it', said one officer, but most considered death simply to be an unavoidable hazard of their chosen profession: 'If I die doing what I'm tasked to do, so be it. It's part of the profession'; 'There's a certain amount of honour and glory in that, but we don't do it for that … you do it for your country, you do it for the cause, you don't do it for the glory'; 'I don't want to die for my country', one even stated.[76]

Methods of burying and honouring the war dead are currently in transition. Many of the British soldiers who died in the Falklands War of 1982 remain in graves in the Falkland Islands, thousands of miles from their homes; their presence there serves a political purpose, committing Britain to continue to defend the islands thereafter. On the other hand, the British dead of the two Iraq Wars of 1991 and 2003 were brought home to be buried, and were interred in civilian cemeteries. Not all favour this. Some feel that the grave of a soldier in a war cemetery is an honoured site, whereas the grave of a soldier in a country churchyard back home risks being seen as just another grave.[77]

Nevertheless, apart from the Falklands War, there does seem to be consensus that the dead should return home. This expectation is especially strong in the United States, whose military now spends about $100 million a year on operations to search for and identify missing war dead in Vietnam and other former battlefields.[78]

Failure to retrieve bodies is considered deeply shameful. In Vietnam, the 2nd Battalion of the 12th Cavalry Regiment had to leave behind the bodies of 11 of its soldiers when it broke out of an encirclement during the Tet Offensive of 1968. The battalion's intelligence officer, Charles Krohn, wrote many years later that though this was 'the right decision', 'we learned later that there was considerable unhappiness over our leaving the dead behind. Some former members of the division haven't forgiven us yet.'[79]

The result is that, as in Ancient Greece, battles are fought to determine the fate of bodies. The most famous example of this is the fighting in Mogadishu in

October 1993. After Somali fighters shot down an American Black Hawk helicopter, the Americans fought a long and desperate battle to rescue the bodies of the helicopter crew. As the American commander, Major General William F. Garrison, said: 'Our creed would not allow us to leave the body of the pilot pinned in the wreckage.'[80] Most American soldiers do not regard this as a mistake. 'Would I risk my life to save your remains and bring them back to your family?', a US officer asked this author. 'Yes, I would', he answered himself, 'Soldiers will fight harder if they know that.'[81]

While the US military considers burying its dead to be a sacrosanct duty, it does not seem to feel a corresponding duty towards the enemy dead. In the First and Second World Wars (excluding the Eastern Front), all belligerents, wherever possible, gave the enemy dead an individual burial, kept records of their names, and informed their opponents via the Red Cross. Before the Iraq war of 2003, US authorities did issue orders concerning the treatment of enemy dead. In practice, says Oliver Poole, American soldiers rapidly forgot the orders to bury Iraqis facing Mecca and simply bulldozed them higgledy-piggledy into mass graves.[82]

Treatment of Vietnamese dead was often much worse. Although it would be a mistake (as well as insulting to the majority who refrained from such abuses) to regard mistreatment of enemy bodies as standard practice in Vietnam, stories of such actions are sufficiently widespread to suggest that it was quite common.

Veteran Alan Camden, for instance, stated that 'I saw officers and sergeants order men to mutilate the bodies of the enemy dead', and Robert Bower described seeing his fellow soldiers bulldozing Vietnamese dead into a hole and then shooting and bayoneting the corpses.[83] Numerous accounts speak of soldiers with collections of ears taken from the bodies of dead Vietnamese – either pickled in jars, or dried and hung on string. Even officers participated in this gruesome practice, which seems to have been perceived as bringing honour to those who could display their martial prowess through such trophies.[84]

Such behaviour does not receive official approval. It represents a sub-culture which is officially disparaged and punished if exposed. Nonetheless, abusive practices persist.

Honour and the conduct of war

Formal codes of law have now replaced informal codes of honour as arbiters of the conduct of war. This change dates back to the Hague Conventions at the end of the nineteenth century. Later additional laws, such as the Geneva Conventions, codified many of the idealistic concepts of chivalry as well as more modern ideas of correct behaviour. But the laws of war are often broken. This is especially true when the enemy hides among the civil population, and it is difficult to distinguish combatant from non-combatant. In these situations, the temptation to target both equally sometimes becomes too great to resist. A notorious example is the massacre by American troops of the population of the village of My Lai in Vietnam. It would be absolutely wrong to consider My Lai typical of American behaviour in Vietnam. It was not, however, unique, and not everybody thought that what happened there was inexcusable. A Major Callicles told Tim O'Brien: 'When you go into My Lai you assume the *worst.* … They're all VC, you should know that. But those so-called children are killers. … Can't you see we're trying to win a war here?'[85]

'We started to burn down all the hootches [huts] with matches and lighters', said Terry Whitmore of a massacre in which he participated in Vietnam:

> There were people inside them. When they tried to come out we shot them. … That was the only massacre I was in. But civilians got killed almost every day if we were about. … Prisoners? We didn't take any prisoners.[86]

Even when Americans did not kill Vietnamese civilians, they humiliated and harassed them. During searches, said Gary Gianninoto, 'we'd go though villages, burning down hootches, trampling the crops, killing the livestock, then throwing grenades in the bunkers.'[87] Another soldier described a typical search operation:

> We would go through a village before dawn, rousting everybody out of bed, and kicking down doors and dragging them out if they didn't move fast enough. They all had underground bunkers inside their huts to protect themselves against bombing and shelling. But to us the bunkers were Vietcong hiding places, and we'd blow them up with dynamite, and blow the huts up too. If we spotted extra rice lying around, we'd confiscate it to keep them from giving it to the Vietcong. … [Villagers were] herded like cattle into a barbed wire compound, and left to sit there in the hot sun for the rest of the day. … they'd be beaten pretty badly, maybe tortured. Or they might be hauled off to jail, and God knows what happened to them. At the end of the day, the villagers would be turned loose. Their homes had been wrecked, their chickens killed, their rice confiscated.[88]

The behaviour of the French and the British in their post-Second War World colonial wars was often much worse. Combatting the Mau Mau guerrillas in Kenya in the 1950s, British troops committed many atrocities.[89] 'I was surprised', said one British witness, 'to find that many reasonable educated people … supported this idea of arresting a hundred people from nowhere, just shooting thirty, and sending the seventy to tell the tale of who was boss.'[90] Police officer Peter Bostock recalled that on one occasion,

> With two other Europeans I was questioning an old man. … One of the white men set his dog at the old fellow. The animal got him to the ground, ripped open his throat, and started mauling his chest and arms. In spite of his screams, my companions just laughed.[91]

Indiscriminate tactics continue. In Iraq, poor intelligence means that it is often difficult to identify men suspected of insurgent activities. Coalition forces have on occasion arrested entire housing blocks when they thought an insurgent might be living somewhere in them. Troops smash open doors in the middle of the night, upturn private belongings, drag out all the men and older boys, bind and hood them, and take them away to unknown destinations for indefinite periods of time. Most are guilty of nothing.

One should note that this does represent restraint of a sort. Coalition forces in Iraq could, if they wished, simply massacre everybody (as American forces in Vietnam could also have done). They do not (and did not). Moreover, there are many soldiers who go out of their way, even at risk to their own lives, to minimize harm to civilians. General Tony Zinni, for example, has described how in Vietnam some Vietcong guerrillas fled on boats among a civilian fishing fleet. When a colleague suggested firing artillery on the fleet, Zinni instead led some South Vietnamese marines on their own boats in pursuit of the Vietcong. This was riskier, but proved successful. The guerrillas were killed, and no civilians were harmed.[92]

In some cases, it is obvious that soldiers consider the use of excessive force to be incompatible with the honour of the profession of arms. In his book *Bravo Two Zero*, Andy McNab of the British Special Air Service tells how his patrol met an old goatherd while on a secret mission deep in Iraq during the 1991 Gulf War. McNab considered killing the man, lest he raise the alarm and summon the Iraqi army, but refrained from doing so, saying, ‘It was the SAS we were in, not the SS.’[93] In Iraq in 2003, Evan Wright repeatedly heard soldiers give instructions not to fire for fear that innocent bystanders might be hit. After a platoon commander told his men to put their own protection first, Sergeant Mike Wynn countermanded him, saying ‘Don’t fucking waste a mother or a kid. … don’t hurt them, even if you can justify it later under our ROE [rules of engagement].’[94] When a battalion commander declared an airfield a free fire zone and said, ‘Everyone on the field is declared hostile’, Captain Paterson told Wright, ‘There’s no fucking way I’m going to pass that on to my men.’[95]

Such high-mindedness is somewhat limited by the modern leadership’s concern for ‘force protection’. Contemporary officer training lays great stress on a style of leadership which suggests that an officer’s primary concern is for his subordinates. This, combined with a political unwillingness to see heavy casualties in war, produces a feeling that an honourable officer is one who brings all his troops home. As Lieutenant Dave Stephen told cadets at West Point about his tour of duty in Bosnia: ‘a lot of stuff over there to me wasn’t worth losing a soldier. So you just gotta remember, in any kind of confrontation, your number one thing is to get all these guys back home.’[96]

The modern officer faces a number of conflicting duties. His honour demands that he complete his mission, that he avoid harming innocent civilians, and that he protect the lives of his own men. Asked whether they would put their troops at risk in order to protect civilians (even ‘enemy’ civilians), officers interviewed for this book gave different answers. Some said that they would put civilians first: ‘If I wasn’t willing to risk my life, I wouldn’t have the uniform on’, ‘I’m paid to risk my life, civilians aren’t. I’m paid to protect them’, and so forth; while others said,

'I would reduce the risk to my troops. Overall, I want to protect my folks', and 'As a commander you have to go with your troops'; and still others saw it as a question of scale: 'One soldier for lots of civilians, yes; but not hundreds of soldiers for one civilian.'[97]

Americans seem to place a much higher value on force protection than other nationalities. One Canadian officer with experience of working with American soldiers told the author, 'I think the Americans go way, way overboard on force protection, to a ridiculous extent. For them force protection is everything.'[98] Many others have made the same observation.[99]

The force protection priority has important effects on military strategy. For instance, during NATO's 1999 military campaign against Yugoslavia, NATO chose to use only air power even though aircraft could not in the short term prevent the atrocities which NATO leaders said were being committed by Yugoslav forces on the ground in Kosovo. In addition, NATO commanders concentrated their bombing on less-defended civilian targets with the aim of forcing the Yugoslav people to put pressure on their government to surrender.[100] The desire to protect servicemen's lives turned a war supposedly fought for humanitarian objectives into a war essentially directed against civilians. Unsurprisingly, many denounced this policy. Canadian military commentator Gwynne Dwyer called it 'a coward's strategy',[101] while the French general Philippe Morillon pointedly asked, 'Who are these soldiers who are ready to kill, but not ready to die?'[102] In conversations with military personnel of all ranks, the author has found many who supported both the war against Yugoslavia and the methods used, but also many others who felt that the methods were unacceptable. There is a sense, at least among some, that it was not quite honourable.

Pursuit of military objectives can also be disrupted, even today, by soldiers engaging in acts of extreme recklessness solely to prove their courage. According to Captain Dane Maddox, who flew the helicopter of Lieutenant Colonel Bob Gregory in Vietnam, Gregory liked to 'fly in harm's way so the enemy could engage his aircraft. … He felt this approach … would enhance his reputation and improve his chance of promotion.' Instead, it got him killed.[103]

During the attack on Baghdad in 2003 Captain Ed Ballanco was ordered to lead a supply convoy up the heavily defended Highway 8 into the city. He understood that it would be best for him to travel in the one available M113 armoured personnel carrier, not just because it was safer but because it had three radios and would help him communicate with the convoy. It was the best place from which to lead. But, as David Zucchino recounts, Ballanco felt that 'he'd look like a coward in front of his men', if he went in the well-protected M113. He travelled instead in a lightly armoured and much more vulnerable vehicle. He survived the journey.[104]

Whole units may base their plans on such logic. During the Vietnam War, the 2nd Battalion, 12 Cavalry Regiment, advanced from its base (named PK-17) towards the city of Hué, only to find itself surrounded. As Charles Krohn recalls: 'The safest thing to do, we thought, would be to retrace our steps to PK-17, but that seemed kind of cowardly.'[105] The battalion instead elected to break out in the direction of Hué, even though this did not contribute to the relief of that city, as the battalion lacked the strength to help in any great way.

During the Vietnam War many Americans were unwilling to 'rock the boat' by questioning things they knew to be wrong or by telling superiors things they knew their superiors did not want to know.[106] The actual (as opposed to theoretical) honour code of the time put more emphasis on loyalty to fellow soldiers than to loyalty to the truth.[107] On occasion, soldiers deliberately deceived their superiors. Tim O'Brien notes that:

> At night we were supposed to send out ambushes ... Sometimes we did, other times we did not. If the officers decided that the men were too tired or too restless for an night's ambush, they would prepare a set of grid coordinates and call them into battalion headquarters. It would be a false report, a fake. ... Phony ambushes were good for morale.[108]

One reason for such behaviour was the absurd pressures exerted by the military system. US commanders in Vietnam were obsessed with the 'body count' of dead Vietcong and their subordinates felt obliged to indicate that they had killed large numbers of guerrillas. As a result they often simply fabricated the figures. 'It was easier to fake than to count', confessed intelligence officer Charles Krohn.[109]

Few if any soldiers were willing to expose the falsifications, for fear of being deemed disloyal. Another intelligence officer, Eric McAllister Smith, discovered this when he reported to his superior that the 'blacklist' containing names of suspected Vietcong was so inaccurate as to be useless. 'Lieutenant Smith, I don't want to hear any more about that', his supervisor told him, 'I'm not going to be the one to tell Saigon that its blacklist system is totally fucked up. Now just go back to what you were doing, and let's pretend you never even came in here.'[110]

Such examples illustrate exactly why military forces preach honesty and integrity to their soldiers. Since Vietnam, the US military has put an admirable effort into improving the moral education of its troops, but some willingness to cover up, lie, or at least to play along with the prevailing current of opinion rather than challenge false assumptions, remains. For instance, US soldiers in Iraq told a journalist from the British newspaper *The Independent on Sunday* that, 'they do not tell their superiors about attacks on them unless they suffer casualties. This avoids bureaucratic hassle and "our generals want to hear about the number of attacks going down not up".'[111] Many of the false prognoses about Iraqi capabilities which preceded the 2003 invasion emerged from the Department of Defense's own Defense Intelligence Agency, which promoted its own version of intelligence to support government policy. When the head of the US Army, General Eric K. Shinseki, rightly said that the United States would need many more men than planned to pacify Iraq after an invasion, almost nobody came to his support. General Zinni commented: 'In the lead-up to the Iraq war and its later conduct, I saw, at a minimum, true dereliction, negligence, and irresponsibility; at worst, lying, incompetence, and corruption.'[112] American soldiers are continuing to pay for that with their lives.

Honour and the enemy

Modern wars are fought within an ideological framework, rather like the religious wars of the sixteenth and seventeenth centuries, or the crusades of the Middle Ages. The word 'duty' which dominated in the nineteenth century has largely disappeared, while talk of freedom and a desire to promote democracy has become more common. Being a 'force for good' has even become an official role of the British armed forces.[113]

As we have seen, the general public in modern Western societies is less sensitive to matters of insulted honour than it once was. For the public to accept a war, it seems that it must be fought to resist and destroy some 'evil'. The usual companion of modern war, therefore, is a propaganda campaign to persuade the public that the enemy are debased and evil people who must be destroyed.

Modern wars often do involve enemies who do not abide by the laws of war, and so we now begin our wars with a perception that our opponents are dishonourable. One consequence of this has been to complete the process of discrediting the practice of parole, since one should obviously not give one's word to 'evil' opponents. The Korean War of 1950–1953 marked the official end of parole. The North Koreans succeeded in persuading some captured Western troops to denounce their own governments. It was then seen as necessary to prohibit troops from treating with the enemy in any fashion after their capture. After the war, President Eisenhower endorsed a new 'Code of Conduct for Members of the Armed Forces of the United States', which stipulates that 'I will not accept parole nor any special favours from the enemy.'[114] A double standard operates, however, as Western armies still extract paroles from their enemies. After the conquest of Iraq in 2003, for instance, thousands of Iraqi troops were released from captivity after signing parole agreements 'in which they pledged not to engage in any "hostile actions" against coalition forces'.[115] In this instance, at least, the British and Americans demanded of enemy soldiers behaviour which they would consider dishonourable in their own.

Some military personnel interviewed for this book felt that their enemies in contemporary wars would not be honourable, but also said that they should not lower their standards as a result. 'It should not affect the way I behave toward them at all', said one. 'It doesn't matter whether they are honourable or not, according to the law of armed conflict. You obey the Geneva Convention regardless of their behaviour', said another. 'We should treat them with respect anyway … barbarity begets barbarity', said a third.[116]

Others are less forgiving. According to Davida Kellogg, who has taught American officer cadets for many years, it has become increasingly difficult to persuade them of the need to treat the enemy with honour and to abide by the laws of war. Some cadets display 'intense and sustained resistance to expectations of their chivalrous behaviour'.[117] 'There is a sense in these young people that winning at all costs is the right answer', an officer at the US Naval Academy also told the author of this book.[118] Some commissioned officers share this perspective. Regarding the use of torture on prisoners, one officer told this author, 'I don't have a problem with working on them to get information. We're in a global war on terror in which our very culture is at stake. … We should keep these prisoners and work on them.'[119]

This attitude translates into the occasional use of excessive force on the battlefield. One American soldier told Oliver Poole during the invasion of Iraq: 'We should be killing everything. It's what they deserve. These people have no regard for human life', while Captain James Montgomery told him: 'The values of the American soldier are ultimately humanitarian. … But we can't abide by the original rules anymore.'[120]

Religious belief cements this attitude, especially among troops of the US armed forces, who are remarkably religious compared with the members of other Western forces. 'The enemy', declared US General William G. Boykin about the 'Global War on Terror', 'is a guy named Satan.'[121] 'The enemy has got a face', agreed a Marine lieutenant-colonel before the November 2004 assault on Fallujah, 'He's called Satan. He lives in Fallujah.'[122] What one does with such evil is exterminate it. Marine Corps Major General James N. Mattis told troops:

> You are helping us to *kill* the enemy. Let's not make any mistakes about this. Let's not try to sugarcoat it. You are assisting my marines to *kill* evil. To *bayonet* it, to *shoot* it with machine guns, to *cut* its eyes out and *shit* in the sockets. And you can take pride in that. You can take pride in knowing that you had a hand in gouging out the eyes and cutting out the tongue of evil.[123]

The most alarming thing about this speech is that the men and women to whom Mattis delivered it were US Army interrogators in Afghanistan. This talk of 'gouging out eyes' and 'cutting out tongues' was directed at personnel charged with handling enemy prisoners of war. It is hardly surprising that it subsequently came to light that US troops abused and occasionally even killed prisoners in both Afghanistan and Iraq.

Pictures showing prisoner abuse at Abu Ghraib prison in Iraq outraged public opinion both in America and throughout the world and made it clear that such behaviour is considered deeply shameful. Still, the prison abuses were at least in part a product of an environment which said to the troops guarding prisoners that these were men who were beyond the bounds of the code of honour. The US government decision to deprive prisoners held in Guantanamo Bay of their rights as prisoners of war, new and looser codes of conduct regarding interrogation techniques issued by the US Department of Defense, and a general endorsement of the view that in the War on Terror 'the gloves must come off', did not explicitly authorize prisoner abuse, but did make it more likely.

On the whole, fortunately, one must recognize that contemporary soldiers treat their opponents in a fashion which by historical standards is extremely humane. Even the most dangerous suspects in the War on Terror, while deprived of their legal rights, live in relative security while in American or British hands. While Oliver Poole cites the US soldiers he lived with during the Iraq war as considering Iraqi soldiers 'barely human', Evan Wright describes an American captain being relieved of his command for attacking a prisoner during the same war, as well as US soldiers extending aid to captured enemies, and providing them with food and water out of their own rations.[124]

Honour and the ending of wars

The tendency to demonize the enemy in modern wars makes it hard to make peace. When fighting 'evil', anything less than absolute victory is unacceptable. Negotiating with an enemy requires a recognition of some form of equality, yet to give such recognition after portraying the enemy as demonic suggests either that one has partially capitulated or that one was not being entirely truthful about the enemy's nature. Neither is compatible with honour and dignity.

As a result, modern Western states prefer to issue ultimata to their opponents. States no longer formally declare war, and they very rarely end their wars through formally negotiated peace treaties. Just like the mediaeval knights, at best they manage to agree on ceasefires. The Korean War has still not officially ended, no peace treaty ever having succeeded the 1953 ceasefire. The United States left Vietnam under the terms of a 1973 ceasefire, which the North subsequently broke, and the war ended only with the North's absolute victory in 1975. The Falklands War of 1982 ended when the British captured all the Argentine troops on the Falkland Islands, but the two sides did not then sit down to formalize the end of hostilities on paper. Fighting in the Gulf War of 1991 officially halted with a ceasefire, but Anglo-American accusations that Iraq was in breach of its terms meant that British and American aircraft continued to bomb Iraq for the next 12 years before invading the country in 2003. At the time of writing, the war begun by that invasion has not ended either. Western states, it seems, are very good at starting wars but extremely bad at ending them.

We fight, apparently, for absolute precedence, and only firm evidence of failure after protracted war (as in Vietnam) is likely to persuade us to settle for anything less. Even then it may be necessary to engage in a certain amount of deceit in order to create the image that one has achieved 'victory'. In a perverse way, it may be necessary to lie in order to make peace.

US President Richard Nixon once told a friend, 'If you can't lie, you'll never go anywhere.'[125] He proclaimed that his goal in Vietnam was not 'victory', but 'peace with honour'. This allowed him to end the war short of winning it. In fact, America suffered a terrible defeat in Vietnam, but in its external sense honour is purely a matter of opinion. Nixon was able to create a temporary impression of partial success which allowed retreat to appear as honourable withdrawal. By the time the bad news was clear, somebody else was president.

As early as December 1966, Robert McNamara was warning that the war could not be won in a military sense, and that a diplomatic solution was necessary. However, many others argued against making any concessions to the North Vietnamese, lest these be interpreted as signs of weakness.[126] Direct negotiations with the North did not begin until May 1968, and dragged on fruitlessly for many years. The real negotiating went on behind the scenes in secret between Secretary of State Henry Kissinger and his Vietnamese counterpart Le Duc Tho – in terms of honour, secret negotiations have the great advantage that one can make concessions without losing face before the public. Eventually, Kissinger settled for a 'standstill ceasefire' in which the US would withdraw its forces, while North and South agreed that their troops would stand where they stood but not take any additional territory from each other.[127] In their hearts the Americans must have known that once their troops were gone, the South would fall to the North, as it did in 1975. But that was something for later. For now, the peace deal could be proclaimed as guaranteeing the South's independence, and that was good enough. Nixon also claimed that the South's army was strong enough to hold its own. After a bungled Southern invasion of Laos in 1971, he had proclaimed that 'Vietnamization has succeeded.'[128] By such distortions of the truth, a peace which might otherwise have appeared shameful could be sold as 'peace with honour'.

In Iraq and elsewhere, the struggle of the next few years will more probably be to find peace with honour than it will be to find a way to achieve victory. The sooner people realize this, as Nixon realized it in Vietnam, the sooner peace is likely to come.

Honour and women

In the three thousand years covered by this book, there have been many changes, but one constant was the masculine nature of war. Now, even this is beginning to change. The war in Iraq has taken the lives of female as well as male combatants. Women remain a minority within Western armed forces, but they have arrived.

The Russians led the way in this regard. In 1914 a factory worker by the name of Maria Bochkareva petitioned Tsar Nicholas II to be allowed to fight in the First World War. Once her request was granted, she served with distinction, winning several medals and rising to the rank of sergeant. In the aftermath of the revolution of March 1917 which overthrew Nicholas II, she observed the disintegration of Russia's army with despair. Thousands of soldiers deserted, and those who stayed in the ranks regularly refused to fight. Bochkareva proposed the creation of a women's unit, and the new government permitted her to form what became known as the Women's Battalion of Death. The unit had little military value. It was meant to appeal to the honour of the men, and shame them back into fighting. It failed dismally. Male soldiers continued to desert, and before long Russia had dropped out of the war.[129]

The women's battalion marked the start of a new trend. In the Second World War, the Soviet Union used numerous women in combat roles, especially as snipers and fighter pilots. Other European states lagged behind, and only in the 1990s began to allow women to serve in front line units (some armed forces still refuse to do so). Gradually, barriers to female personnel are falling away, and it seems likely that before long in most Western countries there will be no branch of the military in which they cannot serve.

Throughout this book, it has been clear that many wars are a product of men's desire to prove themselves to be in accordance with some ideal of the honourable man – to show their strength and courage, to gain precedence over each other, to avenge insult, and so on. As society loses interest in the virtues of the warrior male, the tendency to provoke war in order to display one's manhood should diminish. On the other hand, as women continue to encroach on previously male territory, some men may feel that their maleness is threatened. At the level of states or large populations, this can provoke war. Thus, Osama bin Laden has justified his terrorist activities by referring to the humiliation many Arabs felt when, after Iraq's 1990 invasion of Kuwait, they had to call on Americans (including American women) to defend the holy sites of Islam in Saudi Arabia:

> We believe that we are men. Muslim men who must have the honour of defending [Mecca]. We do not want American women soldiers defending [it] ... The rulers in that region have been deprived of their manhood. And they think that the people are women. By God, Muslim women refuse to be defended by these American and Jewish prostitutes.[130]

The acts of Islamist terrorists sometimes seem to serve no clear political purpose. Often the end may simply be to prove by action that Arab men are still men. Bin Laden supporter Suleiman Abu Gheith explained al-Qaeda's philosophy, saying:

> Tyranny only leaves humiliation. Perhaps they [the Americans] also thought that this [oppressive] atmosphere is sufficient to kill a man's virility, shatter his will and uproot his honour. These people erred twice: once when they ignored [the consequences of] treating man with contempt, and again when they were unaware of man's ability to triumph.[131]

Most people in the West probably regard such attitudes as mediaeval. However, the continued regard for strength in international politics suggests that perhaps the West's own attitudes are not so very different. Perhaps when women truly attain equal power in Western societies the view that one can only win honour through violence will finally wane.

Conclusion

There has been rapid change in the last century. The merging of male and female honour in recent years is possibly the most dramatic development. The expansion of the code of chivalry to include all combatants and now even all non-combatants is also important, and the diminishing importance of religious obligations is noticeable too. All is not as it was in the world of war and honour.

But for all the talk of honour's obsolescence, it clearly remains central to the waging of war. In this sense, nothing has changed since the age of Achilles. The desire to be a person of worth, to win a good reputation in the eyes of others, and to live up to one's own internal standards of honourable conduct, is as strong now as it ever has been. People continue to go to war to defend their honour; that honour still determines how they fight and the manner in which they treat their enemies; and matters of honour still affect the way in which wars are brought to an end.

Notes

1 For instance, Peter Berger, 'On the Obsolescence of the Concept of Honour', in Sandel, Michael J., (ed.), *Liberalism and Its Critics*, Oxford: Basil Blackwell, 1984, p. 151.
2 Robinson, Paul, '"Always with Honour": The Code of the White Russian Officers', *Canadian Slavonic Papers*, 1999, vol. 41, no. 2, 121–41.
3 Hermann, John, *The Knight-Monks of Vichy France: Uriage, 1940–1945*, Montreal and Kingston: McGill-Queen's University Press, 1993.
4 Coombs, William, 'Fatal Attraction: Duelling and the SS', *History Today*, June 1997, 11–16.
5 Interviews with the author.
6 de Botton, Alain, *Status Anxiety*, London: Hamish Hamilton, 2004, p. 85.
7 Miller, William Ian, *Humiliation and Other Essays on Honor, Social Discomfort, and Violence*, Cornell Unversity Press, 1993, pp. ix–x.
8 Marmot, Michael, *Status Syndrome*, London: Bloomsbury, 2004, passim.
9 de Botton, *Status Anxiety*, p. 194.
10 Miller, *Humiliation*, p. 10. See also, Heller, Agnes, *The Power of Shame: A Rational Perspective*, London: Routledge & Kegan Paul, 1985, p. 15.
11 For discussions of the history of the West Point honour code, see: Hansen, Richard P., 'The Crisis of the West Point Honor Code', *Military Affairs*, 1985, vol. 49, no. 2, 59. See also, Knowlton, William, 'Honor – the Setting', *Military Affairs*, 1985, vol. 49, no. 2, 62–4; and Crackel, Theodore J., *West Point: A Bicentennial History*, Lawrence: University Press of Kansas, 2002, passim.
12 *Cadet Honor Code and Honor System*, West Point: Center for the Professional Military Ethic, 2000, p. 1.
13 For a discussion of the honour code at Annapolis, see, for instance, Steffan, Joseph, *Honor Bound: A Gay Midshipman Fights to Serve his Country*, New York: Avon Books, 1992, p. 46.
14 *Cadet Honor Code and Honor System*, p. 1.
15 The information about the honour codes at West Point and Annapolis in this section derives from visits I undertook to those institutions in 2002.
16 For a comment of this sort, see Lipsky, David, *Absolutely American: Four Years at West Point*, New York: Vintage, 2003, p. 214.
17 *Values and Standards of the British Army: Commanders' Edition*, no publication details provided, 2000, pp. 6–11.
18 *Summary of Duty with Honour: The Profession of Arms in Canada*, Canadian Defence Academy, 2003, pp. 16–18.
19 *Values and Standards of the British Army*, pp. 3 and 12–13.
20 Interview with the author. Against this, many others told me that, given a choice, they would prefer a moral soldier to a technically proficient one – 'you must be able to trust people'.
21 O'Neill, Barry, *Honor, Symbols, and War*, Ann Arbor: University of Michigan Press, 2001, p. xii.
22 Ibid, pp. 103–5.
23 George W. Bush, cited in *The North Bay Nugget*, Thursday 5 September 2002, p. A.10.
24 Anthony Storr, cited in *The Sunday Times*, News Review section, 20 October 2002, p. 1.
25 Kaplan, Robert D., *Warrior Politics: Why Leadership Demands a Pagan Ethos*, New York: Vintage, 2002, p. 131.
26 Logevall, Fredrik, *The Origins of the Vietnam War*, Harlow: Pearson Education, 2001, p. 3.

27 Ibid, p. 46.
28 Lyndon Johnson, cited in Wyatt-Brown, Bertram, *The Shaping of Southern Culture: Honor, Grace, and War, 1760s to 1880s*, Chapel Hill: University of North Carolina Press, 2001, p. 299.
29 Karnow, Stanley, *Vietnam: A History*, New York: Penguin, 1984, p. 320.
30 Ibid, p. 375.
31 Mead, Walter Russell, *Special Providence: American Foreign Policy and How it Changed the World*, New York: Alfred A. Knopf, 2001, p. 88.
32 Ibid, p. 231. See also pp. 232–57.
33 Nisbett, Richard E. and Cohen, Dov, *Culture of Honor: The Psychology of Violence in the South*, Boulder: Westview, 1996, pp. 25 and 41.
34 Lind, Michael, *Made in Texas: George W. Bush and the Southern Takeover of American Politics*, New York: Basic Books, 2003, p. 130.
35 Ibid, pp. 159 and 193.
36 For a typical expression of this sentiment, see Steyn, Mark, 'Now it's up to Iraqis', *The Spectator*, 5 July 2004.
37 See Osama bin Laden's comments to this effect: interview with John Miller of ABC News, 1998.
38 Bowman, James, 'Whatever Happened to Honor?', The Bradley Lecture, American Enterprise Institute, 10 June 2002. Available online: http://www.jamesbowman.net/articleDetail.asp?pubID=1169 (accessed 20 July 2005).
39 Jack Straw, Speech to the UN Security Council, 14 February 2003.
40 Interview on BBC Newsnight, 21 April 2005.
41 *The Guardian*, 17 February 2003, p. 1.
42 Wong, Leonard, Kolditz, Thomas A., Millen, Raymond A. and Potter, Terrence M., *Why They Fight: Combat Motivation in the Iraq War*, Carlisle: Strategic Studies Institute, 2003, p. 9.
43 Wright, Evan, *Generation Kill: Living Dangerously on the Road to Baghdad with the Ultraviolent Marines of Bravo Company*, London: Bantam, 2004, p. 24.
44 Poole, Oliver, *Black Knights: On the Bloody Road to Baghdad*, London: Harper Collins, 2003, p. 232.
45 Karnow, *Vietnam*, p. 465.
46 Lane, Mark, *Conversations with Americans*, New York: Simon & Schuster, 1970, p. 229.
47 Shay, Jonathan, *Achilles in Vietnam: Combat Trauma and the Undoing of Character*, New York: Simon & Schuster, 1994, p. 9.
48 Gabriel, Richard A. and Savage, Paul L., *Crisis in Command: Mismanagement in the Army*, New York: Hill & Wang, 1978, p. 9.
49 Ibid, pp. 17 and 30.
50 Karnow, *Vietnam*, p. 466.
51 Poole, *Black Knights*, pp. 47–8.
52 Wong *et al.*, *Why They Fight*, p. 9.
53 Ibid, p. 10.
54 Wright, *Generation Kill*, p. 263.
55 O'Brien, Tim, *If I Die in a Combat Zone*, London: Calder & Boyars, 1973, p. 198.
56 Holmes, Richard, *Acts of War: The Behavior of Men in Battle*, New York: The Free Press, 1985, p. 142.
57 O'Brien, *If I Die*, p. 129.
58 Braudy, Leo, *From Chivalry to Terrorism: War and the Changing Nature of Masculinity*, New York: Alfred A. Knopf, 2003, p. 489.
59 Interviews with author.
60 Wright, *Generation Kill*, p. 23.
61 Ibid, p. 57.
62 Ibid, p. 21.

63 Ibid, pp. 182–3.
64 Danner, Mark, 'Torture and Truth', *The New York Review of Books*, 10 June 2004, 46.
65 Bowman, 'Whatever Happened to Honor?', p. 9.
66 Interview with the author.
67 Interviews with the author.
68 Miller, William Ian, *The Mystery of Courage*, Cambridge: Harvard University Press, 2002, p. 121.
69 Zucchino, David, *Thunder Run: Three Days in the Battle for Baghdad*, London: Atlantic, 2004, pp. 329–46.
70 Gabriel and Savage, *Crisis in Command*, p. 15.
71 O'Brien, *If I Die*, p. 172.
72 Lane, *Conversations*, p. 181.
73 West, Owen, 'Who Really Deserves a Silver Star?', *Slate*, 29 September 2004. Available online: http://slate.msn.com/id/2107438/ (accessed 20 July 2005). Also, Moran, Michael, 'Too many medals?', MSNBC, 12 February 2004. Available online: http://www.msnbc.msn.com/id/4243092/ (accessed 20 July 2005).
74 See Clarkson, Jeremy, 'You won't believe what it takes to get a VC today', *Sunday Times*, 2 November 2003.
75 Barris, Ted, *Deadlock in Korea: Canadians at War, 1950–1953*, Toronto: Macmillan Canada, 1999, pp. 245–7.
76 Interviews with the author.
77 For instance, Campbell, Curt, 'Where the War Dead Go', *National Post*, 3 May 2003, A16.
78 Swift, Earl, *Where They Lay: Searching for America's Lost Soldiers*, Boston and New York: Houghton Mifflin, 2003, p. 7.
79 Krohn, Charles A., *The Lost Battalion: Controversy and Casualties in the Battle for Hue*, Westport: Praeger, 1993, p. 109.
80 See Bowden, Mark, *Black Hawk Down*, London: Corgi, 2000, pp. 416 and 491.
81 Interview with the author.
82 Poole, *Black Knights*, p. 217.
83 Lane, *Conversations*, pp. 65 and 229.
84 O'Brien, *If I Die*, p. 79; Lane, *Conversations*, pp. 60, 65–6, 120–1, 123, 192–3, and 197.
85 O'Brien, *If I Die*, pp. 187–8.
86 Lane, *Conversations*, pp. 73 and 76.
87 Ibid, p. 210.
88 Karnow, *Vietnam*, pp. 467–8.
89 Elkins, Caroline, *Britain's Gulag: The Brutal End of Empire in Kenya*, London: Jonathan Cape, 2005, p. 66.
90 Ibid, p. 87.
91 Ibid, p. 86.
92 Clancy, Tom, with General Tony Zinni, *Battle Ready*, New York: G.P. Putnam's Sons, 2004, p. 61.
93 McNab, Andy, *Bravo Two Zero*, New York: Dell, 1993, p. 155.
94 Wright, *Generation Kill*, pp. 33–4.
95 Ibid, pp. 166–7. For other examples, see pp. 67, 93, 128, and 151–2.
96 Lipsky, *Absolutely American*, p. 14.
97 Interviews with the author.
98 Interview with the author.
99 For instance, Poole, *Black Knights*, pp. 213–14.
100 I have outlined this argument in more detail in '"Ready to Kill but not to Die": NATO Strategy in Kosovo', *International Journal*, 1999, vol. 54, no. 4, 671–82.
101 Dwyer, Gwynne, *Montreal Gazette*, 11 May 1999, B3.
102 Cited in Beevor, Antony, 'The Soldiers Preferred Margaret', *The New Statesman*, 19 April 1999, 11.

103 Krohn, *The Lost Battalion*, p. 35.
104 Zucchino, *Thunder Run*, p. 252.
105 Krohn, *The Lost Battalion*, p. 105.
106 Gabriel and Savage, *Crisis in Command*, p. 98.
107 Ibid, p. 114.
108 O'Brien, *If I Die*, pp. 102–3.
109 Krohn, *The Lost Battalion*, p. 140.
110 McAllister Smith, Eric, *Not by the Book: A Combat Intelligence Officer in Vietnam*, New York: Ivy, 1993, p. 52.
111 Cockburn, Patrick, 'Violent Upsurge in Iraq Destroys US Claims of a Return to Normality', *The Independent on Sunday*, 17 April 2005, 21.
112 Clancy, *Battle Ready*, p. 426.
113 Ministry of Defence, *Delivering Security in a Changing World*, Defence White Paper, December 2003, London: The Stationery Office, 2003, p. 20.
114 Rachaminov, Alon, *POWs and the Great War: Captivity on the Eastern Front*, Oxford and New York: Berg, 2002, p. 84. The code of conduct was subsequently amended in 1975 and 1988. The prohibition on giving parole is included in paragraph III. Oddly, the US Field Manual continues to state that soldiers who violate their parole are subject to punishment. This caters for situations where a soldier may give a temporary parole in special circumstances, such as promising to return to a prison camp after being temporarily released to visit a doctor outside the camp. Axinn, Sidney, *A Moral Military*, Philadelphia: Temple University Press, 1989, pp. 49–51.
115 'Pentagon: Most Iraqi Captives Released', *USA Today*, 9 May 2003, 4A.
116 Interviews with the author.
117 Kellogg, Davida, 'On the Importance of Having an Honorable Enemy'. Paper presented to the 4th Canadian Conference on Ethical Leadership, Royal Military College of Canada, November 2001.
118 Interview with the author.
119 Interview with the author.
120 Poole, *Black Knights*, pp. 109 and 129.
121 Boykin, cited in Lind, *Made in Texas*, p. 189.
122 Cited in Siddiqui, Haroon, 'For Many, Iraq Becoming a Crusade', *Toronto Star*, 11 November 2004.
123 General Mattis, cited in Mackey, Chris and Miller, Greg, *The Interrogators: Inside the Secret War Against Al Qaeda*, New York and Boston: Little Brown, 2004, p. 153.
124 Wright, *Generation Kill*, pp. 67 and 308.
125 Karnow, *Vietnam*, p. 577.
126 Ibid, pp. 481–2.
127 Ibid, pp. 623–7.
128 Ibid, p. 630.
129 Figes, Orlando, *A People's Tragedy: The Russian Revolution 1891–1924*, London: Jonathan Cape, 1996, p. 413.
130 Osama bin Laden, cited in Braudy, *From Chivalry to Terrorism*, p. 547.
131 Suleiman Abu Gheith, 'In the Shadow of the Lances'. Available online: http://www.memri.org/bin/articles.cgi?Area=middleeast&ID=SP38802 (accessed 20 July 2005).

9 Conclusion

The Second World War German Enigma encryption machine looked more or less like a typewriter, but used a series of dials which spun so that every time a letter was pressed, a different letter was printed. If you typed, for instance, 'A' twice, you might get first 'X' then 'Z', or any other combination. War is somewhat similar. It never turns out the same way twice, even when the inputs appear to us to be the same. As a result, it seems irrational. Yet, like the Enigma machine, it is actually quite logical; the problem is that it is far more complicated than it looks, so much so that we still have only the dimmest understanding of the way it works.

Because people fight for abstract notions like honour not as a means to other things (security, wealth, and so on), but as ends in themselves, they go to war even in circumstances where the possible benefits in terms of security, wealth and the rest are far outweighed by the probable losses. Because they are going to war for honour, rather than for some tangible goal, they are in effect fighting for the sake of fighting. The stated material goal of the war, whatever it may be, is merely the issue which put their honour on the line.

Only if this is understood can one begin to decrypt the workings of war. There is, for instance, nothing irrational about recklessness in war. True, it more often serves to undermine the cause than to promote it. Throughout this book, readers will have encountered numerous examples of military disaster resulting from glory-led rashness. But because men fight in order to fight, thereby proving their courage, manliness, and so forth, behaviour of this sort is entirely in keeping with the purpose of war. The immediate conclusion which arises from this is that strategists who like to think that they can use war to achieve material or political objectives, and that military force can be tightly focused on such goals, are suffering from delusions. Wars simply are not fought in that way. War is by its very nature unsuited to be a tool for policy. Alas, efforts in the post-Cold War era of some in the West to re-legitimize war, be it for 'humanitarian intervention', 'regime change', or 'pre-emptive strikes', show that many have failed to understand this.

The paradoxical results of honour's impact on war do not end there. It is often stated that a sense of honour helps limit violence and prevent atrocity. So it does. But it also does the opposite. In the first place, the very same sense of honour makes war likely in the first place, and so creates the conditions which make atrocity possible. Second, the desire to humiliate others, and thereby rise in relative status oneself, is a sad but common result of the sense of honour. Third, in order to show mercy, one first has to have somebody at one's mercy.

There has undoubtedly been progress in the timespan covered by this book. The honour group towards whom soldiers show restraint has grown enormously, so that now most – but still not always all – of humanity belongs to it. Having said that, the picture of war in this book is an almost unrelentingly grim one. Those who have a naïve faith that they can somehow fight in a 'clean' and humane fashion should probably read more history.

The paradoxes continue right through to the ending of wars. As with Flamininus and the Macedonians, or Queen Elizabeth I and the Earl of Tyrone, people may often be more lenient with their defeated enemies than with those they are still fighting. If the purpose of fighting is to defeat one's enemy so that one can impose one's will upon him, this makes no sense. The cause of this paradox is that negotiating with an enemy is a sign of weakness, whereas imposing a settlement on him is a sign of strength and provides an opportunity to display generosity. It is actually better for the victor to impose terms which favour the enemy than to negotiate ones which favour himself.

The only possible conclusion one can draw from these facts is that from a purely material point of view, unless one has actually been attacked and must fight in order to survive, war is a ridiculous activity. The main reason why it continues to happen in the Western world is that many continue to believe that their honour is linked to their willingness to fight. Over the ages, this link has weakened. Virtues other than prowess, strength, physical courage, and the like, have gradually risen in value in our societies. The inclination to war has, therefore, diminished.

Humans will always compete for honour. As peaceful virtues come increasingly to the fore, we can hope that the urge to war will decline still further, and that they will shift their competition to other arenas.

Bibliography

General works on honour

Abrams, Elliott (ed.), *Honor among Nations: Intangible Interests and Foreign Policy*, Washington DC: Ethics and Public Policy Center, 1998.

Bailey, F.G. (ed.), *Gifts and Poison: The Politics of Reputation*, Oxford: Blackwell, 1971.

Bechtel, Lyn M., 'Shame as a Sanction of Social Control in Biblical Israel: Judicial, Political, and Social Shaming', *Journal for the Study of the Old Testament*, 1991, no. 49, 47–76.

Berger, Peter, 'On the Obsolescence of the Concept of Honour', in Michael J. Sandel (ed.), *Liberalism and its Critics*, Oxford: Basil Blackwell, 1984.

Best, Geoffrey, *Honour among Men and Nations: Transformation of an Idea*, Toronto: Toronto University Press, 1982.

Blok, Anton, 'Rams and Billy-goats: A Key to the Mediterranean Code of Honour', *Man*, 1981, vol. 16, 427–40.

Botton, Alain de, *Status Anxiety*, London: Hamish Hamilton, 2004.

Boulay, Juliet du, *Portrait of a Greek Mountain Village*, Limni: Denise Harvey, 1994.

Bourdieu, Pierre, 'From the Rules of Honour to the Sense of Honour', in *Outline of a Theory of Practice*, Cambridge: Cambridge University Press, 1977.

Bowman, James, *Whatever Happened to Honor?* The Bradley Lecture, American Enterprise Institute, 10 June 2002. Online: http://www.jamesbowman.net/articleDetail.asp?pubID=1169 (accessed 20 July 2005).

Braudy, Leo, *The Frenzy of Renown: Fame and its History*, New York: Vintage, 1997.

Campbell, J.K., *Honour, Family, and Patronage: A Study of Institutions and Moral Values in a Greek Mountain Community*, Oxford: Clarendon Press, 1964.

Gray, J. Glenn, 'Ending with Honor', in Edward C. Luck and Stuart Albert (eds), *On the Ending of Wars*, Port Washington: Kennikat Press Corp., 1980, pp. 145–56.

Hatch, Elvin, 'Theories of Social Honor', *American Anthropologist*, 1989, vol. 91, no. 2, 341–53.

Heller, Agnes, *The Power of Shame: A Rational Perspective*, London: Routledge & Kegan Paul, 1985.

Herzfeld, Michael, 'Honour and Shame: Problems in the Comparative Analysis of Moral Systems', *Man*, 1980, vol. 15, no. 2, 339–51.

Honeth, Axel, *The Struggle for Recognition: The Moral Grammar of Social Conflicts*, Cambridge: Polity Press, 1995.

Ignatieff, Michael, *The Warrior's Honor: Ethnic War and the Modern Conscience*, London: Chatto & Windus, 1998.

Kollmann, Nancy Shields, *By Honor Bound: State and Society in Early Modern Russia*, Ithaca and London: Cornell University Press, 1999.

Kressel, Gideon, 'More on Honour and Shame', *Man*, 1988, vol. 23, no. 1, 167–70.

Lever, Alison, 'Honour as a Red Herring', *Critique of Anthropology*, 1986, vol. 6, no. 3, 83–106.

McNamee, Maurice B., *Honor and the Epic Hero: A Study of the Shifting Concept of Magnanimity in Philosophy and Epic Poetry*, New York: Rinehart & Winston, 1959.

Malina, Bruce J., *The New Testament World: Insights from Cultural Anthropology*, 3rd edition, Louisville: Westminster John Knox Press, 2001.

Marmot, Michael, *Status Syndrome: How Your Social Standing Directly Affects Your Health and Life Expectancy*, London: Bloomsbury, 2004.

Miller, William Ian, *Humiliation and Other Essays on Honor, Social Discomfort, and Violence*, Ithaca: Cornell Unversity Press, 1993.

——— *The Mystery of Courage*, Cambridge: Harvard University Press, 2002.

Neyrey, Jerome H., *Honor and Shame in the Gospel of Matthew*, Louisville: Westminster John Knox Press, 1998.

Olyan, Saul M., 'Honor, Shame, and Covenant Relations in Ancient Israel and its Environment', *Journal of Biblical Literature*, 1996, vol. 115, no. 2, 201–18.

O'Neill, Barry, *Honor, Symbols, and War*, Ann Arbor: University of Michigan Press, 2001.

Osiel, Mark J., *Obeying Orders: Atrocity, Military Discipline and the Law of War*, New Brunswick: Transaction, 2002.

Pedersen, John, *Israel: Its Life and Culture*, London: Oxford University Press, 1946.

Peristiany, J.G. (ed.), *Honour and Shame: The Values of a Mediterranean Society*, Chicago: University of Chicago Press, 1968.

Peristiany, J.G. and Pitt-Rivers, Julian (eds), *Honor and Grace in Anthropology*, Cambridge: Cambridge University Press, 1992.

Pitt-Rivers, Julian, 'Honor', in *Encyclopedia of the Social Sciences*, vol. 6, New York: Macmillan, 1968, pp. 503–11.

Scheider, Peter, 'Honor and Conflict in a Sicilian Town', *Anthropological Quarterly*, 1969, vol. 42, 130–54.

Sennett, Richard, *Respect: The Formation of Character in an Age of Inequality*, London: Allen Lane, 2003.

Stewart, Frank Henderson, *Honor*, Chicago: University of Chicago Press, 1994.

Taylor, Charles, 'The Politics of Recognition', in Amy Gutman (ed.), *Multiculturalism: Examining the Politics of Recognition*, Princeton: Princeton University Press, 1994, pp. 25–74.

Taylor, Gabriele, *Pride, Shame, and Guilt: Emotions of Self-Assessment*, Oxford: Clarendon Press, 1985.

Wikan, Unni, 'Shame and Honour: A Contestable Pair', 1984, *Man*, vol. 19, no. 4, 635–52.

General works on war

Axinn, Sidney, *A Moral Military*, Philadelphia: Temple University Press, 1989.

Blainey, Geoffrey, *The Causes of War*, London: Macmillan, 1973.

Borg, Alan, *War Memorials from Antiquity to the Present*, London: Leo Cooper, 1991.

Braudy, Leo, *From Chivalry to Terrorism: War and the Changing Nature of Masculinity*, New York: Alfred A. Knopf, 2003.

Brown, Seyom, *The Causes and Prevention of War*, New York: St. Martin's Press, 1987.

Browning, Christopher R., *Ordinary Men: Reserve Police Battalion 101 and the Final Solution in Poland*, London: Penguin, 2001.
Cashman, Greg, *What Causes Wars? An Introduction to Theories of International Conflict*, San Francisco: Lexington, 1993.
Cohen, Richard, *By the Sword: Gladiators, Musketeers, Samurai, Warriors, Swashbucklers and Olympians*, London: Pan, 2002.
French, Shannon, *The Code of the Warrior: Exploring Warrior Values Past and Present*, Lanham: Rowman and Littlefield, 2003.
Grossman, Lt. Col. Dave, *On Killing: The Psychological Cost of Learning to Kill in War and Society*, Boston and London: Little Brown, 1995.
Hastings, Max, *Warriors: Extraordinary Tales from the Battlefield*, London: HarperCollins, 2005.
Holmes, Richard, *Acts of War: The Behavior of Men in Battle*, New York: The Free Press, 1985.
Howard, Michael, Andreopoulos, George J., and Shulman, Mark R. (eds), *The Laws of War: Constraints on Warfare in the Western World*, New Haven: Yale University Press, 1994.
James, Lawrence, *Warrior Race: A History of the British at War*, London: Little, Brown & Company, 2001.
Kagan, Donald, *On the Origins of War and the Preservation of Peace*, New York: Anchor, 1995.
Keegan, John, *The Face of Battle: A Study of Agincourt, Waterloo and the Somme*, Harmondsworth: Penguin, 1976.
Markey, Daniel, 'Prestige and the Origins of War: Returning to Realism's Roots', *Security Studies*, 1999, vol. 8, no. 4, 126–73.
Robinson, Chione, 'A Theory of War Termination for Peacemakers', *Canadian Forces College Review*, 2000, 81–92.
Robinson, Paul, '"Always with Honour: The Code of the White Russian Officers', *Canadian Slavonic Papers*, 1999, vol. 41, no. 2, 121–41.
——— *The White Russian Army in Exile, 1920–1941*, Oxford: Clarendon Press, 2002.
Schivelbusch, Wolfgang, *The Culture of Defeat: On National Trauma, Mourning, and Recovery*, London: Granta, 2003.
Suganami, Hidemi, *On the Causes of War*, Oxford: Clarendon Press, 1996.
Wilkinson, Frederick, *Militaria*, Bungay: Richard Clay, 1969.

Ancient Greece

Classical sources

Aristotle, *The Art of Rhetoric*, trans. Hugh Lawson-Tancred, London: Penguin, 1991.
——— *Ethics*, trans. J.A.K. Thomson, revised by Hugh Tredennick, London: Penguin, 1976.
Arrian, *The Campaigns of Alexander*, trans. Aubrey de Sélincourt, London: Penguin, 1971.
Demosthenes, *Demosthenes' Public Orations*, trans. A.W. Pickard-Cambridge, London: Dent, 1963.
Euripides, *Euripides Plays: Two*, introduced by J.M. Walton, London: Methuen, 1991.
——— *Euripides Plays: Six*, trans. Frederic Raphael, Kenneth McLeish, and J. Michael Walton, London: Methuen, 1997.
Herodotus, *The Histories*, trans George Rawlinson, New York: Alfred A. Knopf, 1997.

Homer, *The Iliad: A New Prose Translation*, trans. Martin Hammond, Harmondsworth: Penguin, 1987.
——— *The Odyssey*, trans. E.V. Rieu, Harmondsworth: Penguin, 1978.
Pausanias, *Descriptions of Greece*, vol. 1, London: Heinemann, 1918.
Plutarch, *The Age of Alexander: Nine Greek Lives*, trans. Ian Scott-Kilvert, London: Penguin, 1973.
——— *Plutarch on Sparta*, trans. R.J.A. Talbert, London: Penguin, 1988.
——— *The Rise and Fall of Athens: Nine Greek Lives*, trans. Ian Scott-Kilvert, London: Penguin, 1973.
Sophocles, *Electra and Other Plays*, trans E.F. Watling, Harmondsworth: Penguin, 1953.
Thucydides, *History of the Peloponesian War*, trans Rex Warner, London: Penguin, 1972.
Xenophon, *Anabasis*, trans. Carleton L. Browson, Cambridge: Harvard University Press, 1998.
——— *A History of My Times*, trans. Rex Warner, Harmondsworth: Penguin, 1966.

Modern secondary sources

Bowra, C.M., *Early Greek Elegists*, London: Oxford University Press, 1938.
Cairns, Douglas, *Aidos: The Psychology and Ethics of Honour and Shame in Ancient Greek Literature*, Oxford: Oxford University Press, 1992.
Cook, B.F., *Greek Inscriptions*, London: British Museum Publications, 1987.
Dodds, E.R., *The Greeks and the Irrational*, Berkeley: University of California Press, 1951.
Donlon, Walter, 'Reciprocities in Homer', *The Classical World*, 1982, vol. 75, no. 3, 137–75.
Dover, K.J., *Greek Popular Morality in the Time of Plato and Aristotle*, Oxford: Basil Blackwell, 1974.
Finley, M.I., *The World of Odysseus*, London: Pimlico, 1999.
Fisher, N.R.E., *Hybris: A Study in the Values of Honour and Shame in Ancient Greece*, Warminster: Aris & Phillips, 1992.
Forrest, W.G., *A History of Sparta*, London: Hutchinson University Library, 1968.
Garlan, Yvon, *War in the Ancient World: A Social History*, London: Chatto & Windus, 1975.
Garland, Robert, *The Greek Way of Death*, London: Duckworth, 1985.
Higgins, W.E., *Xenophon the Athenian: The Problem of the Individual and the Society of the Polis*, Albany: State University of New York Press, 1977.
Hirsch, Steven W., *The Friendship and the Barbarians: Xenophon and the Persian Empire*, Hanover and London: University Press of New England, 1985.
Lloyd-Jones, Hugh, 'Honour and Shame in Ancient Greek Culture', in *Greek Comedy, Hellenistic Literature, Greek Religion, and Miscellanea*, Oxford: Clarendon Press, 1990, pp. 253–80.
Martin, Thomas R., *Ancient Greece: From Prehistoric to Hellenistic Times*, New Haven and London: Yale Nota Bene, 2000.
Mulroy, David, *Early Greek Lyric Poetry*, Ann Arbor: University of Michigan Press, 1992.
Murray, Gilbert, *Euripides and his Age*, London: Oxford University Press, 1965.
Pomeroy, Sarah B., *Spartan Women*, Oxford: Oxford University Press, 2002.
Pritchett, W. Kendrick, *The Greek State at War*, Parts I, II, III, IV, and V, Berkeley: University of California Press, 1971, 1974, 1979, 1985, and 1991.
Stupperich, Reinhard, 'The Iconography of Athenian State Burials in the Classical Period', in W.D.E. Coulston, O. Palagia, L. Shear Jr., H.A. Shapiro, and F.J. Frost (eds), *The Archeology of Athens and Attica under the Democracy*, Oxford: Oxbow, 1994.

Tritle, Lawrence A., *From Melos to My Lai: War and Survival*, London and New York: Routledge, 2000.

Walcot, Peter, *Envy and the Greeks: A Study in Human Behaviour*, Warminster: Aris & Phillips, 1978.

van Wees, Hans, *Status Warriors: War, Violence and Society in Homer and History*, Amsterdam: J.C. Gieben, 1992.

Rome

Classical sources

Appian, *The Civil Wars*, trans John Carter, London: Penguin, 1996.

Caesar, *The Civil War*, trans. Jane F. Gardner, London: Penguin, 1967.

——— *The Conquest of Gaul*, trans. S.A. Handford, London: Penguin, 1982.

Cassius Dio, *The Roman History: The Reign of Augustus*, trans. Ian Scott-Kilvert, London: Penguin, 1987.

Cicero, *On Moral Obligation*, trans. John Higginbotham, London: Faber & Faber, 1967.

——— *On the Good Life*, trans. Michael Grant, Harmondsworth: Penguin, 1971.

Josephus, *The Jewish War*, trans. G.A. Williamson, revised E. Mary Smallwood, London: Penguin, 1981.

Juvenal, *The Sixteen Satires*, trans. Peter Green, London: Penguin, 1974.

Livy, *The Early History of Rome*, trans. Aubrey de Selincourt, London: Penguin, 2002.

——— *The War with Hannibal*, trans. Aubrey de Selincourt, London: Penguin, 1972.

Lucan, *Civil War*, trans. Susan H. Braund, Oxford: Oxford University Press, 1992.

Marcus Aurelius, *Meditations*, trans. Maxwell Staniforth, London: Penguin, 1964.

Plutarch, *Fall of the Roman Republic*, trans. Rex Warner, London: Penguin, 1972.

——— *Makers of Rome*, trans. Ian Scott-Kilvert, London: Penguin, 1965.

Polybius, *The Rise of the Roman Empire*, trans. Ian Scott-Kilvert, London: Penguin, 1979.

Sallust, *The Jugurthine War/The Conspiracy of Catiline*, trans. S.A. Handford, London: Penguin, 1963.

Suetonius, *The Twelve Caesars*, trans. Robert Graves, revised Michael Grant, London: Penguin, 1989.

Tacitus, *The Agricola and the Germania*, trans. H. Mattingly, Harmondsworth: Penguin, 1970.

——— *The Annals of Imperial Rome*, trans. Michael Grant, revised edition, London: Penguin, 1989.

Virgil, *The Aeneid*, trans. W.F. Jackson Knight, Harmondsworth: Penguin, 1956.

Modern secondary sources

Badian, E., *Roman Imperialism in the Late Republic*, Ithaca: Cornell University Press, 1968.

Barton, Carlin A., *Roman Honor: The Fire in the Bones*, Berkeley: University of California Press, 2001.

Eck, Werner, *The Age of Augustus*, Oxford: Blackwell, 2003.

Eckstein, Arthur M., *Senate and General: Individual Decision-Making and Roman Foreign Policy (264–194 BC)*, Berkeley: University of California Press, 1987.

Flower, Harriet L., 'The Tradition of the *Spolia Opima*: M. Claudius Marcellus and Augustus', *Classical Antiquity*, 2000, vol. 19, no. 1, 34–64.

Goldsworthy, Adrian, *Roman Warfare*, London: Cassell, 2002.

Harris, William V., *War and Imperialism in Republican Rome, 327–70 BC*, Oxford: Clarendon Press, 1979.

Harris, William V. (ed.), *The Imperialism of Mid-Republican Rome*, Rome: American Academy in Rome, 1984.

Holland, Tom, *Rubicon: The Triumph and Tragedy of the Roman Republic*, London: Little Brown, 2003.

Jiminez, Ramon L., *Caesar against the Celts*, Edison: Castle Books, 1996.

Kern, Paul Bentley, *Ancient Siege Warfare*, Bloomington and Indianapolis: Indiana University Press, 1999.

Lendon, J.E., *Empire of Honour: The Art of Government in the Roman World*, Oxford: Oxford University Press, 2001.

Luttwak, Edward N., *The Grand Strategy of the Roman Empire: From the First Century A.D. to the Third*, London: Weidenfeld & Nicolson, 1999.

Mattern, Susan, *Rome and the Enemy: Imperial Strategy in the Principate*, Berkeley: University of California Press, 2002.

Maxfield, Valerie A., *The Military Decorations of the Roman Army*, London: B.T. Batsford, 1981.

North, J.A., 'The Development of Roman Imperialism', *Journal of Roman Studies*, 1981, vol. 71, 1–9.

Payne, Robert, *Rome Triumphant: How the Empire Celebrated its Victories*, New York: Barnes & Noble, 1993.

Pomeroy, Sarah B., *Goddesses, Whores, Wives, & Slaves: Women in Classical Antiquity*, London: Pimlico, 1994.

Rich, John and Shipley, Graham (eds), *War and Society in the Roman World*, London and New York: Routledge, 1995.

Rosenstein, Nathan, *Imperatores Victi: Military Defeat and Aristocratic Competition in the Middle and Late Republic*, Berkeley: University of California Press, 1990.

Santosuosso, Antonio, *Storming the Heavens: Soldiers, Emperors and Civilians in the Roman Empire*, London: Pimlico, 2004.

Sherwin-White, A.N., 'Rome the Aggressor?', *Journal of Roman Studies*, 1980, vol. 70, 177–81.

——— *Roman Foreign Policy in the East, 168 B.C. to A.D. 1*, London: Duckworth, 1984.

Watson, G.R., *The Roman Soldier*, Ithaca: Cornell University Press, 1969.

Chivalry

Mediaeval sources

The Anglo-Saxon Chronicles, trans. and ed. Michael Swanton, London: Phoenix, 2000.

Aquinas, Thomas, *Summa Theologiae*, vols XXIII, XXXVIII, XLI, XLII, and XLIII, New York: Blackfriars, 1972.

Bonet, Honoré, *The Tree of Battles*, with introduction by G.W. Coopland, Liverpool: University Press of Liverpool, 1949.

de Charny, Geoffroi, 'The Book of Chivalry', in Richard W. Kaeuper and Elspeth Kennedy (eds), *The Book of Chivalry of Geoffroi de Charny: Text, Context, and Translation*, Philadelphia: Philadelphia University Press, 1996.

Froissart, *Chronicles*, trans. Geoffrey Brereton, London: Penguin, 1978.

Joinville and Villehardouin, *Chronicles of the Crusades*, trans. M.R.B. Shaw, London: Penguin, 1963.

Jordan Fantosme's Chronicle, ed. R.C. Johnston, Oxford: Clarendon Press, 1981.

Life and Campaigns of the Black Prince, ed. Richard Barber, Woodbridge: The Boydell Press, 1979.

Lull, Ramon, *The Book of the Ordre of Chyvalry*, trans. William Caxton, ed. Alfred T.P. Byles, London: Oxford University Press, 1926.

Malory, Sir Thomas, *Le Morte Darthur*, ed. Helen Cooper, Oxford: Oxford University Press, 1998.

de Pizan, Christine, *The Book of Deeds of Arms and Chivalry*, trans. Sumner Willard, University Park: Pennsylvania State University Press, 1999.

Raoul de Cambrai, ed. and trans. Sarah Key, Oxford: Clarendon Press, 1992.

The Song of Roland, trans. Gerard J. Brault, University Park: Pennsylvania State University Press, 1981.

de Troyes, Chrétien, *Arthurian Romances*, trans. William W. Kibler, London: Penguin, 1991.

Modern secondary sources

Allmand, Christopher, *The Hundred Years War: England and France at War, c. 1300 – c. 1450*, Cambridge: Cambridge University Press, 1988.

Allmand, Christopher (ed.), *Society at War: The Experience of England and France During the Hundred Years War*, Woodbridge: The Boydell Press, 1998.

Asbridge, Thomas, *The First Crusade: A New History*, London: The Free Press, 2004.

Barber, Richard, *The Knight and Chivalry*, 2nd edition, Ipswich: The Boydell Press, 1974.

Barnie, John, *War in Medieval Society: Social Values and the Hundred Years War, 1337–99*, London: Weidenfeld and Nicolson, 1974.

Bouchard, Constance Brittain, *'Strong of Body, Brave and Noble': Chivalry and Society in Medieval France*, Ithaca and London: Cornell University Press, 1998.

Bumke, Joachim, *The Concept of Knighthood in the Middle Ages*, New York: AMS Press, 1982.

Carpenter, David, *The Struggle for Mastery: Britain 1066–1284*, London: Allen Lane, 2003.

Chickering, Howell, and Seiler, Thomas H. (eds), *The Study of Chivalry: Resources and Approaches*, Kalamazoo: Medieval Institute Publications, 1988.

Contamine, Philippe, *War in the Middle Ages*, Oxford: Basil Blackwell, 1984.

Coss, Peter, *The Knight in Medieval England, 1000–1400*, Stroud: Alan Sutton, 1995.

Crouch, David, *William Marshal: Knighthood, War, and Chivalry, 1147–1219*, 2nd edition, London: Pearson, 2002.

Foss, Michael, *Chivalry*, London: Michael Joseph, 1975.

France, John, *Western Warfare in the Age of the Crusades, 1000–1300*, London and New York: Routledge, 1999.

Gillingham, John, 'War and Chivalry in the *History* of William the Marshal', in P.R. Cross and S.D. Lloyd (eds), *Thirteenth Century England II: Proceedings of the Newcastle Upon Tyne Conference, 1989*, Woodbridge: The Boydell Press, 1988, pp. 1–13.

——— '1066 and the Introduction of Chivalry into England', in George Garnett and John Hudson (eds), *Law and Government in Medieval England and Normandy*, Cambridge: Cambridge University Press, 1994, pp. 31–55.

Harper-Bill, Christopher, and Harvey, Ruth (eds), *The Ideals and Practice of Medieval Knighthood*, Dover, New Hampshire: The Boydell Press, 1986.

——— *Medieval Knighthood IV*, Woodbridge: The Boydell Press, 1992.

Huizinga, Johan, *Homo Ludens: A Study of the Play Element in Culture*, London: Routledge & Kegan Paul, 1949.
——— 'The Political and Military Significance of Chivalric Ideas in the Late Middle Ages', in Johan Huizinga, *Men and Ideas: History, the Middle Ages, the Renaissance*, trans. James S. Holmes and Hans van Marle, London: Eyre & Spottiswoode, 1960, pp. 196–206.
——— *The Waning of the Middle Ages*, Harmondsworth: Penguin, 1972.
Kaeuper, Richard W., *Chivalry and Violence in Medieval Europe*, Oxford: Oxford University Press, 1999.
Keen, Maurice, 'Brotherhood in Arms', *History*, 1962, vol. 47, 1–17.
——— 'Chivalry, Nobility, and the Man-at-Arms', in C.T. Allmand (ed.), *War, Literature, and Politics in the Late Middle Ages*, Liverpool: Liverpool University Press, 1976, pp. 32–45.
——— *Chivalry*, New Haven and London: Yale University Press, 1984.
——— *The Laws of War in the Late Middle Ages*, Aldershot: Gregg Revivals, 1993.
Painter, Sidney, *William Marshal: Knight-Errant, Baron, and Regent of England*, Baltimore: Johns Hopkins Press, 1933.
——— *French Chivalry: Chivalric Ideas and Practices in Mediaeval France*, Baltimore: Johns Hopkins Press, 1940.
Prestage, Edgar (ed.), *Chivalry*, London: Kegan Paul, Trench, Trubner & Co., 1928.
Prestwich, Michael, *Armies and Warfare in the Middle Ages: The English Experience*, New Haven and London: Yale University Press, 1996.
Seward, Desmond, *The Monks of War: The Military Religious Orders*, London: Penguin, 1995.
Squibb, G.D., *The High Court of Chivalry: A Study of the Civil Law in England*, Oxford: Clarendon Press, 1959.
Strickland, Matthew, *War and Chivalry: The Conduct and Perception of War in England and Normandy, 1066–1217*, Cambridge: Cambridge University Press, 1996.
Tuchman, Barbara, *A Distant Mirror: The Calamitous 14th Century*, New York: Ballantine, 1978.
Vale, Malcolm, *War and Chivalry: Warfare and Aristocratic Culture in England, France and Burgundy at the End of the Middle Ages*, London: Duckworth, 1981.
——— *The Origins of the Hundred Years War: The Angevin Legacy, 1250–1340*, Oxford: Clarendon Press, 1996.

Elizabethan England

Elizabethan sources

Ashley, Robert, *Of Honour*, with introduction and commentary by Virgil B. Heltzel, San Marino: The Huntington Library, 1947.
Churchyard, Thomas, 'A Generall Rehearsall of Warres', in *Churchyard's Choise*, London: Edward White, 1579.
The Courtyer of Count Baldessar Castilio, trans. Thomas Hoby, London, 1561.
Donne, John, *The Complete English Poems*, ed. A.J. Smith, Harmondsworth: Penguin, 1971.
Elyot, Sir Thomas, *The Boke Named the Governour*, London: J.M. Dent, 1907; first published: London, 1531.
Gates, Geffrey, *The Defence of Militarie Profession*, London: Henry Middleton, 1579.

Greville, Fulke, 'A Dedication to Sir Philip Sidney', in John Gouws (ed.), *The Prose Works of Fulke Greville, Lord Brooke*, Oxford: Clarendon Press, 1986, pp. 3–135.

——— *The Friend of Sir Philip Sidney: Being Selections from the Works in Verse and Prose of Fulke Greville*, ed. Alexander B. Grosart, London: Elliot Stock, 1894.

——— 'An Inquisition upon Fame and Honour', in Geoffrey Bullough (ed.), *The Poems and Dramas of Fulke Greville*, vol. 1, New York: Oxford University Press, 1945, pp. 192–213.

The Institucion of a Gentleman, London: Thomas Marshe, 1568.

Markham, Gervase, 'The Most Honourable Tragedie of Sir Richard Grinville, Knight' (first published, London: I. Roberts, 1595), in Edward Arber (ed.), *The Last Fight of the Revenge*, Westminster: A. Constable & Co., 1895.

Norden, John, *The Mirror of Honour*, London: Thomas Man, 1597.

Raleigh, Sir Walter, 'A Report of the Fight about the Iles of Acores' (first published, London: William Ponsonbie, 1591), in Edward Arber (ed.), *The Last Fight of the Revenge*, Westminster: A. Constable & Co., 1895.

Riche, Barnabe, *Allarme to England*, London, 1578.

Segar, William, *The Booke of Honor and Armes*, London: Richard Jhones, 1590.

——— *Honor Military and Civill*, London: Robert Baker, 1602.

Shakespeare, William, *The Complete Works*, ed. Charles Jasper Sisson, London: Odhams Press, 1953.

Sidney, Sir Philip, *Arcadia*, Harmondsworth: Penguin, 1977.

Spenser, Edmund, *The Faerie Queene*, Harmondsworth: Penguin, 1978.

Whetstone, George, *The Honorable Reputation of a Souldier*, London: Richard Jones, 1585.

Williams, Sir Roger, *The Works of Sir Roger Williams*, ed. John X. Evans, Oxford: Clarendon Press, 1972.

Modern secondary sources

Adamson, J.H., and Holland, H.F., *The Shepherd of the Ocean: An Account of Sir Walter Ralegh and his Times*, London: Bodley Head, 1969.

Andrews, Kenneth R., *Elizabethan Privateering: English Privateering during the Spanish War, 1585–1603*, Cambridge: Cambridge University Press, 1964.

Barber, Charles, *The Theme of Honour's Tongue: A Study of Social Attitudes in the English Drama from Shakespeare to Dryden*, Gothenburg: Gothenburg Studies in English, 1985.

Boynton, Lindsay, *The Elizabethan Militia, 1558–1638*, London: Routledge & Kegan Paul, 1967.

Canny, Nicholas P., 'The Ideology of English Colonization: From Ireland to America', *The William and Mary Quarterly*, 3rd Ser., 1973, vol. 30, no. 4, 575–98.

Council, Norman, *When Honour's at Stake: Ideas of Honour in Shakespeare's Plays*, London: George Allen & Unwin, 1973.

Day, J.F.R., 'Death be Very Proud: Sidney, Subversion, and Elizabethan Heraldic Funerals', in Dale Hoak (ed.), *Tudor Political Culture*, Cambridge: Cambridge University Press, 1995, pp. 179–203.

Elias, Norbert, *The Civilizing Process: The History of Manners*, Oxford: Basil Blackwell, 1978.

——— *The Civilizing Process: State Formation and Civilization*, Oxford: Basil Blackwell, 1982.

Fraser, Antonia, 'Elizabetha Triumphans', in *The Warrior Queens*, Markham: Penguin Canada, 1990.

Greaves, Margaret, *The Blazon of Honour: A Study in Renaissance Magnanimity*, London: Methuen, 1964.

Herrup, Cynthia, '"To Pluck Bright Honour from the Pale-faced Moon": Gender and Honour in the Castlehaven Story', *Transactions of the Royal Historical Society*, sixth series, no. 6., 137–59.

Hughes-Hallett, Lucy, 'Francis Drake', in *Heroes: Saviours, Traitors and Supermen*, London: Fourth Estate, 2004, pp. 225–326.

James, Mervyn, 'English Politics and the Concept of Honour, 1485–1642', *Past and Present*, supplement 3, 1978.

——— 'At a Crossroads of Political Culture: the Essex Revolt, 1601', in *Society, Politics and Culture: Studies in Early Modern England*, Cambridge: Cambridge University Press, 1986, pp. 416–65.

Kelso, Ruth, 'The Doctrine of the English Gentleman in the Sixteenth Century', *University of Illinois Studies in Language and Literature*, 1929, vol. 14, no. 1–2, 1–288.

Kenny, Robert W., *Elizabeth's Admiral: The Political Career of Charles Howard, Earl of Nottingham, 1536–1624*, Baltimore and London: Johns Hopkins Press, 1970.

Kipling, Gordon, *The Triumph of Honour: Burgundian Origins of the Elizabethan Renaissance*, The Hague: Leiden University Press, 1977.

Lacey, Robert, *Robert Earl of Essex: An Elizabethan Icarus*, London: Weidenfeld and Nicolson, 1971.

Lenman, Bruce P., *England's Colonial Wars 1550–1688: Conflicts, Empire and National Identity*, Harlow: Longman, 2001.

Llewellyn, Nigel, 'Honour in Life, Death and in the Memory: Funeral Monuments in Early Modern England', *Transactions of the Royal Historical Society*, sixth series, no. 6, pp. 179–200.

MacCaffrey, Wallace T., *Elizabeth I: War and Politics, 1588–1603*, Princeton: Princeton University Press, 1992.

Martin, Paula, *Spanish Armada Prisoners*, Exeter: University of Exeter Publications, 1988.

Mattingly, Garrett, *The Defeat of the Spanish Armada*, London: Jonathan Cape, 1959.

Meron, Theodor, *Bloody Constraint: War and Chivalry in Shakespeare*, New York and Oxford: Oxford University Press, 1998.

Neale, J.E., *Queen Elizabeth I*, St Albans: Triad, 1979.

Norman, Andrew, *Sir Francis Drake: Behind the Pirate's Mask*, Tiverton: Halsgrove, 2004.

Oosterhoff, F.G., *Leicester and the Netherlands, 1586–1587*, Utrecht: HES, 1988.

Peltonen, Markku, *The Duel in Early Modern England: Civility, Politeness and Honour*, Cambridge: Cambridge University Press, 2003.

Ramsey, G.D., 'The Foreign Policy of Elizabeth I', in Christopher Haigh (ed.), *The Reign of Elizabeth I*, Basingstoke: Macmillan, 1984, pp. 147–68.

Rebholz, Ronald A., *The Life of Fulke Greville, First Lord Brooke*, Oxford: Clarendon Press, 1971.

Rowse, A.L., *Sir Richard Grenville of the Revenge: An Elizabethan Hero*, London: Jonathan Cape, 1937.

——— *The Expansion of Elizabethan England*, 2nd edition, reissued with foreword by Michael Portillo, Basingstoke: Palgrave Macmillan, 2003.

Shalin, Alice, *The Relationship of Renaissance Concepts of Honour to Shakespeare's Problem Plays*, Salzburg: Institut fur Englische Sprache und Literatur, 1972.

Siegel, Paul N., 'Shakespeare and the Neo-Chivalric Cult of Honor', *The Centennial Review*, 1964, vol. 8, 39–70.

Watson, Curtis Brown, *Shakespeare and the Renaissance Concept of Honour*, Princeton: Princeton University Press, 1960.
Wernham, R.B., *The Making of Elizabethan Foreign Policy, 1558–1603*, Berkeley: University of California Press, 1980.
——— *After the Armada: Elizabethan England and the Struggle for Western Europe, 1588–1595*, Oxford: Clarendon Press, 1984.

Southern honour and the American Civil War

Archival sources

Eleanor S. Brockenbrough Library, The Museum of the Confederacy, Richmond:
William F. Slemons, Papers.
J.Q.A. Nadenbousch, Papers.
William Samuel Woods, Letters.
Pvt Daniel Gilley, Letters.
John H. Inglis, Letters.
Sgt Archie Livingstone, Letters.

Southern Historical Collection, University of North Carolina at Chapel Hill:
John Bramblett Beall, Letters.
John Brooks, Letters.
Given Campbell, Letters.
George Phifer Erwin collection.
John Hooper, Letters.
Calvin Leach, Diary.
William Nelson Pendleton, Papers.

Contemporary documents

War of the Rebellion: A Compilation of the Official Records of the Union and Confederate Armies, Series 1, Volume 20, Part 1 (General Orders, no. 93, 22 November 1862, and no. 131, 3 October 1863), and Series 4, Volume 2 (General Orders, no. 52, 23 July 1862).

Secondary sources

Beringer, Richard E., Hattaway, Herman, Jones, Archer, and Still, William N. Jr., *Why the South Lost the Civil War*, Athens and London: University of Georgia Press, 1986.
Berry, Stephen W., *All that Makes a Man: Love and Ambition in the Civil War South*, New York: Oxford University Press, 2003.
Bonner, Robert E., *Colors & Blood: Flag Passions of the Confederate South*, Princeton: Princeton University Press, 2002.
Breen, T.H., 'Horses and Gentlemen: The Cultural Significance of Gambling among the Gentry of Virginia', *William and Mary Quarterly*, 1977, vol. 34, 239–57.
Bruce, Dickson D., *Violence and Culture in the Antebellum South*, Austin: University of Texas Press, 1979.
Buell, Thomas B., *The Warrior Generals: Combat Leadership in the Civil War*, New York: Three Rivers Press, 1997.

Clemmer, Gregg S., *Valor in Gray: The Recipients of the Confederate Medal of Honor*, Staunton: Hearthside, 1998.

Crowther, Edward R., 'Holy Honor: Sacred and Secular in the Old South', *The Journal of Southern History*, 1992, vol. 58, no. 4, 619–36.

Davis, Burke, *The Long Surrender*, New York: Random House, 1985.

Davis, William C., *An Honorable Defeat: The Last Days of the Confederate Government*, San Diego: Harcourt, 2002.

Earle, Peter, *Robert E. Lee*, London: Weidenfeld & Nicolson, 1973.

Evans, David (ed.), *Random Acts of Kindness: True Stories of America's Civil War*, Wilmington: Broadfoot, 2001.

Franklin, John Hope, *The Militant South, 1800–1861*, Cambridge: Harvard University Press, 1956.

Fraser, John, *America and the Patterns of Chivalry*, Cambridge: Cambridge University Press, 1982.

Freeman, Douglas Southall, *Lee*, abridged by Richard Harwell, New York: Collier Books, 1993.

Freeman, Joanne B., *Affairs of Honor: National Politics in the New Republic*, New Haven: Yale University Press, 2002.

Gallagher, Gary W., *The Confederate War*, Cambridge: Harvard University Press, 1999.

Greenberg, Kenneth. S., *Honor and Slavery: Lies, Duels, Noses, Masks, Dressing as a Woman, Gifts, Strangers, Humanitarianism, Death, Slave Rebellions, the Proslavery Argument, Baseball, Hunting, Gambling in the Old South*, Princeton: Princeton University Press, 1996.

Grimsley, Mark, and Simpson, Brooks D. (eds), *The Collapse of the Confederacy*, Lincoln and London: University of Nebraska Press, 2001.

Groom, Winston, *Shrouds of Glory: From Atlanta to Nashville: The Last Great Campaign of the Civil War*, New York: Pocket Books, 1995.

Hartigan, Richard Shelly (ed.), *Lieber's Code and the Law of War*, Chicago: Precedent, 1983.

Leslie, Edward E., *The Devil Knows How to Ride: The True Story of William Clarke Quantrill and his Confederate Raiders*, New York: Da Capo Press, 1996.

McMurry, Richard M., *John Bell Hood and the War for Southern Independence*, Lincoln and London: University of Nebraska Press, 1982.

McNamara, Peter (ed.), *The Noblest Minds: Fame, Honor, and the American Founding*, Lanham: Rowman & Littleman, 1999.

McPherson, James M., *Battle Cry of Freedom: The Civil War Era*, New York and Oxford: Oxford University Press, 1988.

——— *For Cause and Comrades: Why Men Fought in the Civil War*, New York and Oxford: Oxford University Press, 1997.

McWhiney, Grady, *Confederate Crackers and Cavaliers*, Abilene: McWhiney Foundation Press, 2003.

McWhiney, Grady, and Jamieson, Perry D., *Attack and Die: Civil War Military Tactics and the Southern Heritage*, Tuscaloosa: University of Alabama Press, 1982.

Martin, Bessie, *A Rich Man's War, a Poor Man's Fight: Desertion of Alabama Troops from the Confederate Army*, Tuscaloosa: University of Alabama Press, 2003.

Mikaelian, Allen, *Medal of Honor: Profiles of American Military Heroes from the Civil War to the Present*, New York: Hyperion, 2002.

Olsen, Christopher J., *Political Culture and Secession in Mississippi: Masculinity, Honor, and the Antiparty Tradition*, New York: Oxford University Press, 2000.

Perkins, Bradford (ed.), *The Causes of the War of 1812: National Honor or National Interest*, New York: Holt, Rinehart & Winston, 1962.

Risjord, Norman K., '1812: Conservatives, War Hawks and the Nation's Honor', *William and Mary Quarterly*, 1961, vol. 18, no. 2, 196–210.

Smith, Gene, *Lee and Grant*, New York: McGraw-Hill, 1984.

Sword, Wiley, *Southern Invincibility: A Study of the Confederate Heart*, New York: St. Martin's Press, 1999.

Vandiver, Frank E., *Their Tattered Flags: The Epic of the Confederacy*, New York: Harper's, 1970.

Weitz, Mark A., *A Higher Duty: Desertion Among Georgia Troops during the Civil War*, Lincoln: University of Nebraska Press, 2000.

——— 'Shoot Them All: Chivalry, Honour and the Confederate Army Officer Corps', in D.J.B. Trim, *The Chivalric Ethos and the Development of Military Professionalism*, Leiden and Boston: Brill, 2003, pp. 321–47.

West, Jeffry D., *Mosby's Rangers*, New York: Touchstone, 1990.

Winik, Jay, *April 1865: The Month that Saved America*, New York: Perennial, 2002.

Wyatt-Brown, Bertram, *Southern Honor: Ethics and Behavior in the Old South*, New York and Oxford: Oxford University Press, 1982.

——— *The Shaping of Southern Culture: Honor, Grace, and War, 1760s to 1880s*, Chapel Hill: University of North Carolina Press, 2001.

Imperial Britain

Archival sources

Liddle Collection, University of Leeds. Papers of:

G.D. Archer.
W.R. Adams.
L.W. Batten.
S.H. Burt.
J. Charter.
R.J.T. Evans.
W.H. Gardner.
F.B. Hirsch.
P.L. Ibbetson.
P.G. Kennedy.
Walter R. Ludlow.
Jasper Mayne.
H.R. Osbourne.
E.W. Pennell.
R. Ross-Douglas.
A. Sager.
J.R. Tibbles.
R.H.D. Tompson.
J.C. Wakeford.
A. Douglas Wills.
George Worthington.
T. Worthington.

Other contemporary sources

Baden-Powell, Robert, *Scouting for Boys*, London: Horace Cox, 1908. Reprinted, Oxford: Oxford University Press, 2004.

Digby, Kenelm, *The Broad Stone of Honour: Or Rules for the Gentlemen of England*, London: C. & J. Rivington, 1823.

Graves, Robert, *Goodbye to All That*, revised edition, London: Penguin, 1957.

Henty, G.A., *The Dash for Khartoum*, London: Blackie & Son, 1892.

Hibberd, Dominic and Onions, John (eds), *Poetry of the Great War: An Anthology*, Basingstoke: Macmillan, 1986.

Hughes, Thomas, *Tom Brown's Schooldays*, London: W. Foulsham & Co., no date given.

Junger, Ernst, *Storm of Steel*, trans. Michael Hoffmann, London: Allen Lane, 2003.

Kipling, Rudyard, *Complete Verse*, New York: Doubleday, 1940.

Molter, Bennett A., *Knights of the Air*, New York and London: D. Appleton and Company, 1918.

Smiles, Samuel, *Character*, London: John Murray, 1897.

——— *Duty*, London: John Murray, 1897.

——— *Self-Help*, London: John Murray, 1897.

Modern secondary sources

Abrams, Elliott (ed.), *Honor among Nations: Intangible Interests and Foreign Policy*, Washington, DC: Ethics and Public Policy Center, 1998.

Anderson, Olive, 'The Growth of Christian Militarism in Mid-Victorian Britain', *English Historical Review*, 1971, vol. 84, no. 338, 46–72.

Andrew, Donna T., 'The Code of Honour and its Critics: the Opposition to Duelling in England, 1700–1850', *Social History*, 1980, vol. 5, no. 3, 409–34.

Ascoli, David, *A Companion to the British Army*, London: Harrap, 1983.

Bond, Brian (ed.), *Victorian Military Campaigns*, London: Hutchinson, 1967.

Borg, Alan, *War Memorials from Antiquity to the Present*, London: Leo Cooper, 1991.

Brodsky, G.W. Stephen, *Gentlemen of the Blade: A Social and Literary History of the British Army since 1660*, Westport: Greenwood Press, 1988.

Chamberlain, M.E., *The New Imperialism*, London: Historical Association, 1970.

Crook, M.J., *The Evolution of the Victoria Cross: A Study in Administrative History*, Tunbridge Wells: Midas, 1975.

Dawson, Graham, *Soldier Heroes: British Adventure, Empire, and the Imagining of Masculinities*, London and New York: Routledge, 1994.

Dougan, Andy, *The Hunting of Man: A History of the Sniper*, London: Fourth Estate, 2004.

Eldridge, C.C., *Victorian Imperialism*, London: Hodder & Stoughton, 1978.

Farwell, Byron, *For Queen and Country*, London: Allen Lane, 1981.

Ferguson, Niall, *The Pity of War*, London: Allen Lane, 1998.

Flanders, Judith, *The Victorian House: Domestic Life from Childbirth to Deathbed*, London: HarperCollins, 2003.

Girouard, Mark, *The Return to Camelot: Chivalry and the English Gentleman*, New Haven: Yale University Press, 1981.

Grayzel, Susan R., *Women and the First World War*, London: Longman, 2002.

Gullace, Nicoletta F., 'Sexual Violence and Family Honor: British Propaganda and International Law during the First World War', *The American Historical Review*, 1997, vol. 102, no. 3, 714–47.

——— 'White Feathers and Wounded Men: Female Patriotism and the Memory of the Great War', *Journal of British Studies*, 1997, vol. 36, 178–206.

Hall, Donald E., *Muscular Christianity*, Cambridge: Cambridge University Press, 1994.

Hobson, J.A., *Imperialism: a Study*, 3rd edition, London: G. Allen & Unwin, 1938.

Holmes, Richard, *Redcoat: The British Soldier in the Age of Horse and Musket*, London: HarperCollins, 2001.

——— *Tommy: The British Soldier on the Western Front, 1914–1918*, London: HarperCollins, 2004.

Hopkirk, Peter, *Trespassers on the Roof of the World: The Race for Lhasa*, Oxford: Oxford University Press, 1982.

James, Lawrence, *The Rise and Fall of the British Empire*, London: Abacus, 1998.

Johnson, Robert, *British Imperialism*, Basingstoke: Palgrave, 2003.

Lendon, J.E., *Empire of Honor: The Art of Government in the Roman World*, Oxford: Oxford University Press, 2001.

Longworth, Philip, *The Unending Vigil: A History of the Commonwealth War Graves Commission, 1917–1967*, London: Constable, 1967.

Macmillan, Margaret, *Peacemakers: The Paris Peace Conference of 1919 and its Attempt to End War*, London: John Murray, 2001.

Mason, Philip, *A Matter of Honour: An Account of the Indian Army, its Officers and Men*, London: Macmillan, 1974.

Melancon, Glenn, 'Honour in Opium: The British Declaration of War on China, 1839–1840', *The International History Review*, 1999, vol. 21, no. 4, 854–74.

Morris, James, *Pax Brittanica: The Climax of an Empire*, London: Faber & Faber, 1968.

Mosse, George, *Fallen Soldiers: Reshaping the Memory of the World Wars*, New York and Oxford: Oxford University Press, 1990.

Offer, Avner, 'Going to War in 1914: A Matter of Honor?', *Politics and Society*, 1995, vol. 23, no. 2, 213–41.

Ouditt, Sharon, *Fighting Forces, Writing Women: Identity and Ideology in the First World War*, London and New York: Routledge, 1994.

Pakenham, Thomas, *The Boer War*, London: Futura, 1982.

——— *The Scramble for Africa*, London: Abacus, 1992.

Peck, John, *War, the Army and Victorian Literature*, Basingstoke: Palgrave, 1998.

Porter, Bernard, *The Lion's Share: A Short History of British Imperialism, 1850–1983*, London: Longman, 1984.

Rachamimov, Alon, *POWs and the Great War: Captivity on the Eastern Front*, Oxford and New York: Berg, 2002.

Robbins, Keith, *Sir Edward Grey*, London: Cassell, 1971.

Robinson, Ronald, and Gallacher, John, *Africa and the Victorians: The Official Mind of Imperialism*, London: Macmillan, 1961.

Rutherford, Jonathan, *Forever England: Reflections on Race, Masculinity and Empire*, London: Lawrence & Wishart, 1997.

Smith, Simon C., *British Imperialism, 1750–1970*, Cambridge: Cambridge University Press, 1998.

Spiers, Edward M., *The Army and Society, 1815–1914*, London and New York: Longman, 1980.

——— *The Late Victorian Army, 1868–1902*, Manchester and New York: Manchester University Press, 1992.

Strawson, John, *Beggars in Red: The British Army 1789–1889*, London: Hutchinson, 1991.

Trevelyan, G.M., *Grey of Falloden*, London: Longman, Greens & Co., 1937.

Winter, Denis, *Death's Men: Soldiers of the Great War*, London: Penguin, 1979.

Winter, Jay, *Sites of Memory, Sites of Mourning: The Great War in European Cultural History*, Cambridge: Cambridge University Press, 1995.

The Cold War and after

Interviews

22 Wing North Bay, January 2003.

USNA Annapolis, May 2003.

USMA West Point, September 2003.

UK, US and Canadian Delegations, NATO, Brussels, January–April 2005.

Contemporary documents

Cadet Honor Code and Honor System, West Point: Center for the Professional Military Ethic, 2000.

Delivering Security in a Changing World, UK Defence White Paper, December 2003, London: The Stationery Office, 2003.

Report to the Secretary of the Army by the Special Commission of the United States Military Academy, 15 December 1976.

Summary of Duty with Honour: The Profession of Arms in Canada, Canadian Defence Academy, 2003.

Values and Standards of the British Army: Commander's Edition, no publication details given, 2000.

Secondary sources

Abu Gheith, Suleiman, 'In the Shadow of the Lances'. Available online: http://www.memri.org/bin/articles.cgi?Area=middleeast&ID=SP38802 (accessed 20 July 2005).

Barris, Ted, *Deadlock in Korea: Canadians at War, 1950–1953*, Toronto: Macmillan Canada, 1999.

Beevor, Antony, 'The Soldiers Preferred Margaret', *The New Statesman*, 19 April 1999, 11.

Bowden, Mark, *Black Hawk Down*, London: Corgi, 2000.

Bowman, James, 'Whatever Happened to Honor?', The Bradley Lecture, American Enterprise Institute, 10 June 2002. Available online: http://www.jamesbowman.net/articleDetail.asp?pubID=1169.

Campbell, Curt, 'Where the War Dead Go', *National Post*, 3 May 2003, A16.

Clancy, Tom, with General Tony Zinni, *Battle Ready*, New York: G.P. Putnam's Sons, 2004.

Clarkson, Jeremy, 'You Won't Believe What it Takes to Get a VC Today', *Sunday Times*, 2 November 2003.

Cockburn, Patrick, 'Violent Upsurge in Iraq Destroys US Claim of a Return to Normality', *The Independent on Sunday*, 17 April 2005, 21.

Coombs, William, 'Fatal Attraction: Duelling and the SS', *History Today*, June 1997, 11–16.

Crackel, Theodore J., *West Point: A Bicentennial History*, Lawrence: University Press of Kansas, 2002.

Danner, Mark, 'Torture and Truth', *The New York Review of Books*, 10 June 2004, 46–50.

Elkins, Caroline, *Britain's Gulag: The Brutal End of Empire in Kenya*, London: Jonathan Cape, 2005.

Figes, Orlando, *A People's Tragedy: The Russian Revolution, 1891–1924*, London: Jonathan Cape, 1996.

Gabriel, Richard A., and Savage, Paul L., *Crisis in Command: Mismanagement in the Army*, New York: Hill & Wang, 1978.

Hansen, Richard P., 'The Crisis of the West Point Honor Code', *Military Affairs*, 1985, vol. 49, no. 2, 57–62.

Hermann, John, *The Knight-Monks of Vichy France: Uriage, 1940–1945*, Montreal & Kingston: McGill-Queen's University Press, 1993.

Kaplan, Robert, *Warrior Politics: Why Leadership Demands a Pagan Ethos*, New York: Vintage, 2002.

Karnow, Stanley, *Vietnam: A History*, New York: Penguin, 1984.

Kellogg, Davida, 'On the Importance of Having an Honorable Enemy–Moral Asymmetry in Modern Warfare and the End of the Just War Tradition', paper presented to the 4th Conference on Ethical Leadership, held at the Royal Military College of Canada, November 2001.

Knowlton, William A., 'Honor - the Setting', *Military Affairs*, 1985, vol. 49, no. 2, 62–4.

Krohn, Charles A., *The Lost Battalion: Controversy and Casualties in the Battle of Hue*, Westport: Praeger, 1993.

Lane, Mark, *Conversations with Americans*, New York: Simon & Schuster, 1970.

Lind, Michael, *Made in Texas: George W. Bush and the Southern Takeover of American Politics*, New York: Basic Books, 2003.

Lipsky, David, *Absolutely American: Four Years at West Point*, New York: Vintage, 2003.

Logevall, Fredrik, *The Origins of the Vietnam War*, Harlow: Pearson Education, 2001.

Mackey, Chris, and Miller, Greg, *The Interrogators: Inside the Secret War against Al Qaeda*, New York and Boston: Little Brown, 2004.

McNab, Andy, *Bravo Two Zero*, New York: Dell, 1993.

Mead, Walter Russell, *Special Providence: American Foreign Policy and How it Changed the World*, New York: Alfred A. Knopf, 2001.

Moran, Michael, 'Too many medals?', MSNBC, 12 February 2004. Available online: http://www.msnbc.msn.com/id/4243092/ (accessed 20 July 2005).

Nisbett, Richard E., and Cohen, Dov, *Culture of Honor: The Psychology of Violence in the South*, Boulder: Westview, 1996.

O'Brien, Tim, *If I Die in a Combat Zone*, London: Calder & Boyars, 1973.

'Pentagon: Most Iraqi Captives Released', *USA Today*, 9 May 2003, 4A.

Poole, Oliver, *Black Knights: On the Bloody Road to Baghdad*, London: Harper Collins, 2003.

Robinson, Paul, '"Ready to Kill but not to Die": NATO Strategy in Kosovo', *International Journal*, 1999, vol. 54, no. 4, 671–82.

Shay, Jonathan, *Achilles in Vietnam: Combat Trauma and the Undoing of Character*, New York: Simon & Schuster, 1994.

Siddiqui, Haroon, 'For Many, Iraq Becoming a Crusade', *Toronto Star*, 11 November 2004.

Smith, Eric McAllister, *Not by the Book: A Combat Intelligence Officer in Vietnam*, New York: Ivy, 1993.

Steffan, Joseph, *Honor Bound: A Gay Naval Midshipman Fights to Serve his Country*, New York: Avon Books, 1992.

Steyn, Mark, 'Now it's up to Iraqis', *The Spectator*, 5 July 2004.

Swift, Earl, *Where They Lay: Searching for America's Lost Soldiers*, Boston and New York: Houghton Mifflin, 2003.

West, Owen, 'Who Really Deserves a Silver Star?', *Slate*, 29 September 2004. Available online: http://slate.msn.com/id/2107438/ (accessed 20 July 2005).

Wong, Leonard, Kolditz, Thomas A., Millen, Raymond A., and Potter, Terrence M., *Why They Fight: Combat Motivation in the Iraq War*, Carlisle: Strategic Studies Institute, 2003.

Wright, Evan, *Generation Kill: Living Dangerously on the Road to Baghdad with the Ultraviolent Marines of Bravo Company*, London: Bantam, 2004.

Zucchino, David, *Thunder Run: Three Days in the Battle for Baghdad*, London: Atlantic, 2004.

Index

Lightning Source UK Ltd.
Milton Keynes UK
UKOW050709130313

207539UK00003B/121/P

9 780415 545099